MAN-THING

WHATEVER KNOWS FEAR...

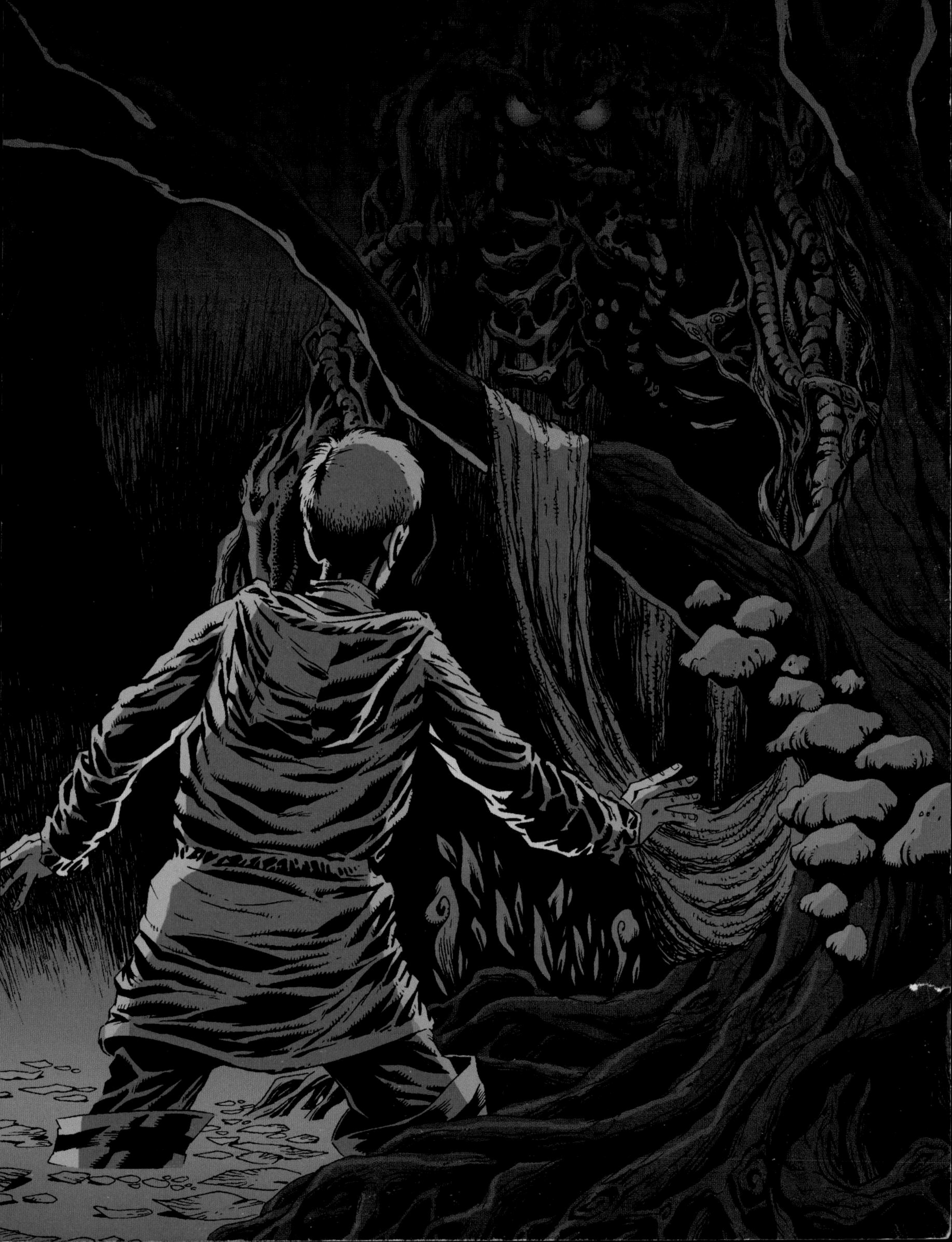

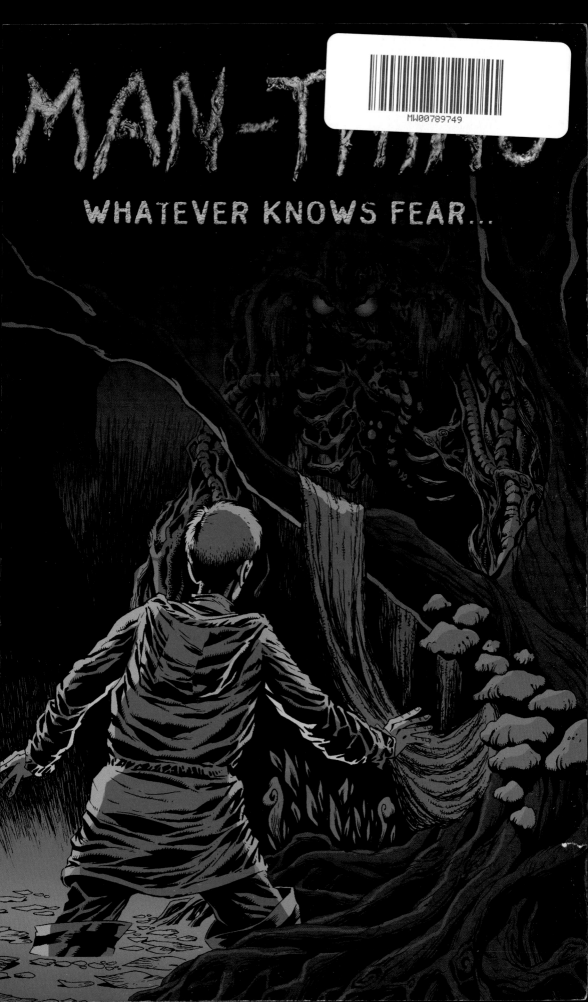

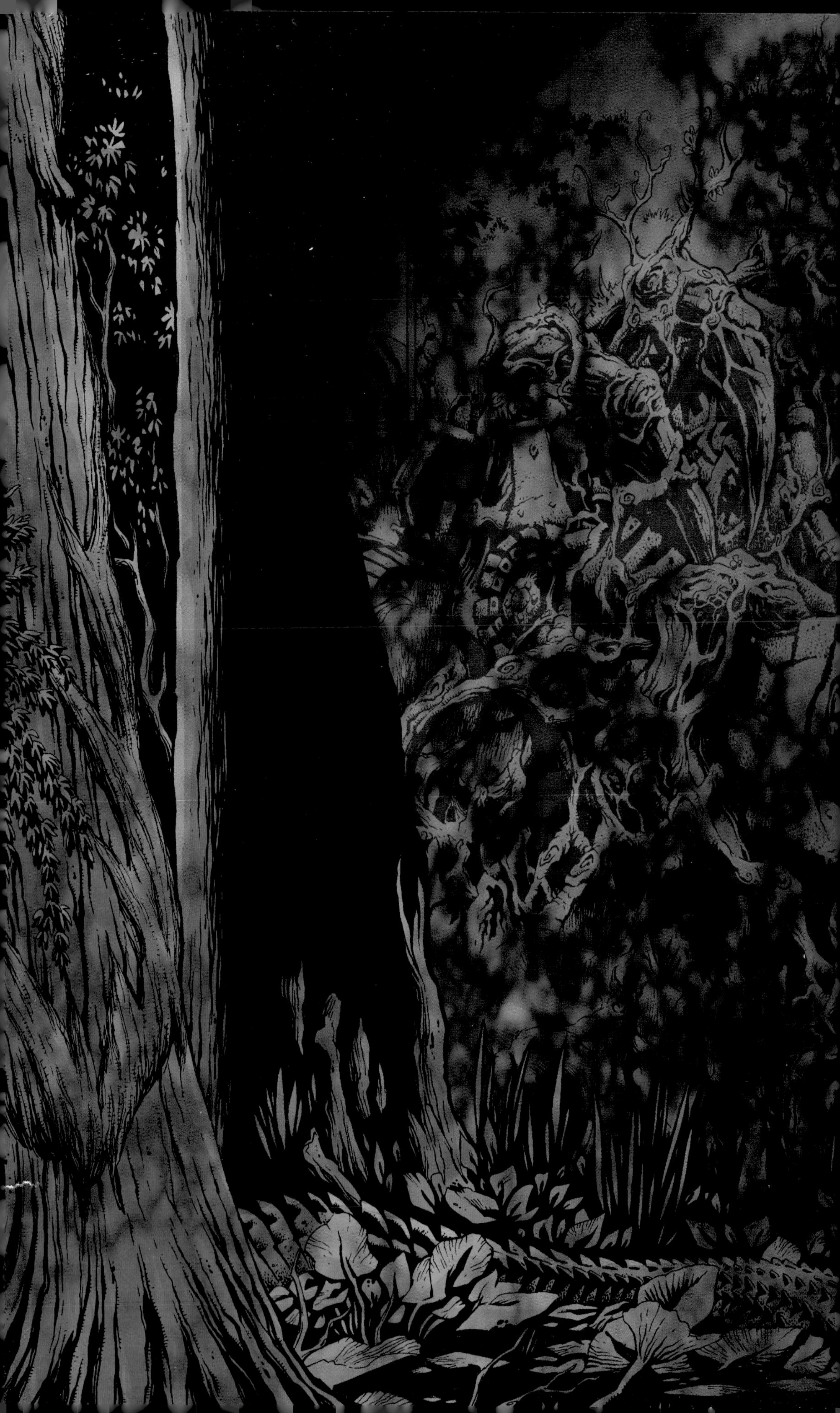

MAN-THING

WHATEVER KNOWS FEAR...

writer: Hans Rodionoff
artist: Kyle Hotz
colorist: Lee Loughridge
letterer: Virtual Calligraphy's Rus Wooton
editor: Jennifer Lee
executive editor: Axel Alonso

SAVAGE TALES #1

writers: Roy Thomas & Gerry Conway (Script)
artist: Gray Morrow

ADVENTURE INTO FEAR #16

writer: Steve Gerber
penciler: Val Mayerik
inker: Sal Trapani
letterer: Artie Simek
colorist: Petra Goldberg
editor: Roy Thomas
color reconstruction: Jerron Quality Color

collection editor: Jennifer Grünwald
senior editor, special projects: Jeff Youngquist
director of sales: David Gabriel
book designer: Patrick McGrath
art director: Tom Marvelli

editor in chief: Joe Quesada
publisher: Dan Buckley

Dedicated to Kelley Jones, Berni Wrightson, Matt
Roach, and Charles Pierce. Each in their own way
encouraged my love of the boggy monsters.
                                                    —Kyle Hotz

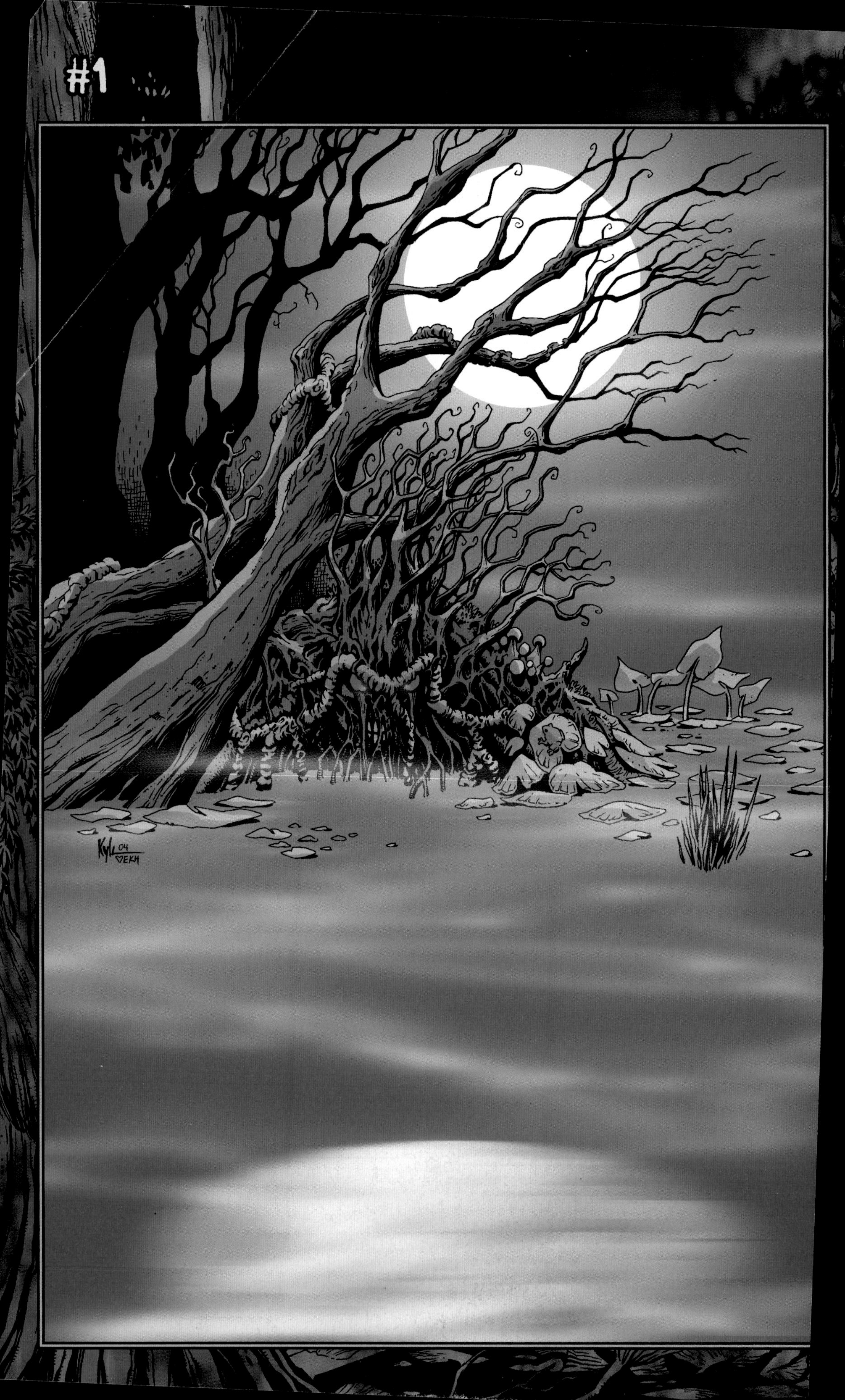
#1

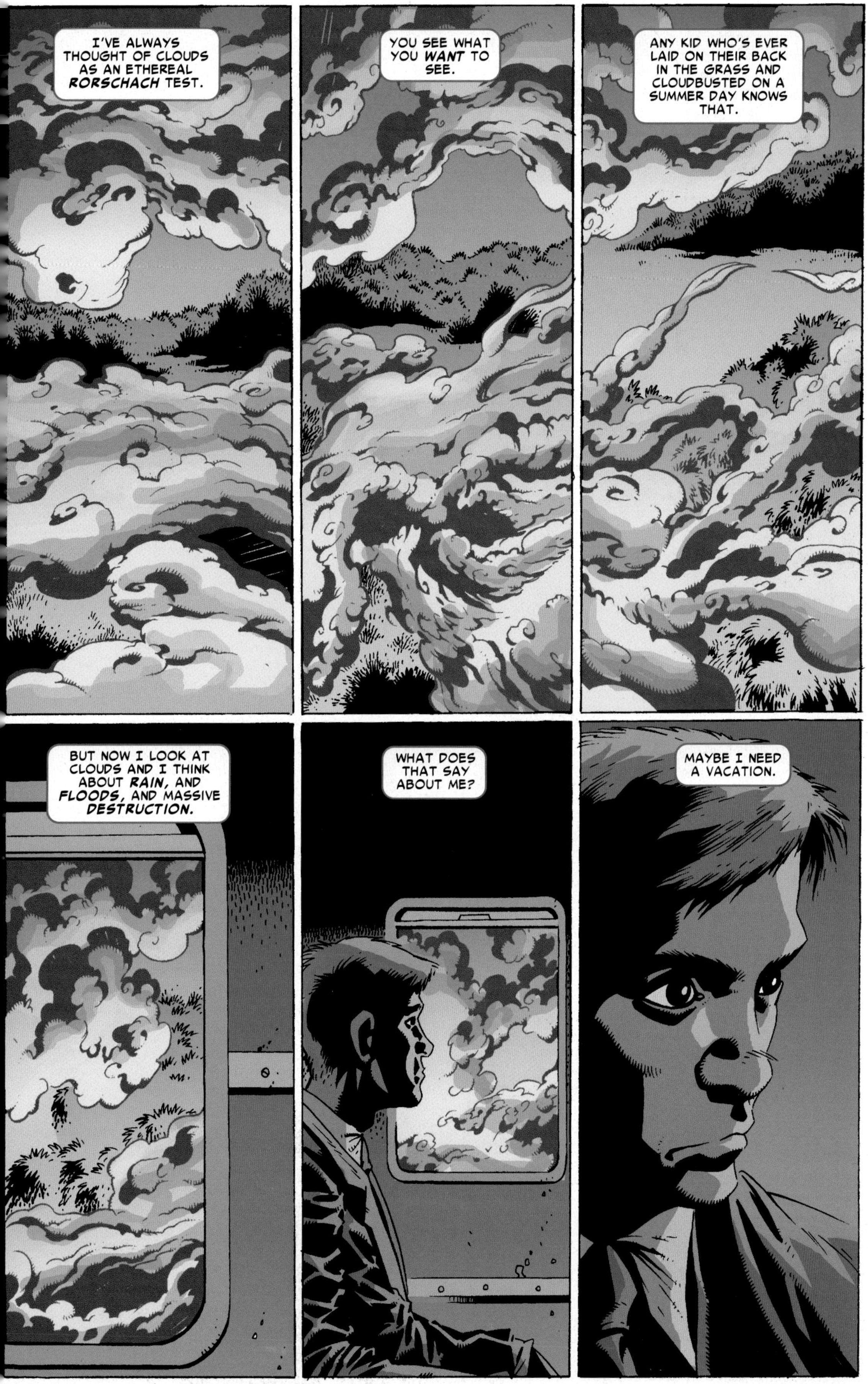
I'VE ALWAYS THOUGHT OF CLOUDS AS AN ETHEREAL RORSCHACH TEST.
YOU SEE WHAT YOU WANT TO SEE.
ANY KID WHO'S EVER LAID ON THEIR BACK IN THE GRASS AND CLOUDBUSTED ON A SUMMER DAY KNOWS THAT.
BUT NOW I LOOK AT CLOUDS AND I THINK ABOUT RAIN, AND FLOODS, AND MASSIVE DESTRUCTION.
WHAT DOES THAT SAY ABOUT ME?
MAYBE I NEED A VACATION.

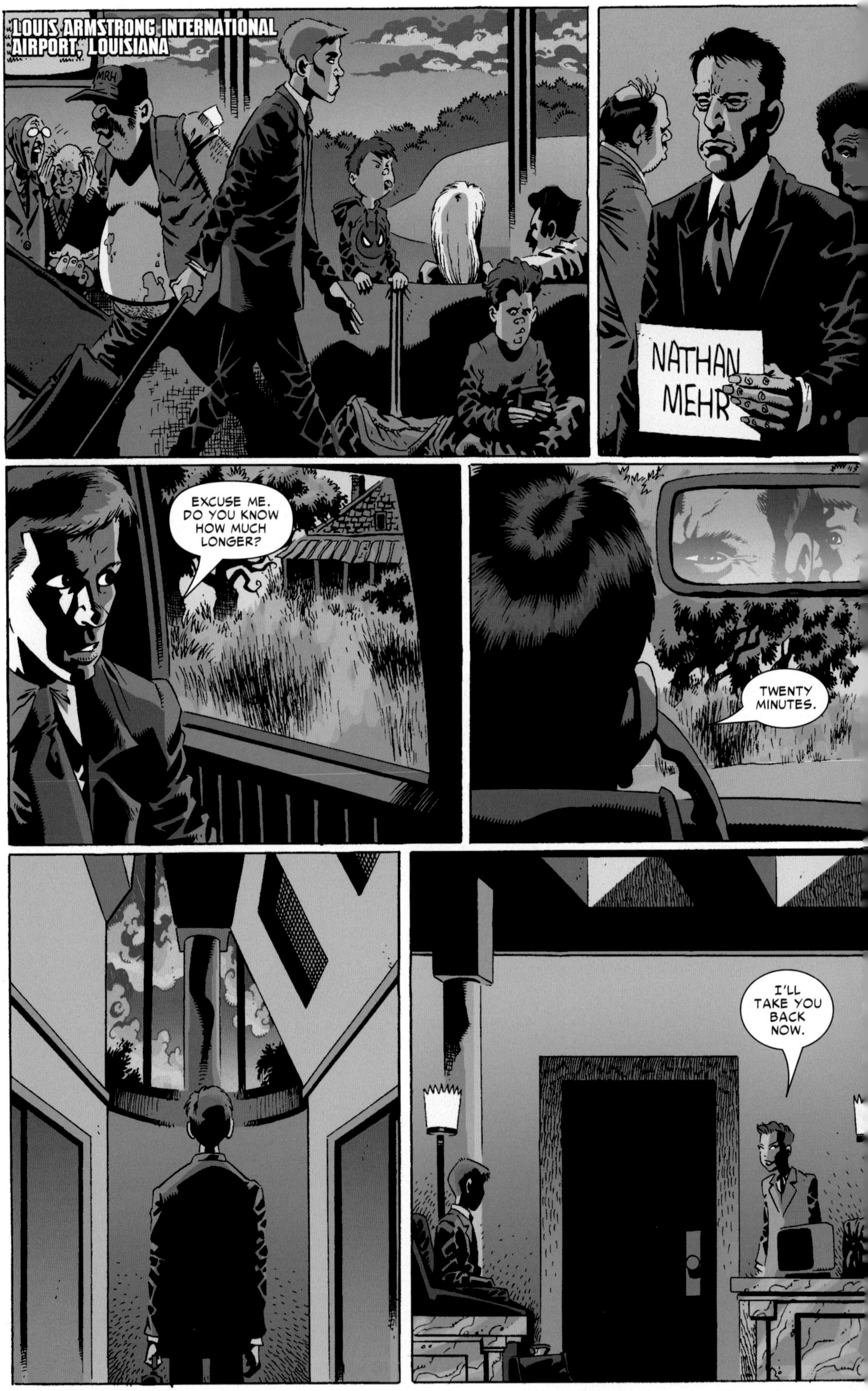

LOUIS ARMSTRONG INTERNATIONAL AIRPORT, LOUISIANA
MRH
NATHAN MEHR
EXCUSE ME. DO YOU KNOW HOW MUCH LONGER?
TWENTY MINUTES.
I'LL TAKE YOU BACK NOW.

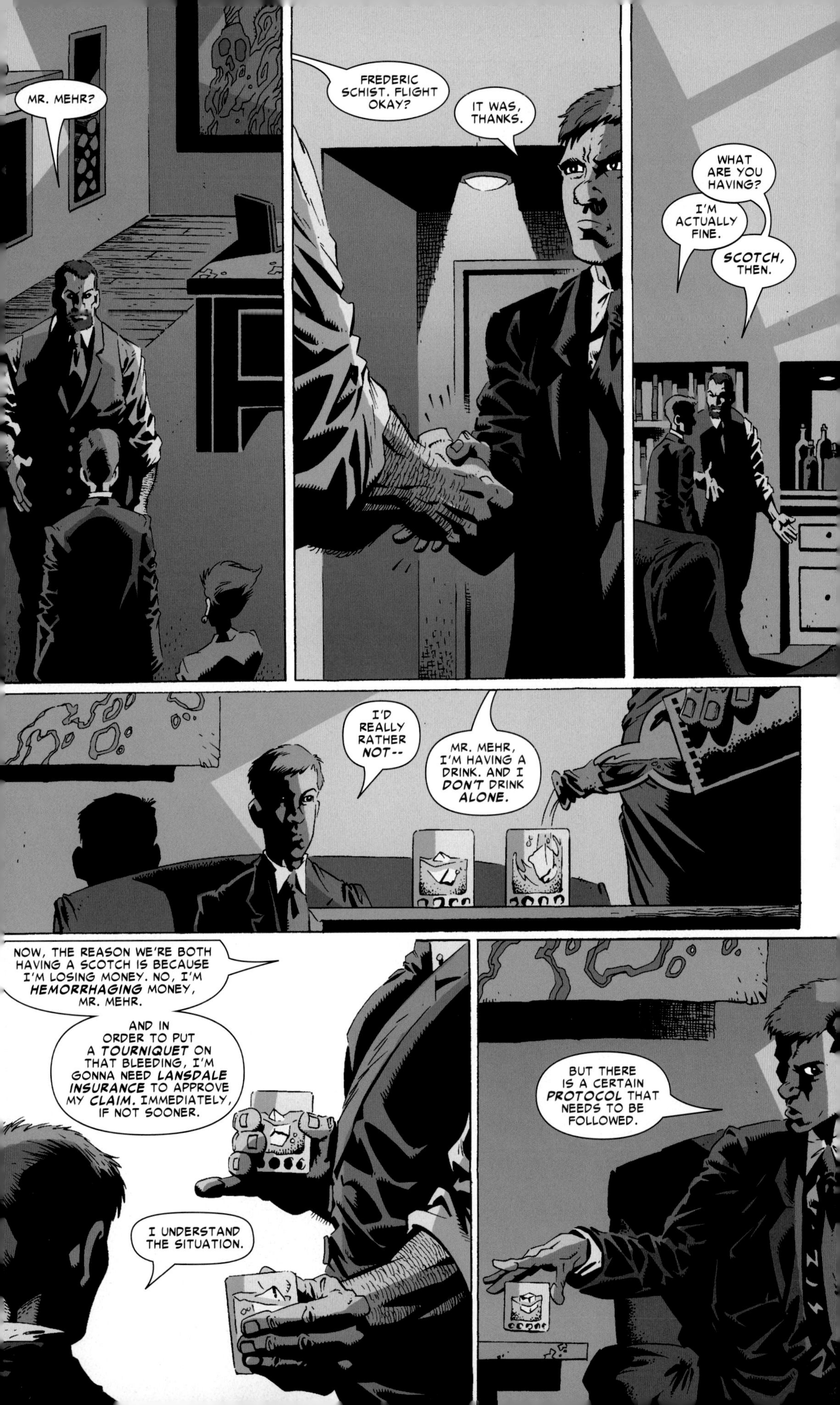
MR. MEHR?
FREDERIC SCHIST. FLIGHT OKAY?
IT WAS, THANKS.
WHAT ARE YOU HAVING?
I'M ACTUALLY FINE.
SCOTCH, THEN.
I'D REALLY RATHER NOT--
MR. MEHR, I'M HAVING A DRINK. AND I DON'T DRINK ALONE.
NOW, THE REASON WE'RE BOTH HAVING A SCOTCH IS BECAUSE I'M LOSING MONEY. NO, I'M HEMORRHAGING MONEY, MR. MEHR.
AND IN ORDER TO PUT A TOURNIQUET ON THAT BLEEDING, I'M GONNA NEED LANSDALE INSURANCE TO APPROVE MY CLAIM. IMMEDIATELY, IF NOT SOONER.
I UNDERSTAND THE SITUATION.
BUT THERE IS A CERTAIN PROTOCOL THAT NEEDS TO BE FOLLOWED.

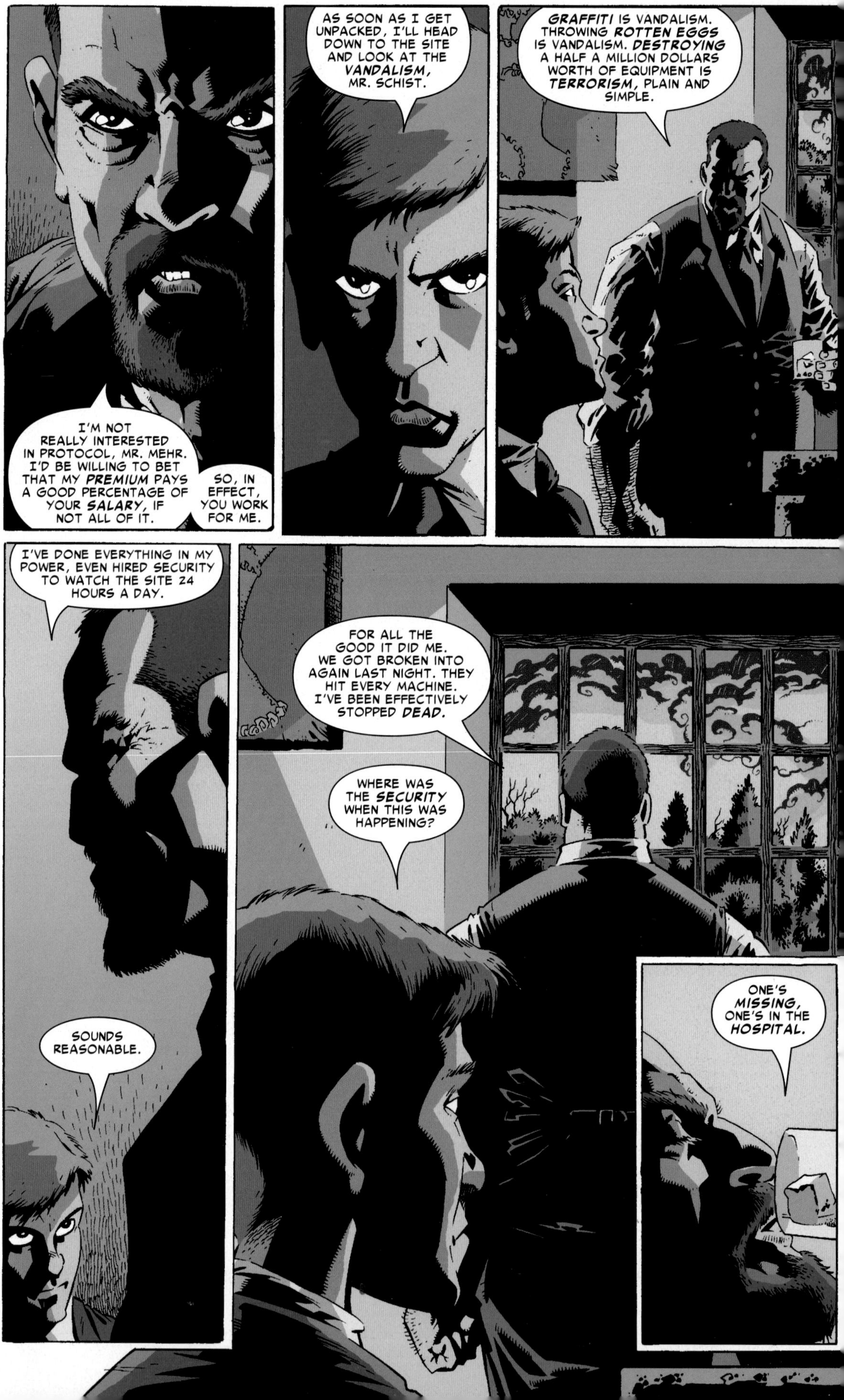
I'M NOT REALLY INTERESTED IN PROTOCOL, MR. MEHR. I'D BE WILLING TO BET THAT MY PREMIUM PAYS A GOOD PERCENTAGE OF YOUR SALARY, IF NOT ALL OF IT.
SO, IN EFFECT, YOU WORK FOR ME.
AS SOON AS I GET UNPACKED, I'LL HEAD DOWN TO THE SITE AND LOOK AT THE VANDALISM, MR. SCHIST.
GRAFFITI IS VANDALISM. THROWING ROTTEN EGGS IS VANDALISM. DESTROYING A HALF A MILLION DOLLARS WORTH OF EQUIPMENT IS TERRORISM, PLAIN AND SIMPLE.
I'VE DONE EVERYTHING IN MY POWER, EVEN HIRED SECURITY TO WATCH THE SITE 24 HOURS A DAY.
SOUNDS REASONABLE.
FOR ALL THE GOOD IT DID ME. WE GOT BROKEN INTO AGAIN LAST NIGHT. THEY HIT EVERY MACHINE. I'VE BEEN EFFECTIVELY STOPPED DEAD.
WHERE WAS THE SECURITY WHEN THIS WAS HAPPENING?
ONE'S MISSING, ONE'S IN THE HOSPITAL.

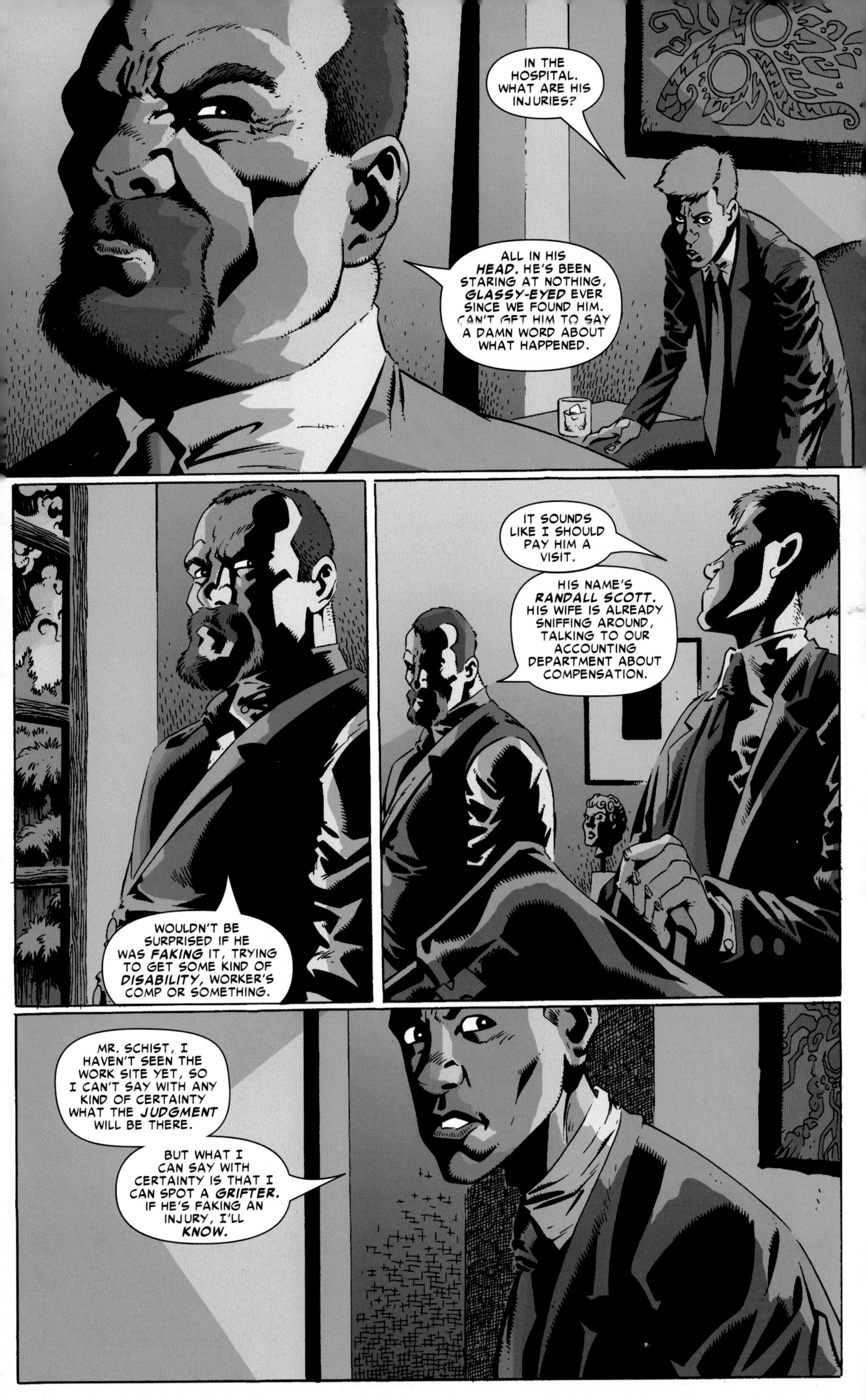
IN THE HOSPITAL. WHAT ARE HIS INJURIES?
ALL IN HIS HEAD. HE'S BEEN STARING AT NOTHING, GLASSY-EYED EVER SINCE WE FOUND HIM. CAN'T GET HIM TO SAY A DAMN WORD ABOUT WHAT HAPPENED.
WOULDN'T BE SURPRISED IF HE WAS FAKING IT, TRYING TO GET SOME KIND OF DISABILITY, WORKER'S COMP OR SOMETHING.
IT SOUNDS LIKE I SHOULD PAY HIM A VISIT.
HIS NAME'S RANDALL SCOTT. HIS WIFE IS ALREADY SNIFFING AROUND, TALKING TO OUR ACCOUNTING DEPARTMENT ABOUT COMPENSATION.
MR. SCHIST, I HAVEN'T SEEN THE WORK SITE YET, SO I CAN'T SAY WITH ANY KIND OF CERTAINTY WHAT THE JUDGMENT WILL BE THERE.
BUT WHAT I CAN SAY WITH CERTAINTY IS THAT I CAN SPOT A GRIFTER. IF HE'S FAKING AN INJURY, I'LL KNOW.

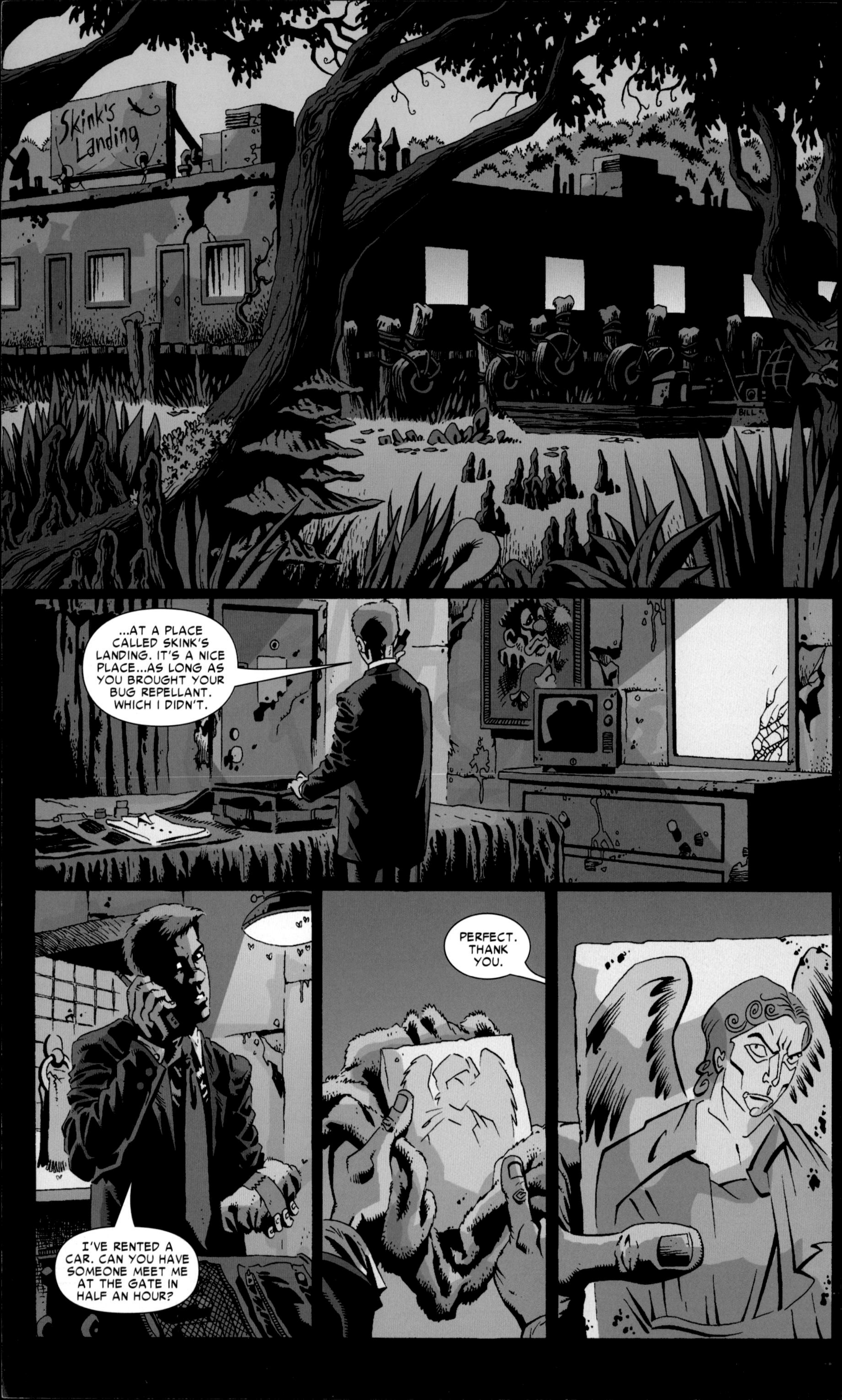
Skink's Landing
BILL
...AT A PLACE CALLED SKINK'S LANDING. IT'S A NICE PLACE...AS LONG AS YOU BROUGHT YOUR BUG REPELLANT. WHICH I DIDN'T.
I'VE RENTED A CAR. CAN YOU HAVE SOMEONE MEET ME AT THE GATE IN HALF AN HOUR?
PERFECT. THANK YOU.

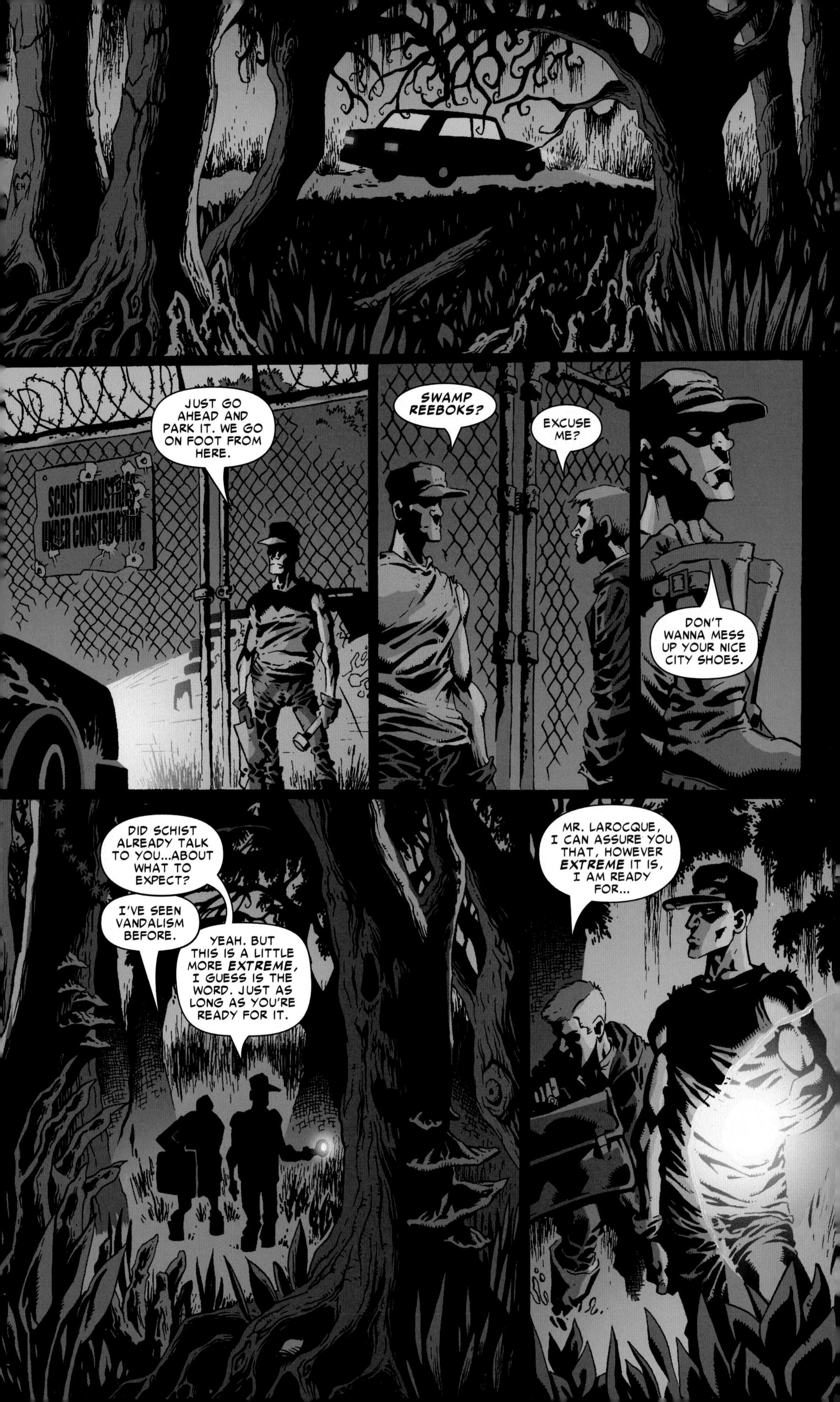

JUST GO AHEAD AND PARK IT. WE GO ON FOOT FROM HERE.
SCHIST INDUSTRIES UNDER CONSTRUCTION
SWAMP REEBOKS?
EXCUSE ME?
DON'T WANNA MESS UP YOUR NICE CITY SHOES.
DID SCHIST ALREADY TALK TO YOU...ABOUT WHAT TO EXPECT?
I'VE SEEN VANDALISM BEFORE.
YEAH. BUT THIS IS A LITTLE MORE EXTREME, I GUESS IS THE WORD. JUST AS LONG AS YOU'RE READY FOR IT.
MR. LAROCQUE, I CAN ASSURE YOU THAT, HOWEVER EXTREME IT IS, I AM READY FOR...

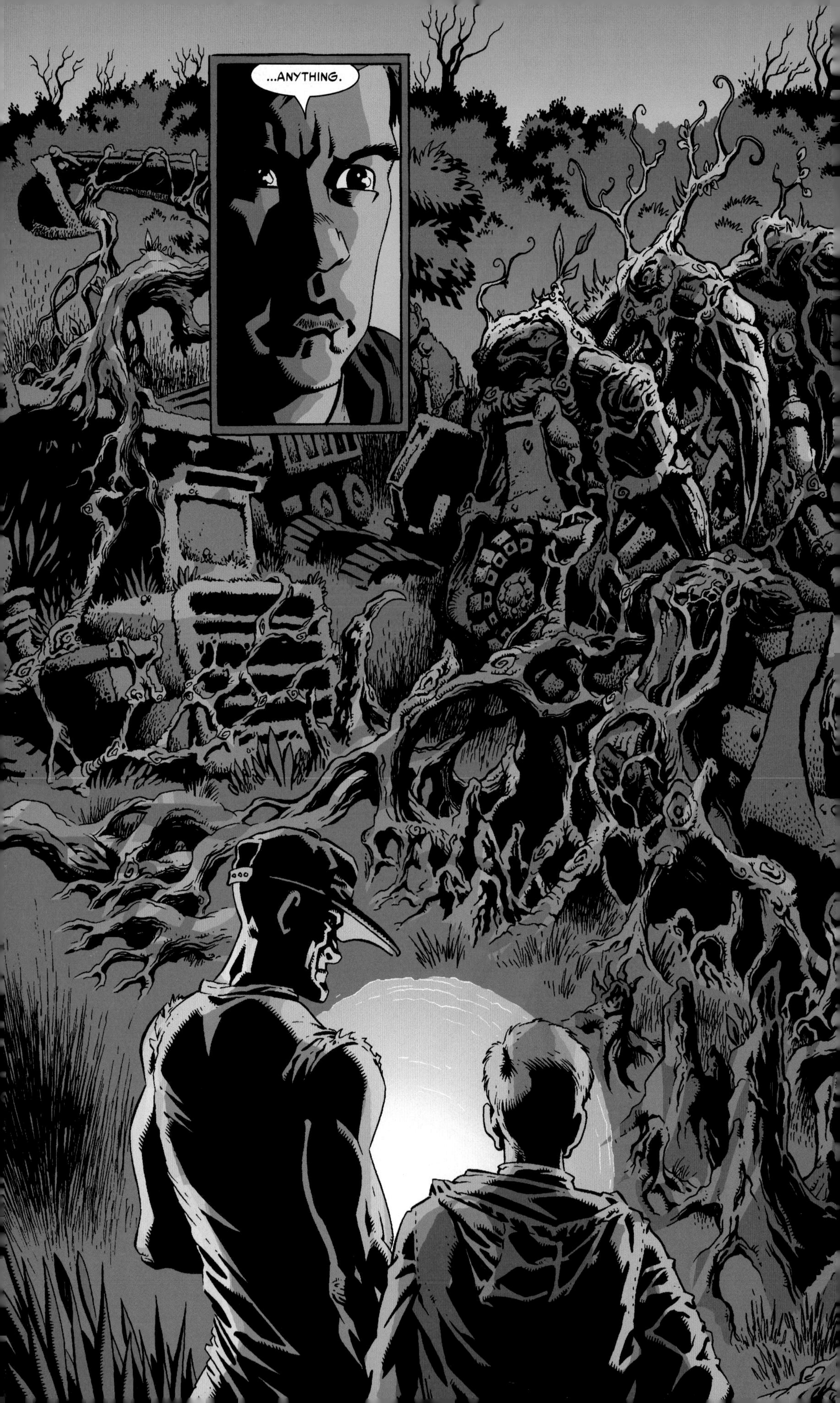
...ANYTHING.

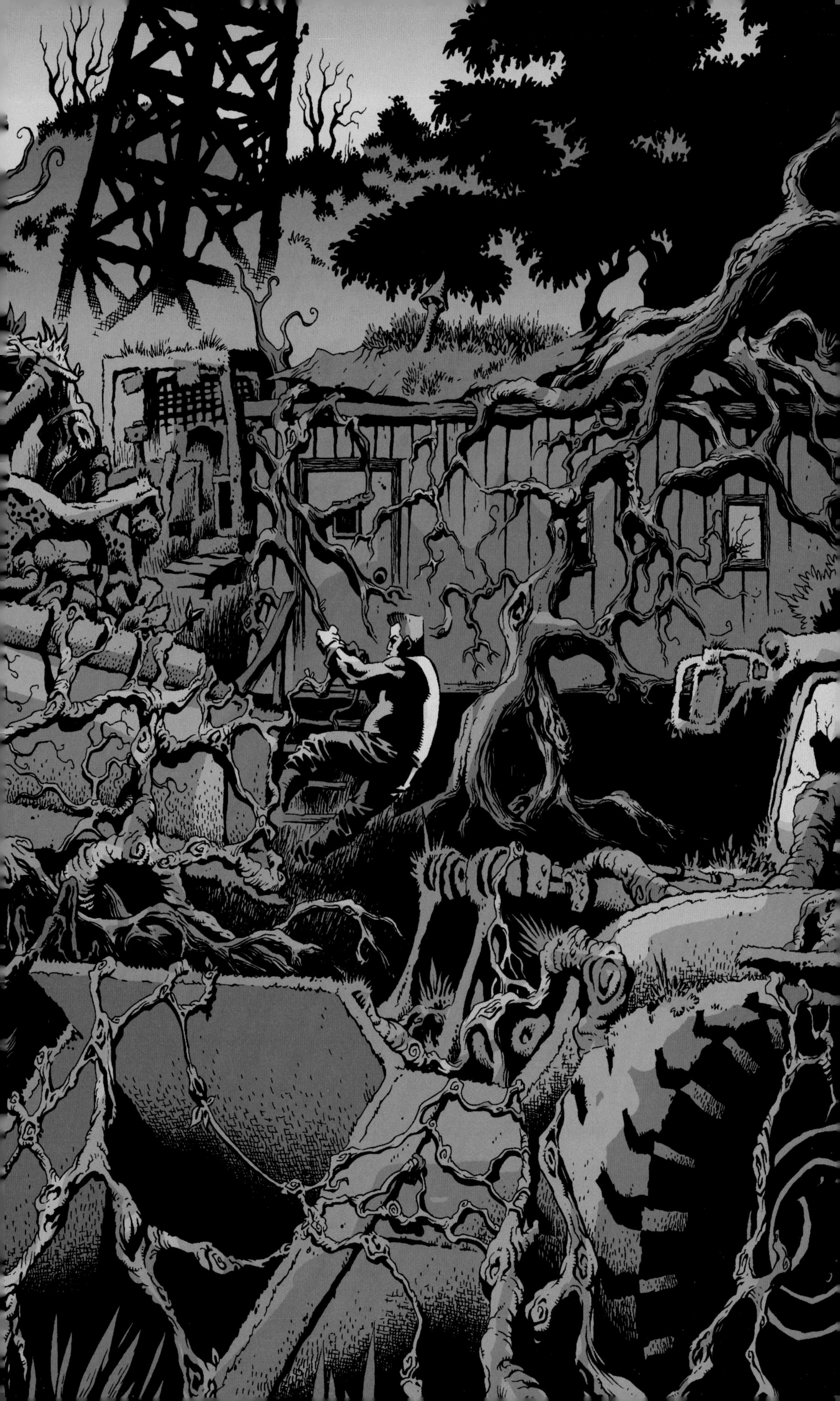

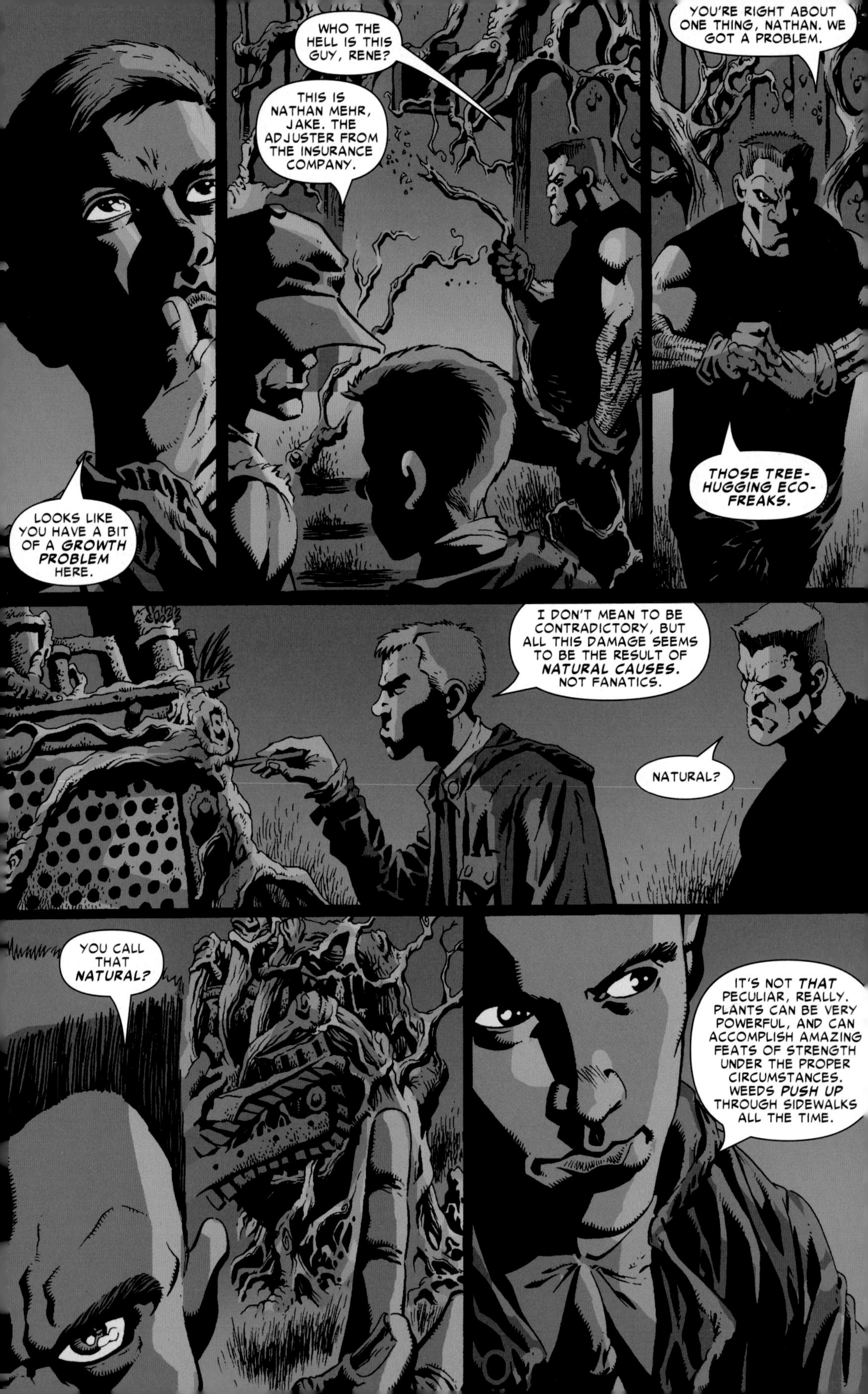
LOOKS LIKE YOU HAVE A BIT OF A *GROWTH PROBLEM* HERE.
WHO THE HELL IS THIS GUY, RENE?
THIS IS NATHAN MEHR, JAKE. THE ADJUSTER FROM THE INSURANCE COMPANY.
YOU'RE RIGHT ABOUT ONE THING, NATHAN. WE GOT A PROBLEM.
THOSE TREE-HUGGING ECO-FREAKS.
I DON'T MEAN TO BE CONTRADICTORY, BUT ALL THIS DAMAGE SEEMS TO BE THE RESULT OF *NATURAL CAUSES.* NOT FANATICS.
NATURAL?
YOU CALL THAT *NATURAL?*
IT'S NOT *THAT* PECULIAR, REALLY. PLANTS CAN BE VERY POWERFUL, AND CAN ACCOMPLISH AMAZING FEATS OF STRENGTH UNDER THE PROPER CIRCUMSTANCES. WEEDS *PUSH UP* THROUGH SIDEWALKS ALL THE TIME.

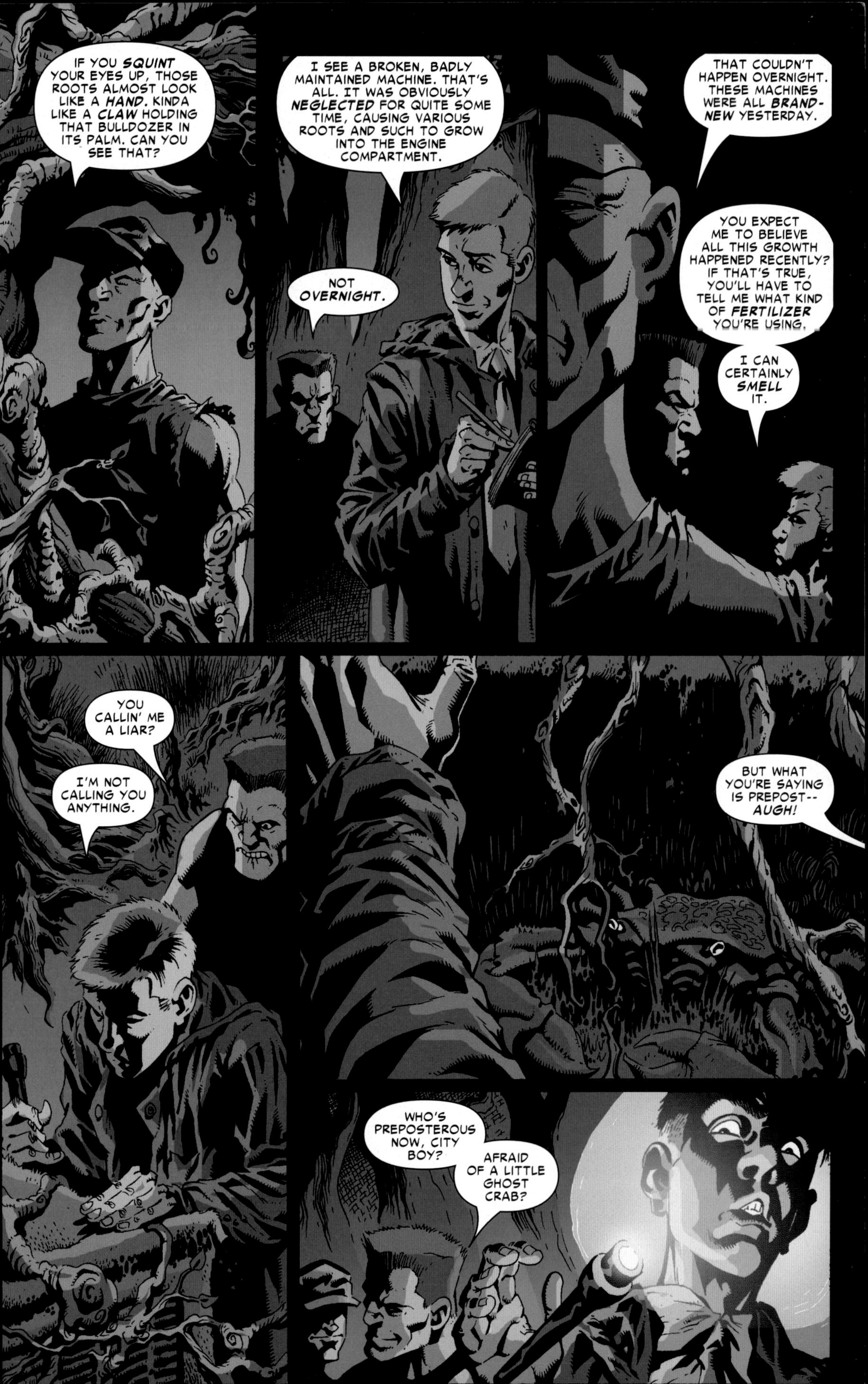
IF YOU SQUINT YOUR EYES UP, THOSE ROOTS ALMOST LOOK LIKE A HAND. KINDA LIKE A CLAW HOLDING THAT BULLDOZER IN ITS PALM. CAN YOU SEE THAT?
I SEE A BROKEN, BADLY MAINTAINED MACHINE. THAT'S ALL. IT WAS OBVIOUSLY NEGLECTED FOR QUITE SOME TIME, CAUSING VARIOUS ROOTS AND SUCH TO GROW INTO THE ENGINE COMPARTMENT.
NOT OVERNIGHT.
THAT COULDN'T HAPPEN OVERNIGHT. THESE MACHINES WERE ALL BRAND-NEW YESTERDAY.
YOU EXPECT ME TO BELIEVE ALL THIS GROWTH HAPPENED RECENTLY? IF THAT'S TRUE, YOU'LL HAVE TO TELL ME WHAT KIND OF FERTILIZER YOU'RE USING.
I CAN CERTAINLY SMELL IT.
YOU CALLIN' ME A LIAR?
I'M NOT CALLING YOU ANYTHING.
BUT WHAT YOU'RE SAYING IS PREPOST-- AUGH!
WHO'S PREPOSTEROUS NOW, CITY BOY?
AFRAID OF A LITTLE GHOST CRAB?

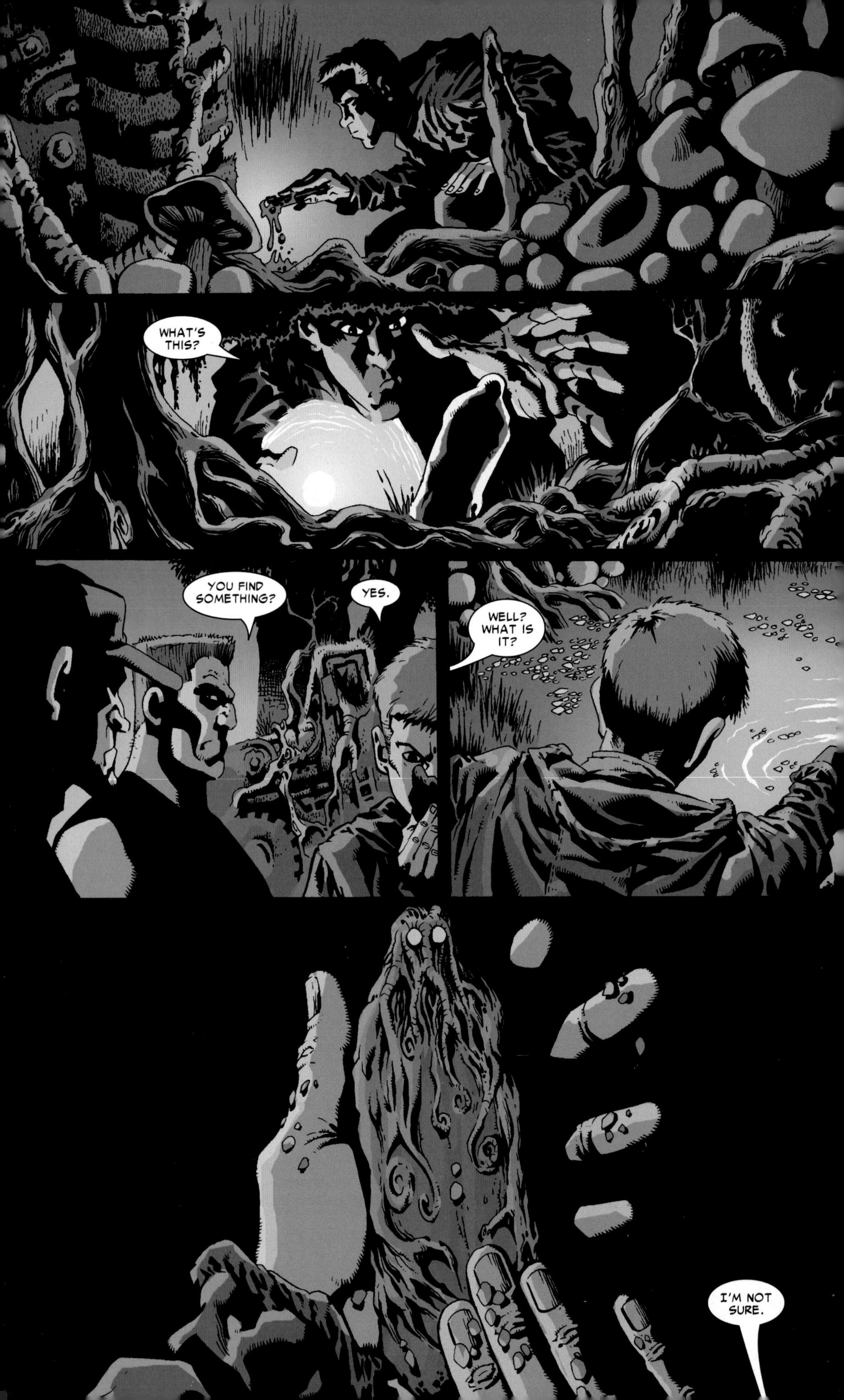
WHAT'S THIS?
YOU FIND SOMETHING?
YES.
WELL? WHAT IS IT?
I'M NOT SURE.

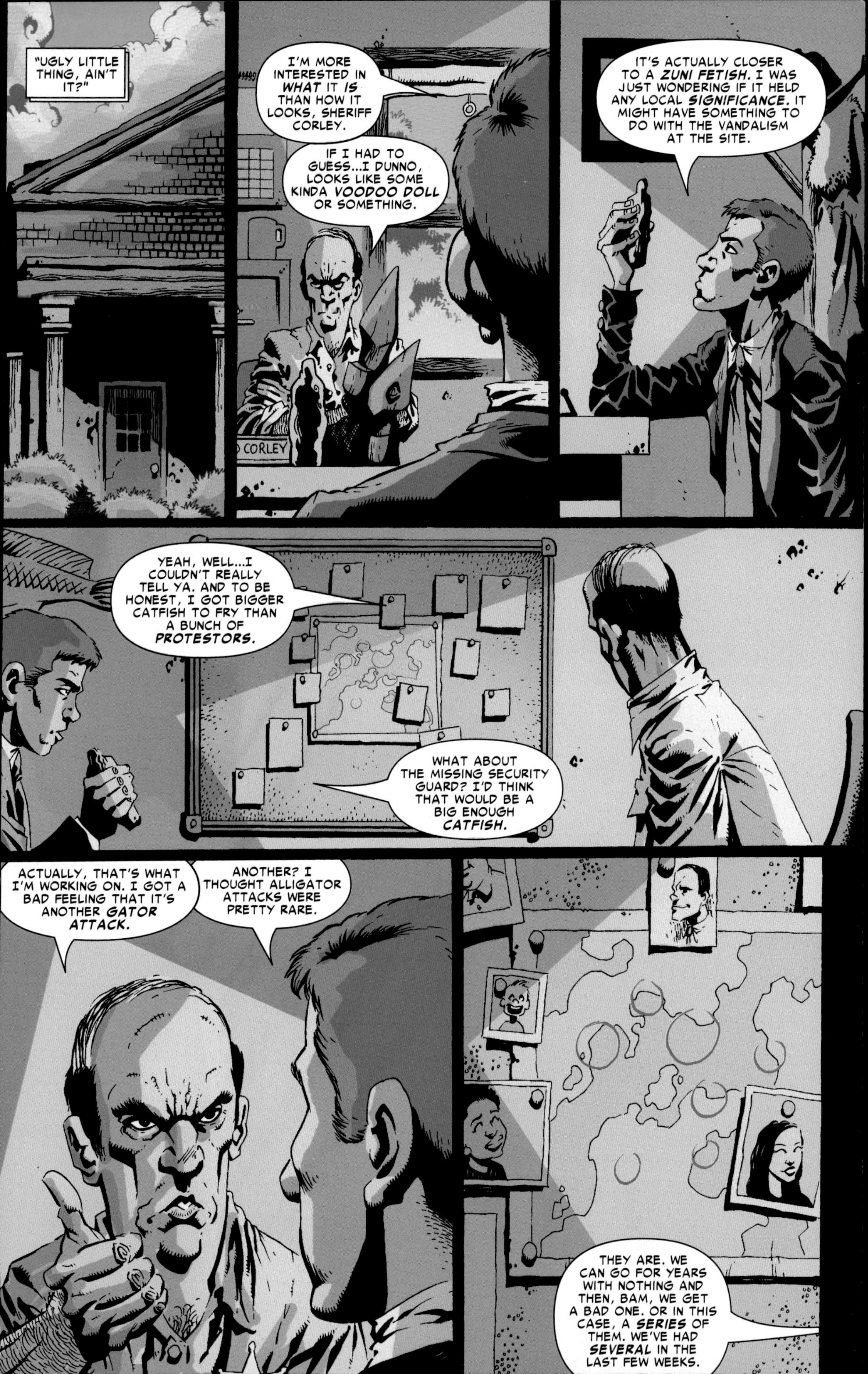
"UGLY LITTLE THING, AIN'T IT?"
I'M MORE INTERESTED IN *WHAT* IT *IS* THAN HOW IT LOOKS, SHERIFF CORLEY.
IF I HAD TO GUESS...I DUNNO, LOOKS LIKE SOME KINDA *VOODOO DOLL* OR SOMETHING.
CORLEY
IT'S ACTUALLY CLOSER TO A *ZUNI FETISH*. I WAS JUST WONDERING IF IT HELD ANY LOCAL *SIGNIFICANCE*. IT MIGHT HAVE SOMETHING TO DO WITH THE VANDALISM AT THE SITE.
YEAH, WELL...I COULDN'T REALLY TELL YA. AND TO BE HONEST, I GOT BIGGER CATFISH TO FRY THAN A BUNCH OF *PROTESTORS*.
WHAT ABOUT THE MISSING SECURITY GUARD? I'D THINK THAT WOULD BE A BIG ENOUGH *CATFISH*.
ACTUALLY, THAT'S WHAT I'M WORKING ON. I GOT A BAD FEELING THAT IT'S ANOTHER *GATOR ATTACK*.
ANOTHER? I THOUGHT ALLIGATOR ATTACKS WERE PRETTY RARE.
THEY ARE. WE CAN GO FOR YEARS WITH NOTHING AND THEN, BAM, WE GET A BAD ONE. OR IN THIS CASE, A *SERIES* OF THEM. WE'VE HAD *SEVERAL* IN THE LAST FEW WEEKS.

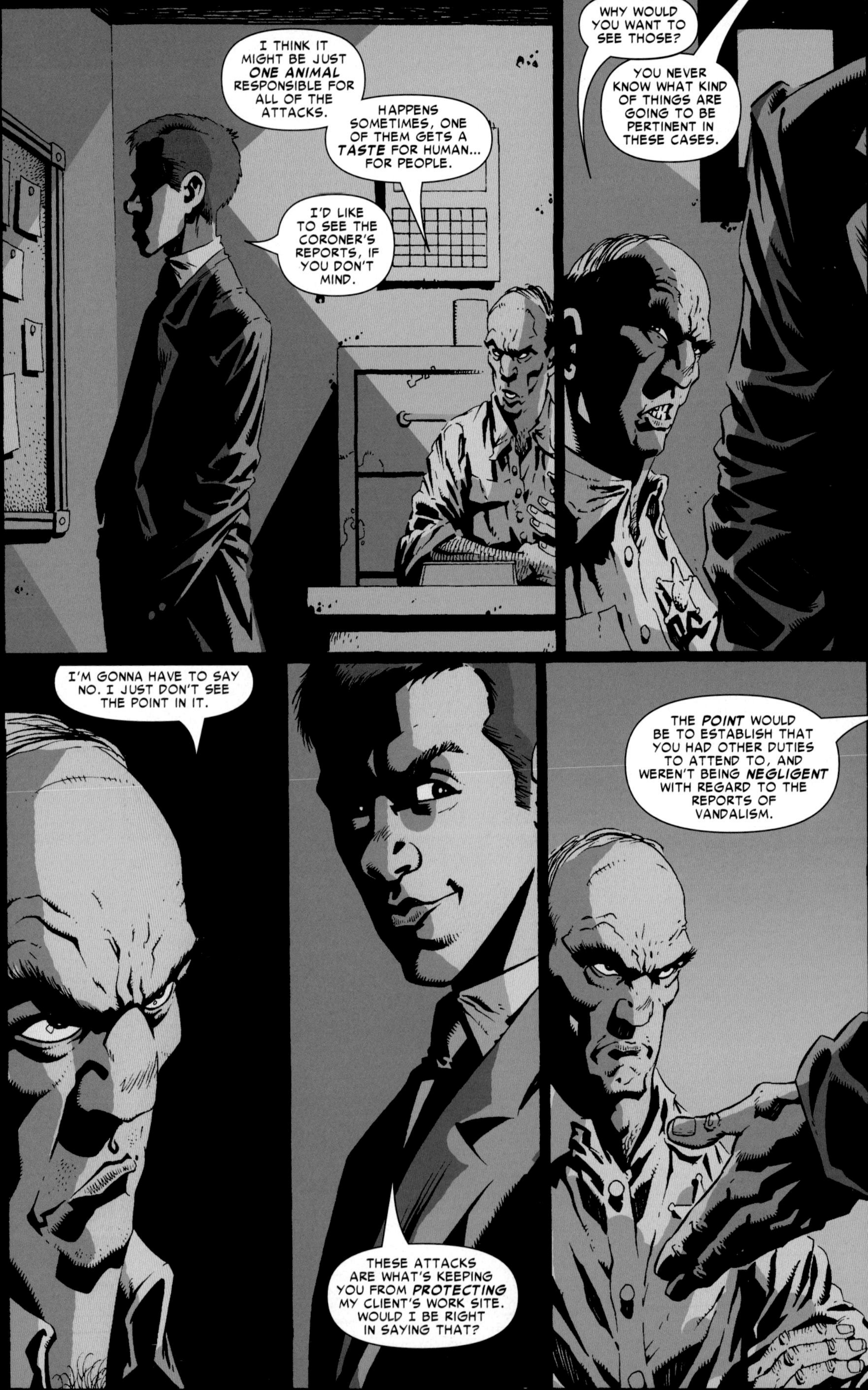
I THINK IT MIGHT BE JUST ONE ANIMAL RESPONSIBLE FOR ALL OF THE ATTACKS.
HAPPENS SOMETIMES, ONE OF THEM GETS A TASTE FOR HUMAN... FOR PEOPLE.
I'D LIKE TO SEE THE CORONER'S REPORTS, IF YOU DON'T MIND.
WHY WOULD YOU WANT TO SEE THOSE?
YOU NEVER KNOW WHAT KIND OF THINGS ARE GOING TO BE PERTINENT IN THESE CASES.
I'M GONNA HAVE TO SAY NO. I JUST DON'T SEE THE POINT IN IT.
THESE ATTACKS ARE WHAT'S KEEPING YOU FROM PROTECTING MY CLIENT'S WORK SITE. WOULD I BE RIGHT IN SAYING THAT?
THE POINT WOULD BE TO ESTABLISH THAT YOU HAD OTHER DUTIES TO ATTEND TO, AND WEREN'T BEING NEGLIGENT WITH REGARD TO THE REPORTS OF VANDALISM.

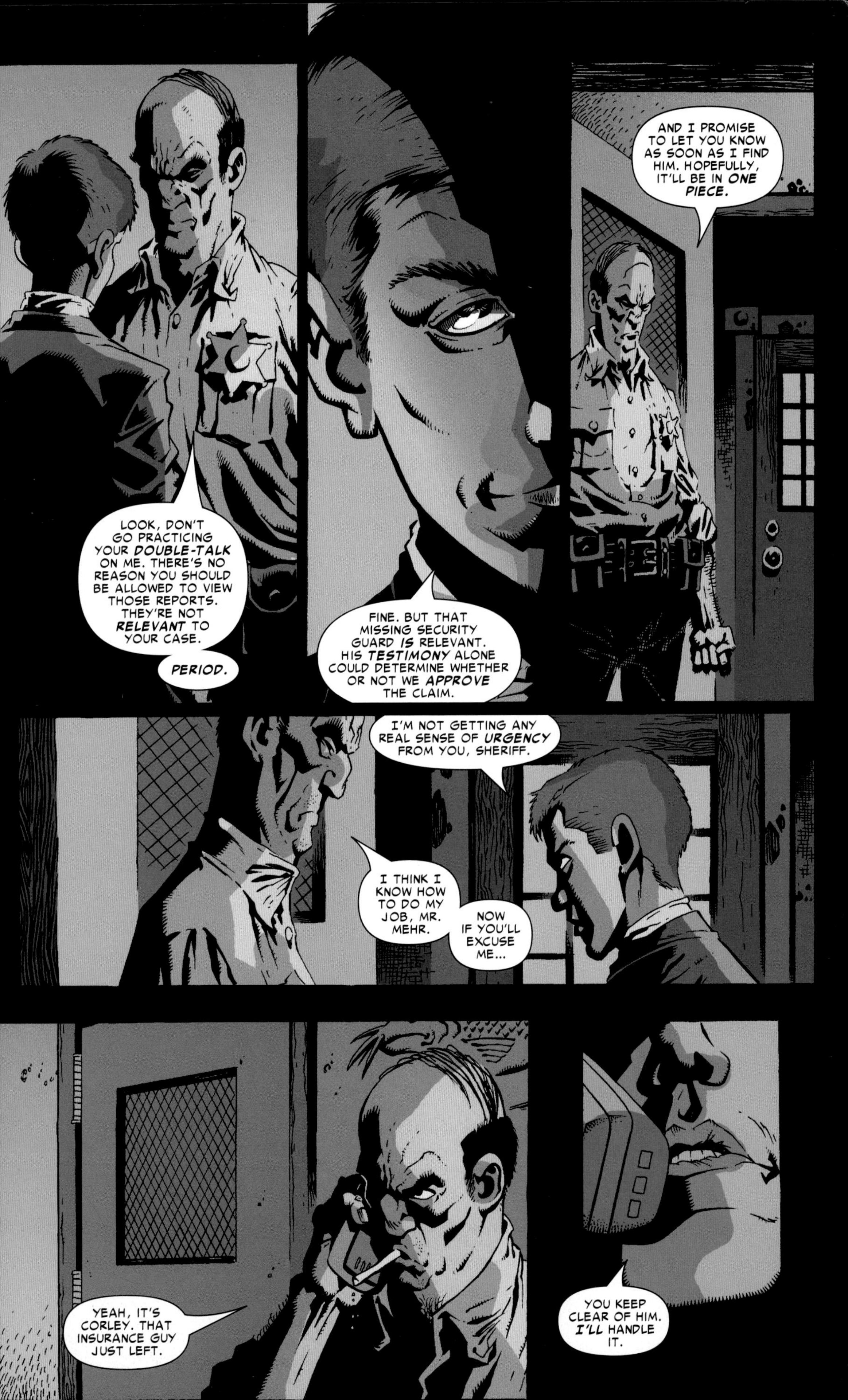
LOOK, DON'T GO PRACTICING YOUR DOUBLE-TALK ON ME. THERE'S NO REASON YOU SHOULD BE ALLOWED TO VIEW THOSE REPORTS. THEY'RE NOT RELEVANT TO YOUR CASE.
PERIOD.
FINE. BUT THAT MISSING SECURITY GUARD IS RELEVANT. HIS TESTIMONY ALONE COULD DETERMINE WHETHER OR NOT WE APPROVE THE CLAIM.
AND I PROMISE TO LET YOU KNOW AS SOON AS I FIND HIM. HOPEFULLY, IT'LL BE IN ONE PIECE.
I'M NOT GETTING ANY REAL SENSE OF URGENCY FROM YOU, SHERIFF.
I THINK I KNOW HOW TO DO MY JOB, MR. MEHR.
NOW IF YOU'LL EXCUSE ME...
YEAH, IT'S CORLEY. THAT INSURANCE GUY JUST LEFT.
YOU KEEP CLEAR OF HIM. I'LL HANDLE IT.

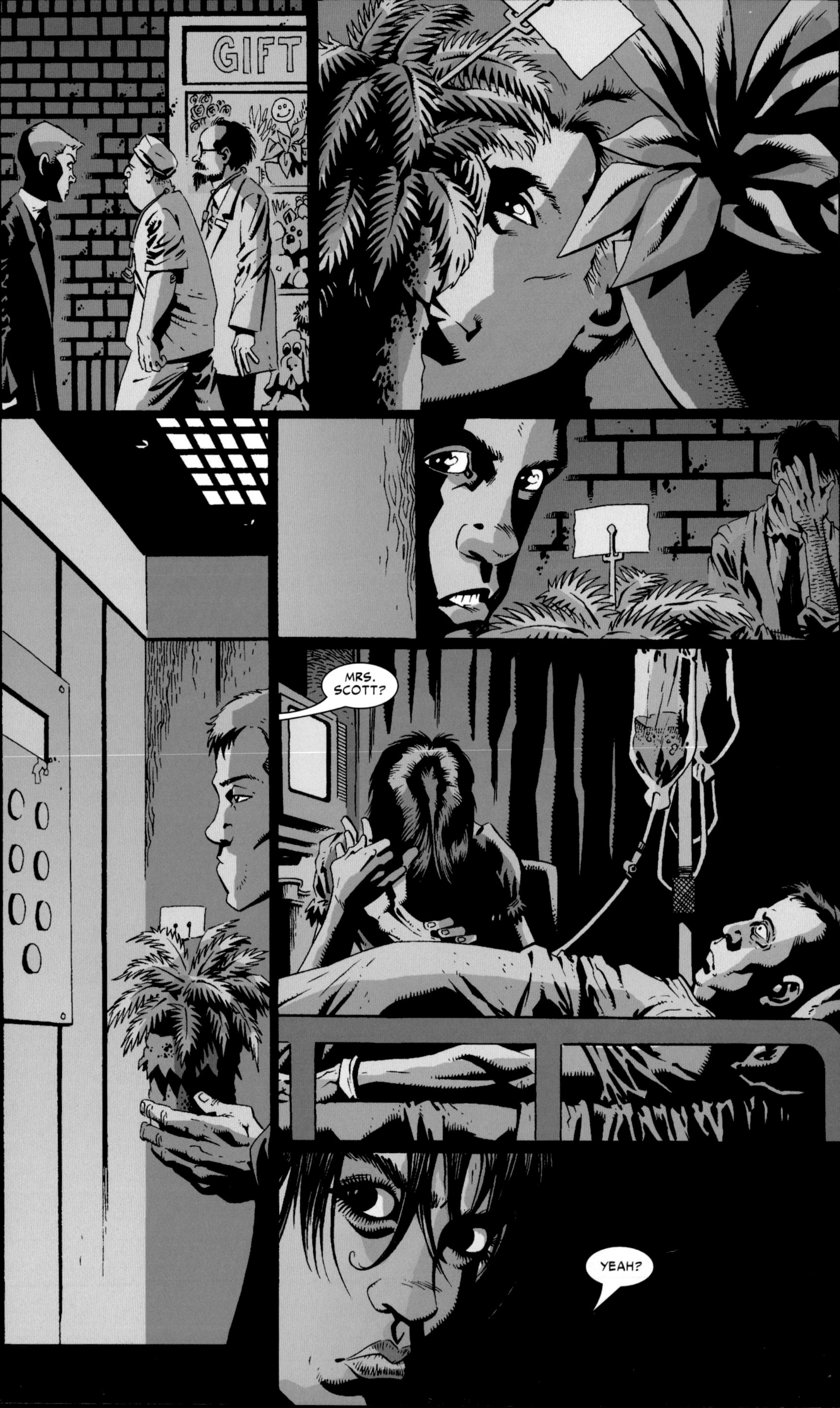
GIFT
MRS. SCOTT?
YEAH?

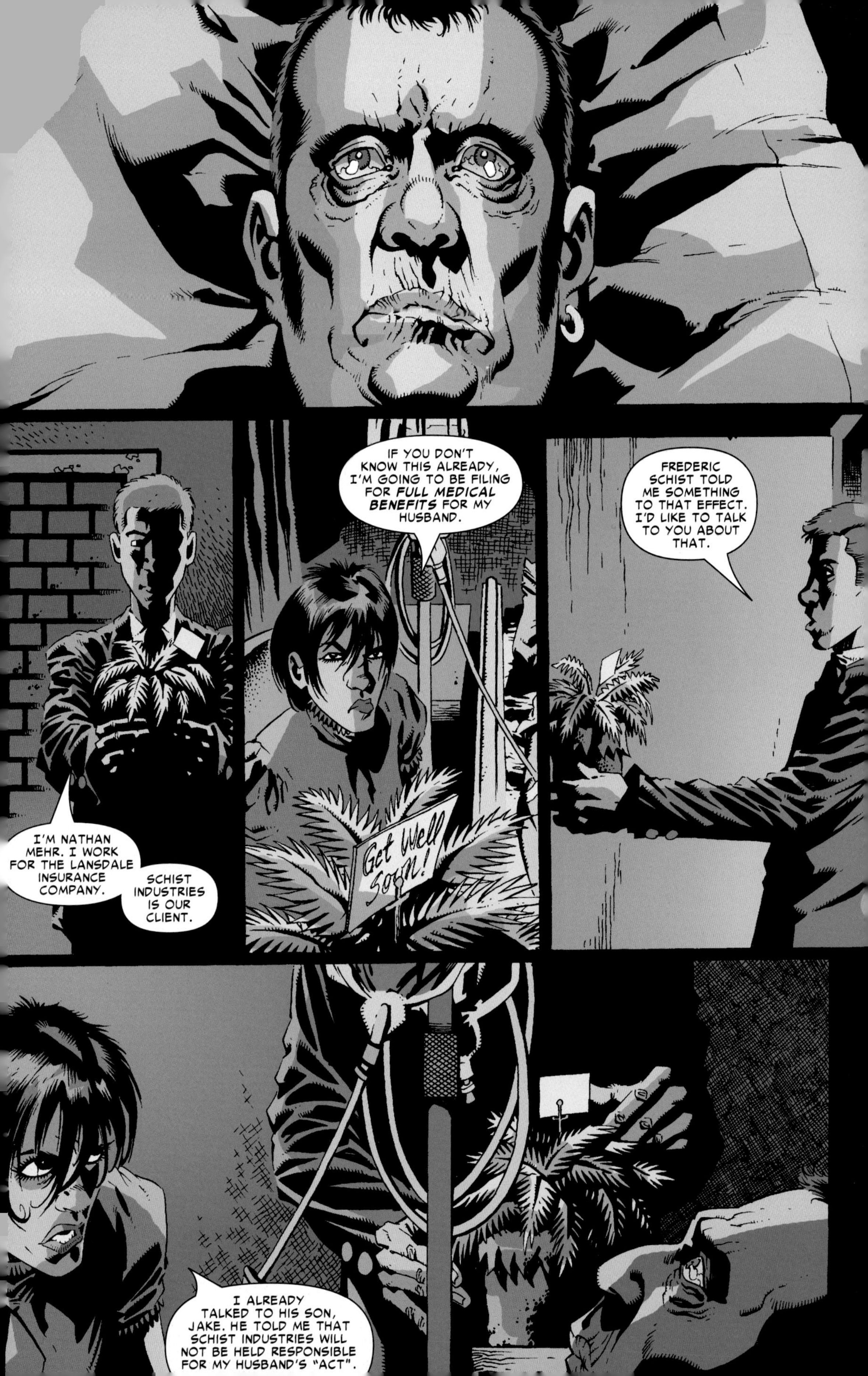
I'M NATHAN MEHR. I WORK FOR THE LANSDALE INSURANCE COMPANY.
SCHIST INDUSTRIES IS OUR CLIENT.
IF YOU DON'T KNOW THIS ALREADY, I'M GOING TO BE FILING FOR FULL MEDICAL BENEFITS FOR MY HUSBAND.
Get Well Soon!
FREDERIC SCHIST TOLD ME SOMETHING TO THAT EFFECT. I'D LIKE TO TALK TO YOU ABOUT THAT.
I ALREADY TALKED TO HIS SON, JAKE. HE TOLD ME THAT SCHIST INDUSTRIES WILL NOT BE HELD RESPONSIBLE FOR MY HUSBAND'S "ACT".

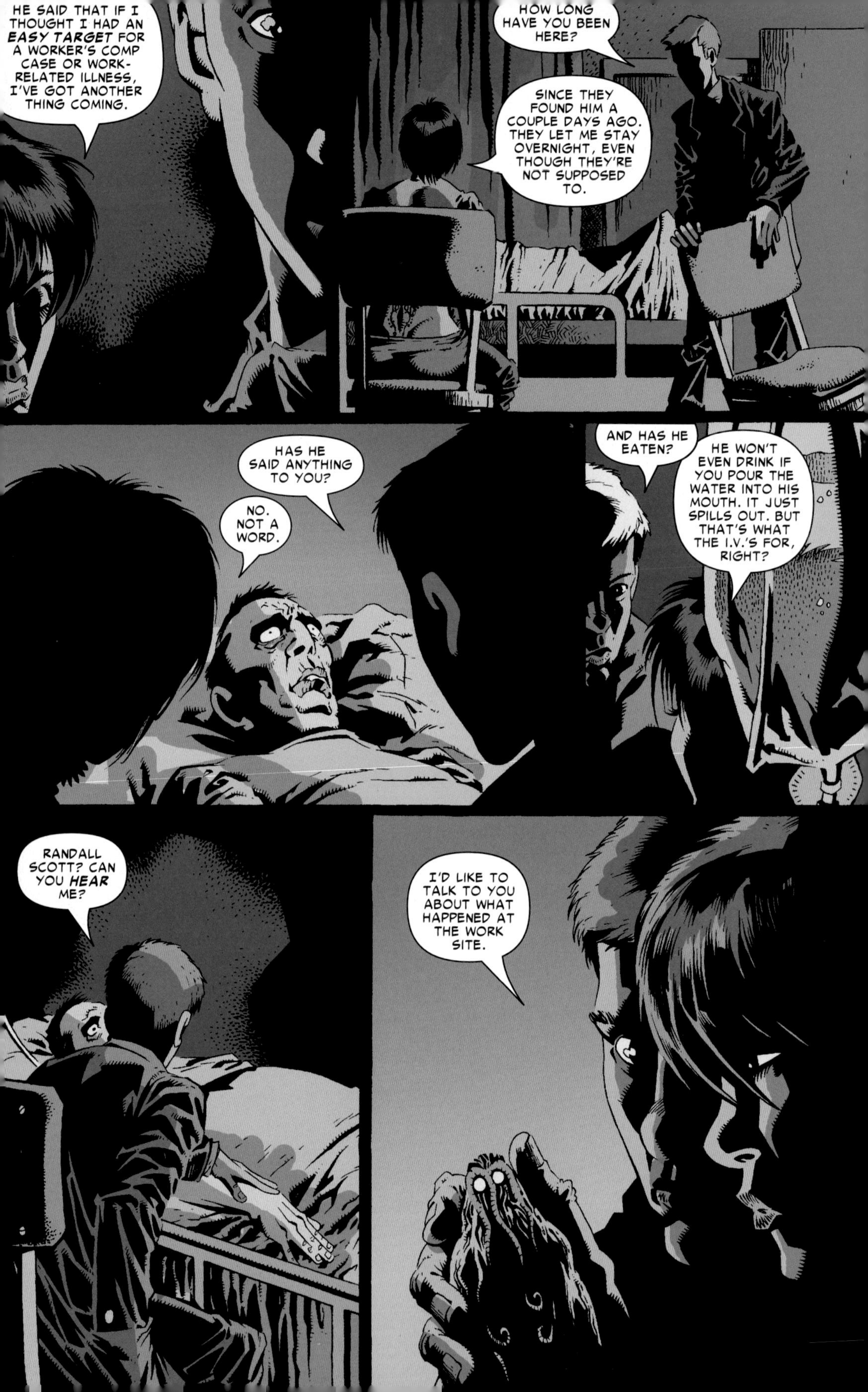
HE SAID THAT IF I THOUGHT I HAD AN *EASY TARGET* FOR A WORKER'S COMP CASE OR WORK-RELATED ILLNESS, I'VE GOT ANOTHER THING COMING.
HOW LONG HAVE YOU BEEN HERE?
SINCE THEY FOUND HIM A COUPLE DAYS AGO. THEY LET ME STAY OVERNIGHT, EVEN THOUGH THEY'RE NOT SUPPOSED TO.
HAS HE SAID ANYTHING TO YOU?
NO. NOT A WORD.
AND HAS HE EATEN?
HE WON'T EVEN DRINK IF YOU POUR THE WATER INTO HIS MOUTH. IT JUST SPILLS OUT. BUT THAT'S WHAT THE I.V.'S FOR, RIGHT?
RANDALL SCOTT? CAN YOU *HEAR* ME?
I'D LIKE TO TALK TO YOU ABOUT WHAT HAPPENED AT THE WORK SITE.

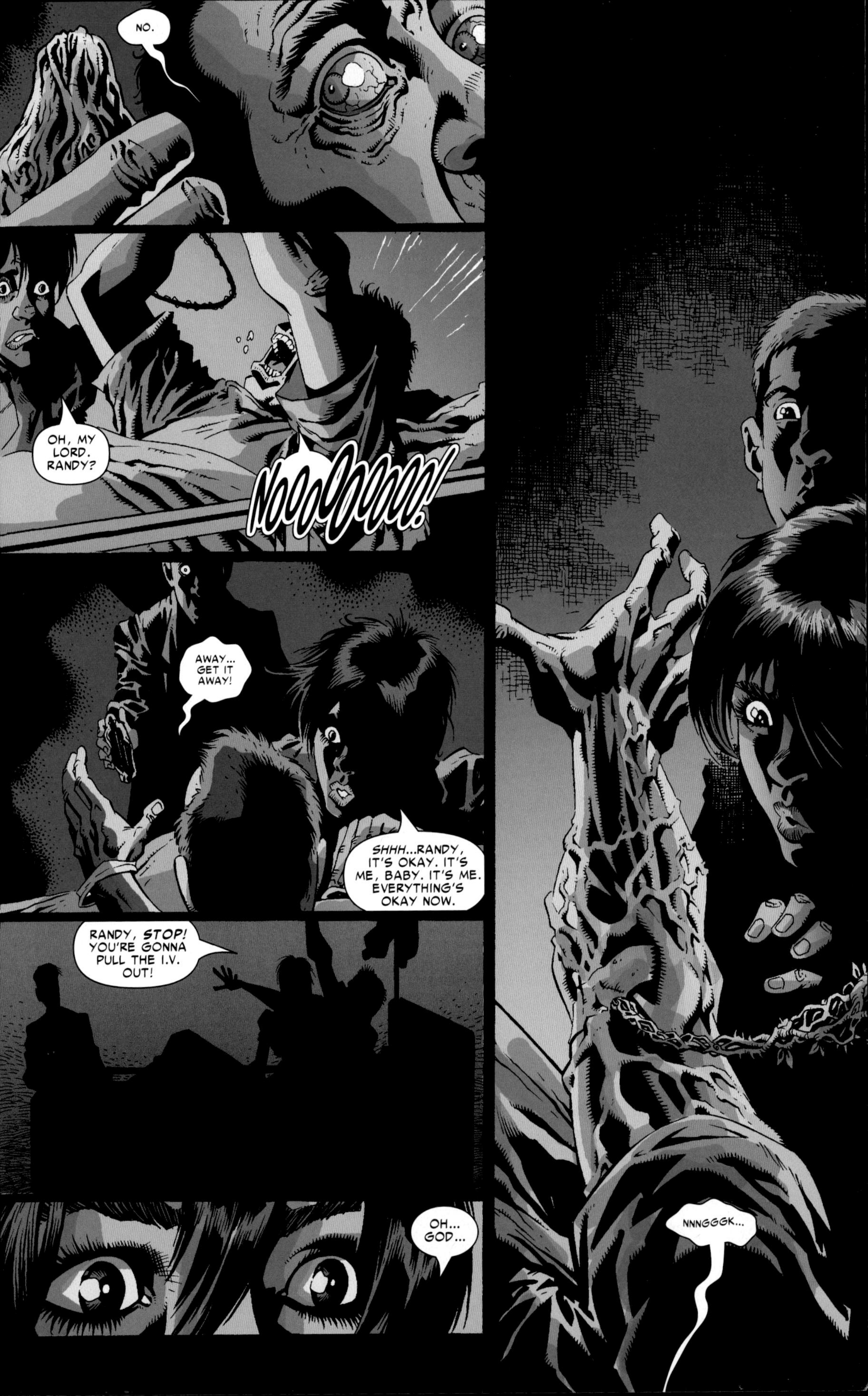
NO.
OH, MY LORD. RANDY?
NOOOOOOOO!
AWAY... GET IT AWAY!
SHHH...RANDY, IT'S OKAY. IT'S ME, BABY. IT'S ME. EVERYTHING'S OKAY NOW.
RANDY, STOP! YOU'RE GONNA PULL THE I.V. OUT!
OH... GOD...
NNNGGGK...

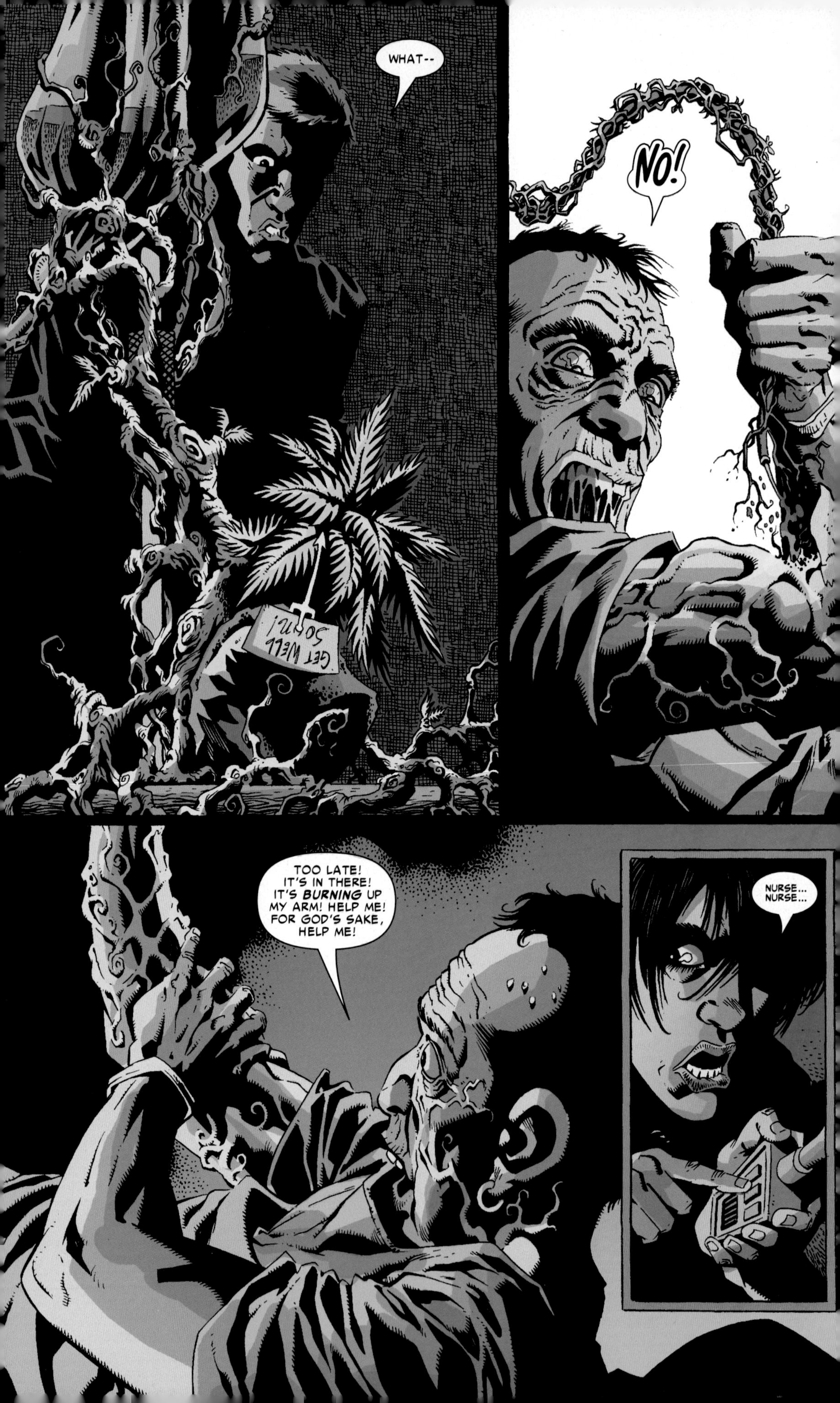
WHAT--
NO!
TOO LATE! IT'S IN THERE! IT'S BURNING UP MY ARM! HELP ME! FOR GOD'S SAKE, HELP ME!
NURSE... NURSE...

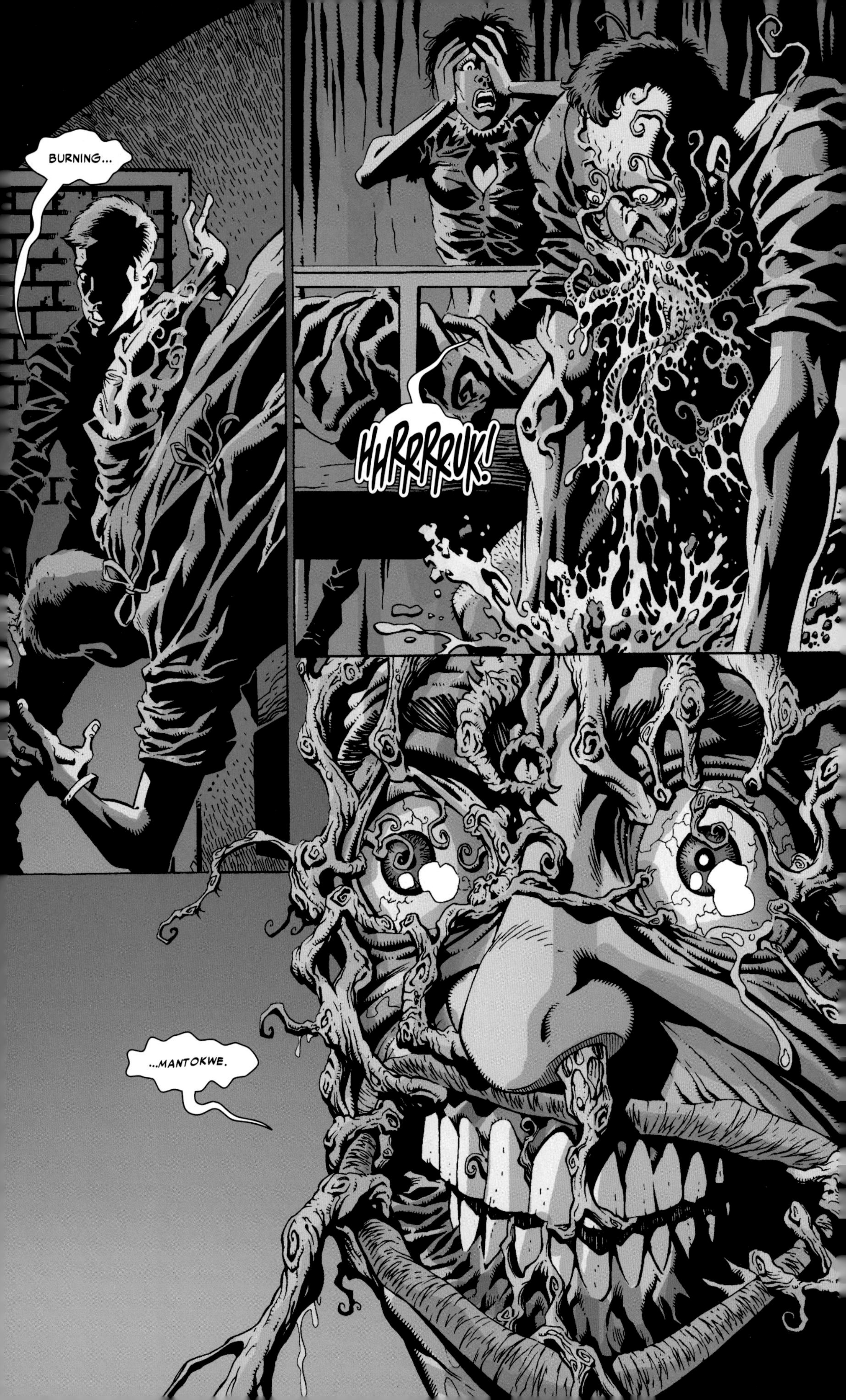
BURNING...
HHRRRRUK!
...MANTOKWE.

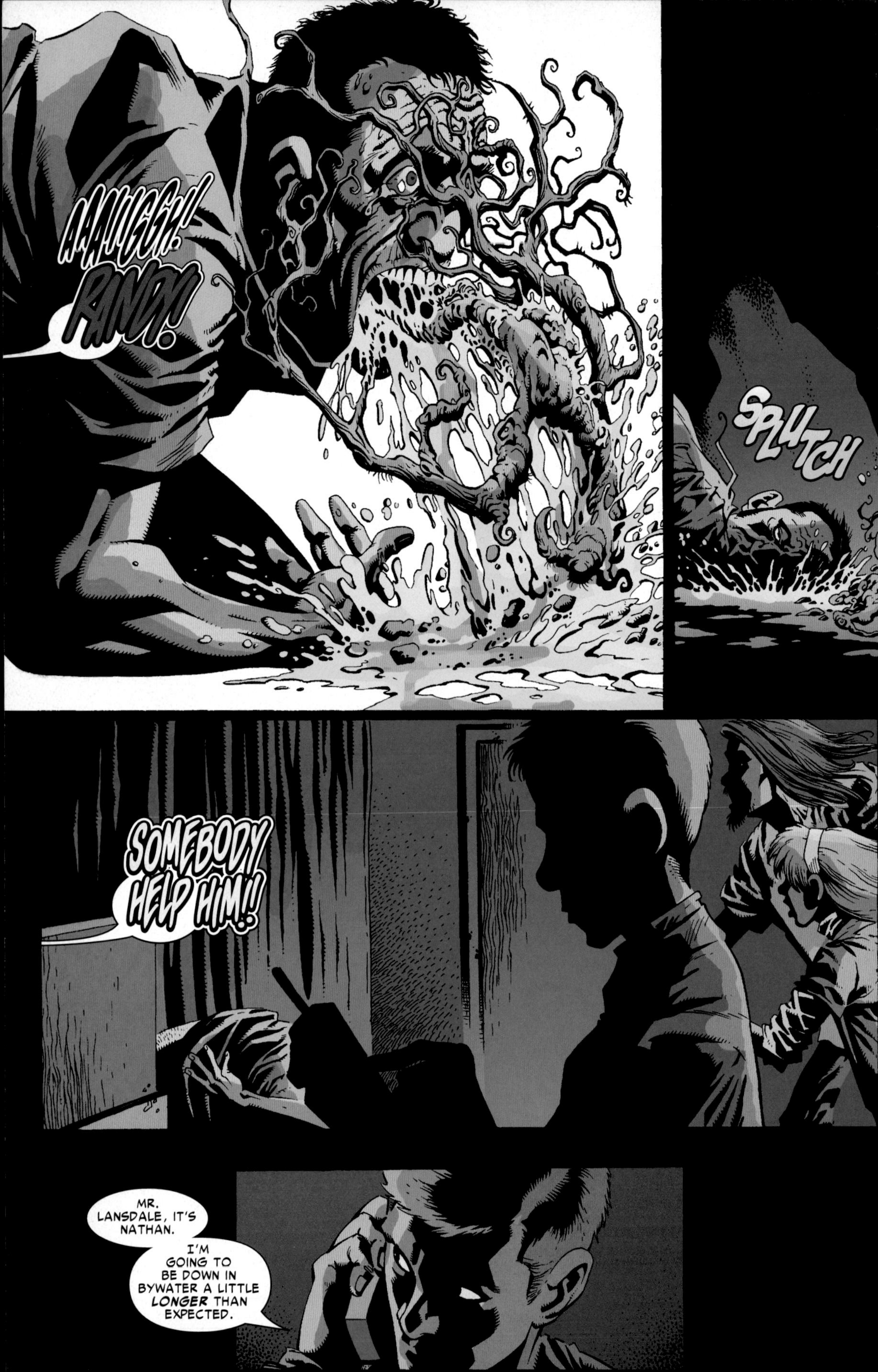
AAAUUGGH! RANDY!
SPLUTCH
SOMEBODY HELP HIM!!
MR. LANSDALE, IT'S NATHAN.
I'M GOING TO BE DOWN IN BYWATER A LITTLE LONGER THAN EXPECTED.

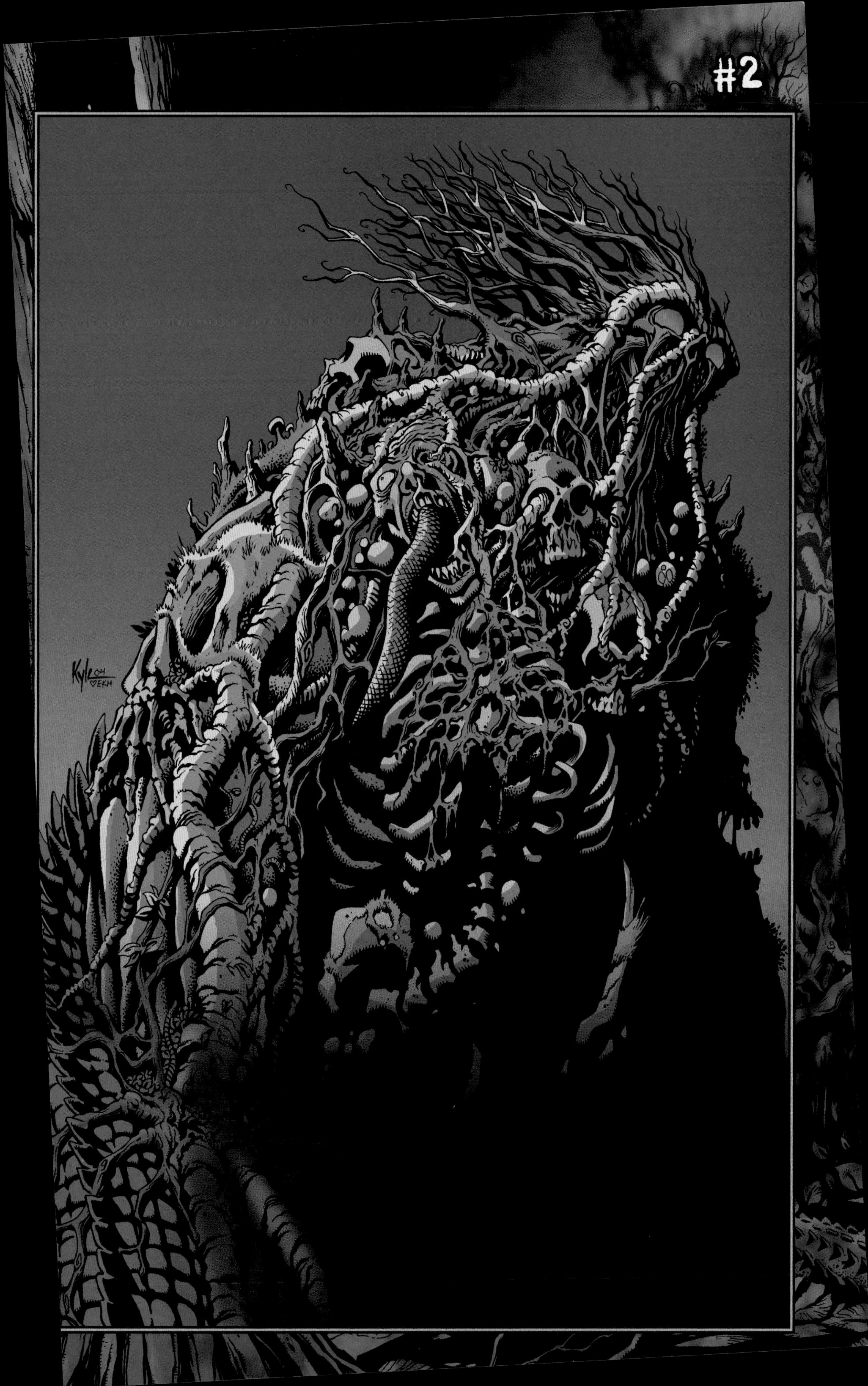
#2

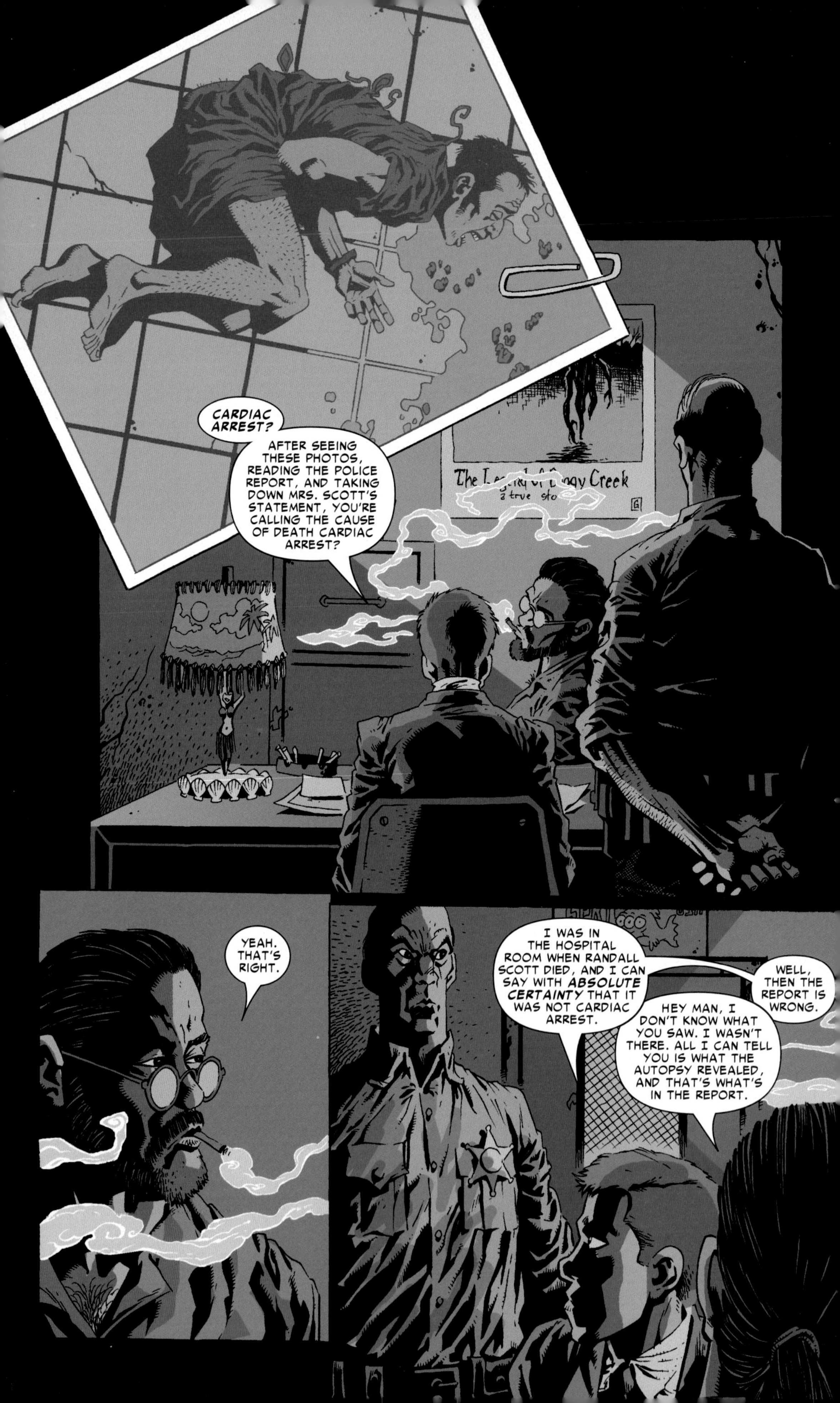
CARDIAC ARREST?
AFTER SEEING THESE PHOTOS, READING THE POLICE REPORT, AND TAKING DOWN MRS. SCOTT'S STATEMENT, YOU'RE CALLING THE CAUSE OF DEATH CARDIAC ARREST?
YEAH. THAT'S RIGHT.
I WAS IN THE HOSPITAL ROOM WHEN RANDALL SCOTT DIED, AND I CAN SAY WITH *ABSOLUTE CERTAINTY* THAT IT WAS NOT CARDIAC ARREST.
HEY MAN, I DON'T KNOW WHAT YOU SAW. I WASN'T THERE. ALL I CAN TELL YOU IS WHAT THE AUTOPSY REVEALED, AND THAT'S WHAT'S IN THE REPORT.
WELL, THEN THE REPORT IS WRONG.

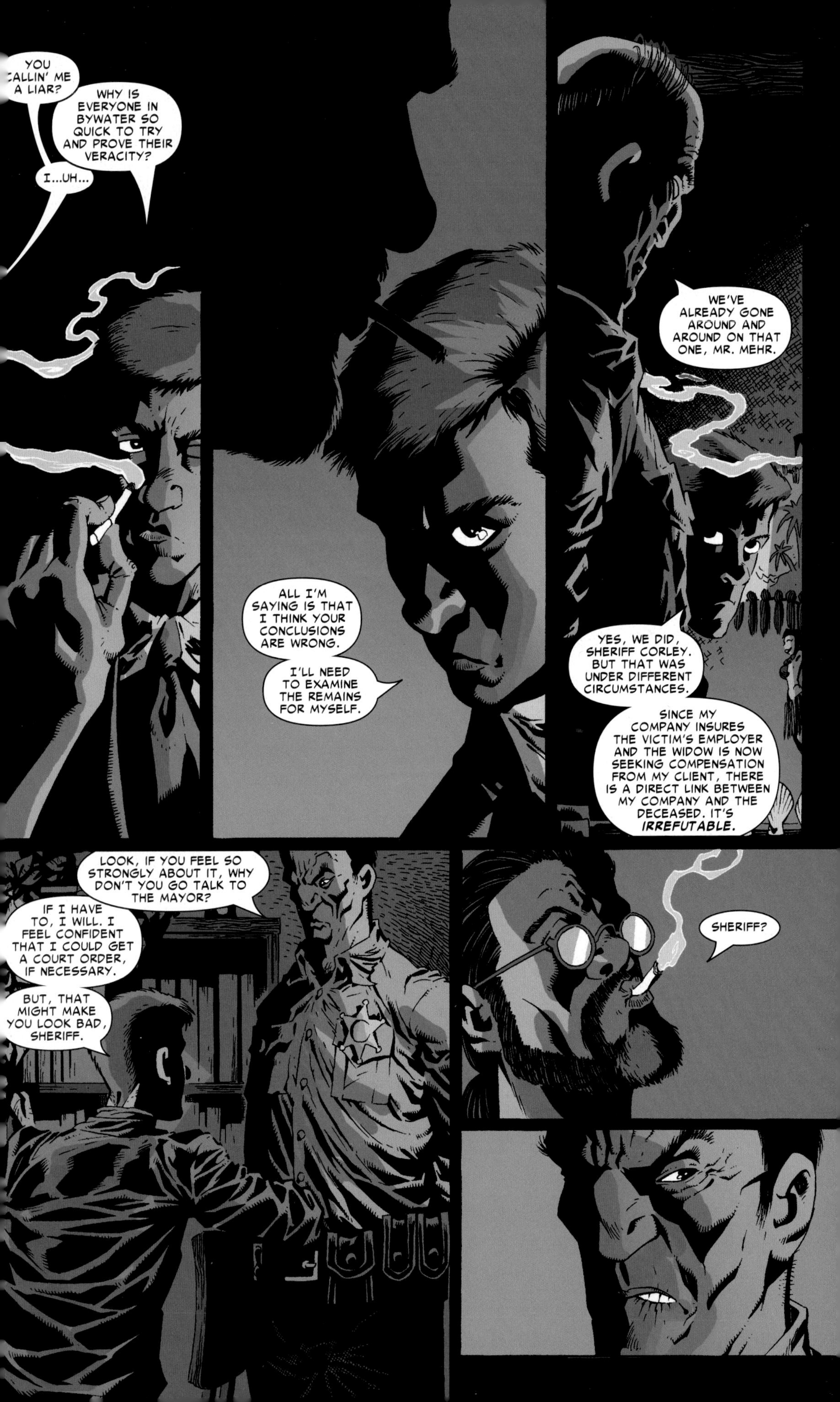
YOU CALLIN' ME A LIAR?
WHY IS EVERYONE IN BYWATER SO QUICK TO TRY AND PROVE THEIR VERACITY?
I...UH...
ALL I'M SAYING IS THAT I THINK YOUR CONCLUSIONS ARE WRONG.
I'LL NEED TO EXAMINE THE REMAINS FOR MYSELF.
WE'VE ALREADY GONE AROUND AND AROUND ON THAT ONE, MR. MEHR.
YES, WE DID, SHERIFF CORLEY. BUT THAT WAS UNDER DIFFERENT CIRCUMSTANCES.
SINCE MY COMPANY INSURES THE VICTIM'S EMPLOYER AND THE WIDOW IS NOW SEEKING COMPENSATION FROM MY CLIENT, THERE IS A DIRECT LINK BETWEEN MY COMPANY AND THE DECEASED. IT'S IRREFUTABLE.
LOOK, IF YOU FEEL SO STRONGLY ABOUT IT, WHY DON'T YOU GO TALK TO THE MAYOR?
IF I HAVE TO, I WILL. I FEEL CONFIDENT THAT I COULD GET A COURT ORDER, IF NECESSARY.
BUT, THAT MIGHT MAKE YOU LOOK BAD, SHERIFF.
SHERIFF?

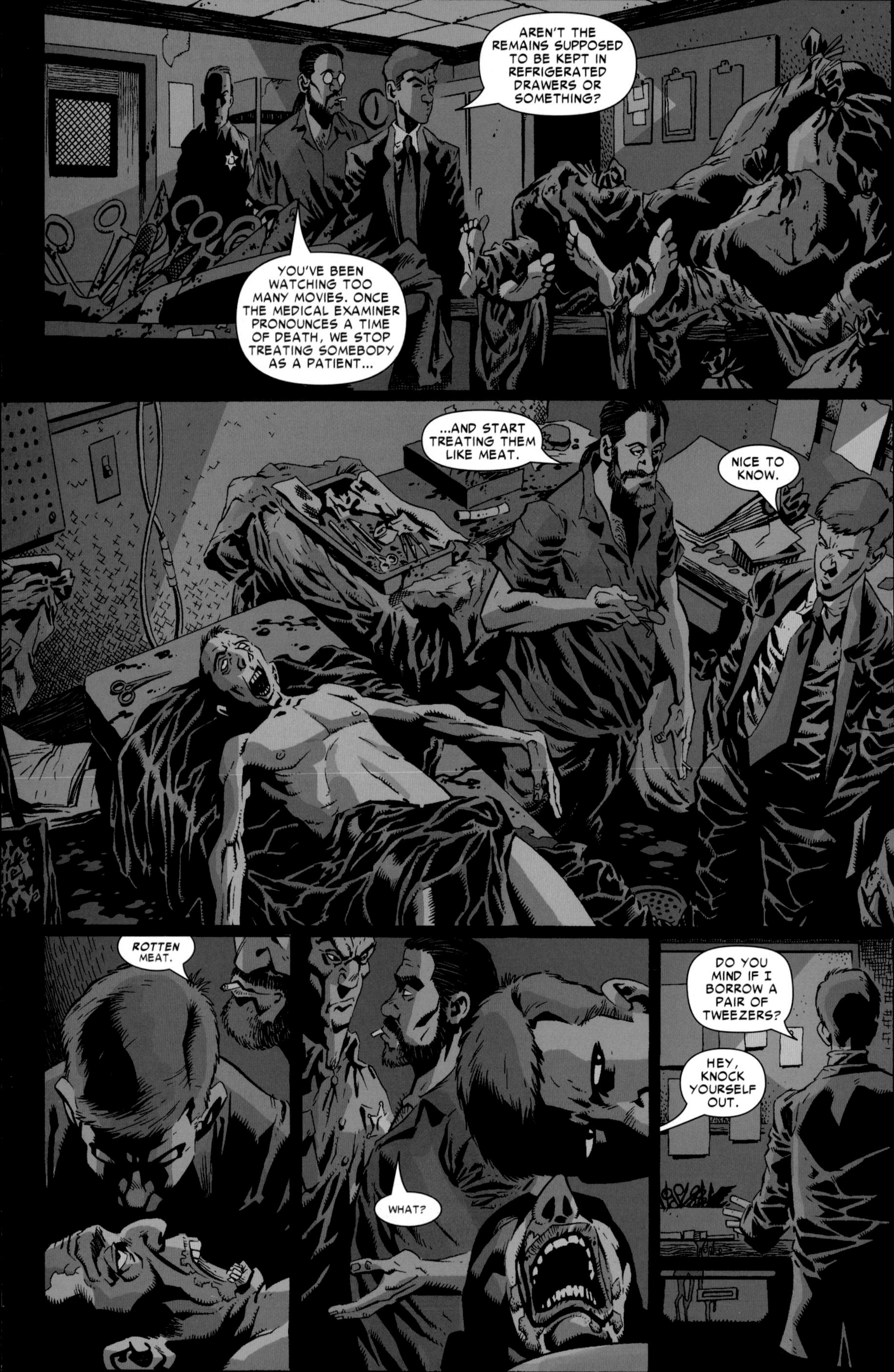
AREN'T THE REMAINS SUPPOSED TO BE KEPT IN REFRIGERATED DRAWERS OR SOMETHING?
YOU'VE BEEN WATCHING TOO MANY MOVIES. ONCE THE MEDICAL EXAMINER PRONOUNCES A TIME OF DEATH, WE STOP TREATING SOMEBODY AS A PATIENT...
...AND START TREATING THEM LIKE MEAT.
NICE TO KNOW.
ROTTEN MEAT.
WHAT?
DO YOU MIND IF I BORROW A PAIR OF TWEEZERS?
HEY, KNOCK YOURSELF OUT.

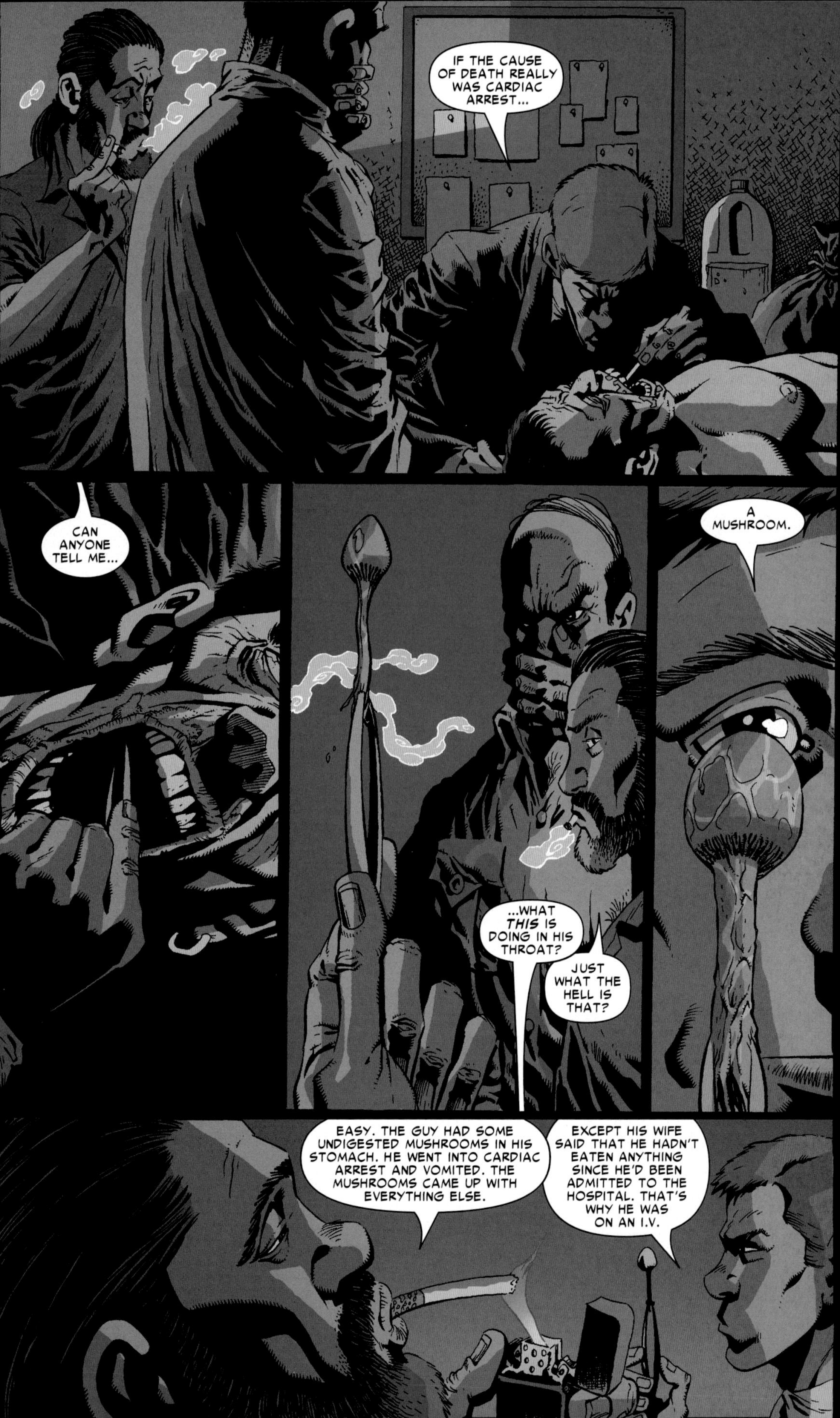

IF THE CAUSE OF DEATH REALLY WAS CARDIAC ARREST...
CAN ANYONE TELL ME...
...WHAT *THIS* IS DOING IN HIS THROAT?
JUST WHAT THE HELL IS THAT?
A MUSHROOM.
EASY. THE GUY HAD SOME UNDIGESTED MUSHROOMS IN HIS STOMACH. HE WENT INTO CARDIAC ARREST AND VOMITED. THE MUSHROOMS CAME UP WITH EVERYTHING ELSE.
EXCEPT HIS WIFE SAID THAT HE HADN'T EATEN ANYTHING SINCE HE'D BEEN ADMITTED TO THE HOSPITAL. THAT'S WHY HE WAS ON AN I.V.

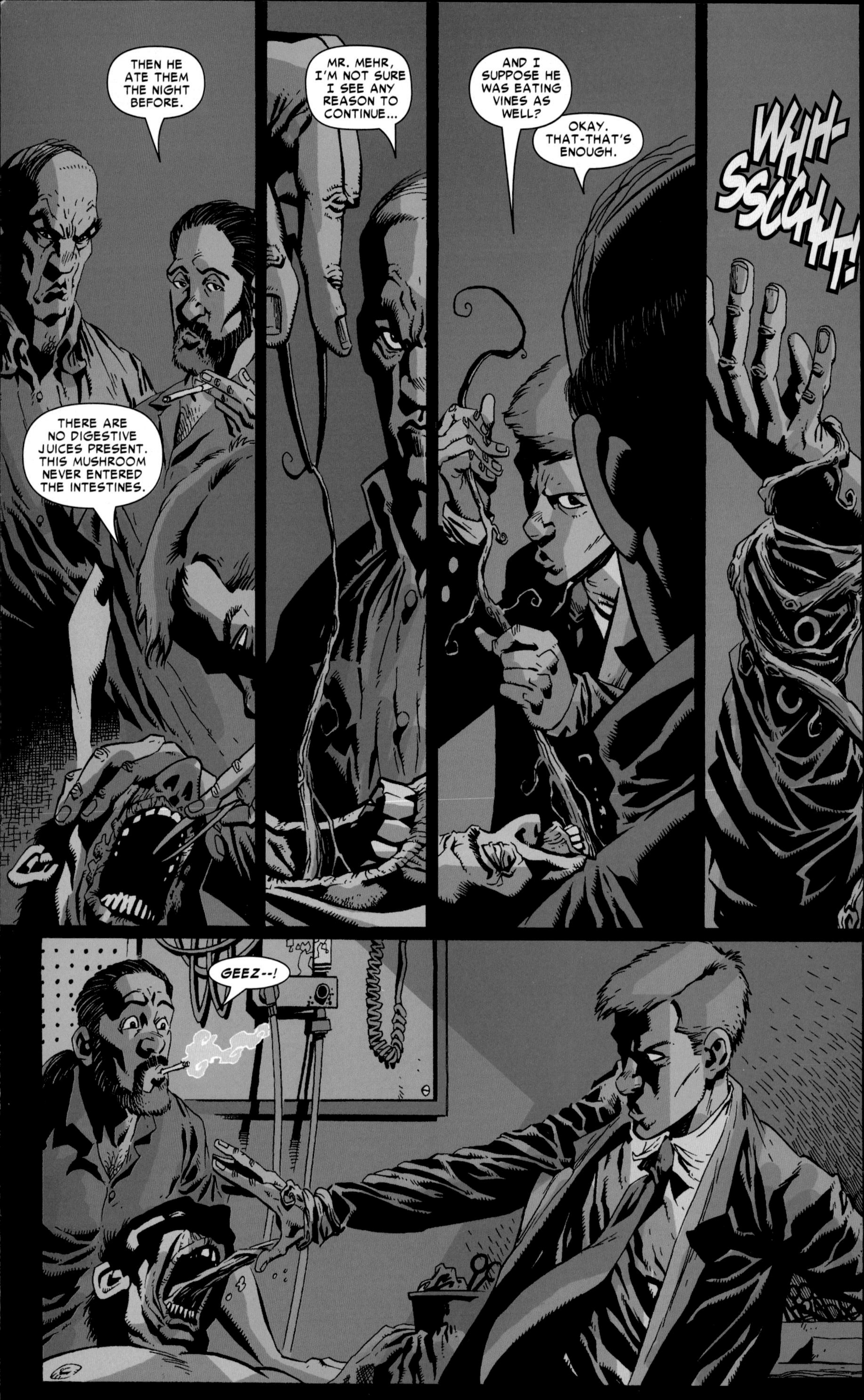
THEN HE ATE THEM THE NIGHT BEFORE.
THERE ARE NO DIGESTIVE JUICES PRESENT. THIS MUSHROOM NEVER ENTERED THE INTESTINES.
MR. MEHR, I'M NOT SURE I SEE ANY REASON TO CONTINUE...
AND I SUPPOSE HE WAS EATING VINES AS WELL?
OKAY. THAT-THAT'S ENOUGH.
WHH-SSCHHT!
GEEZ--!

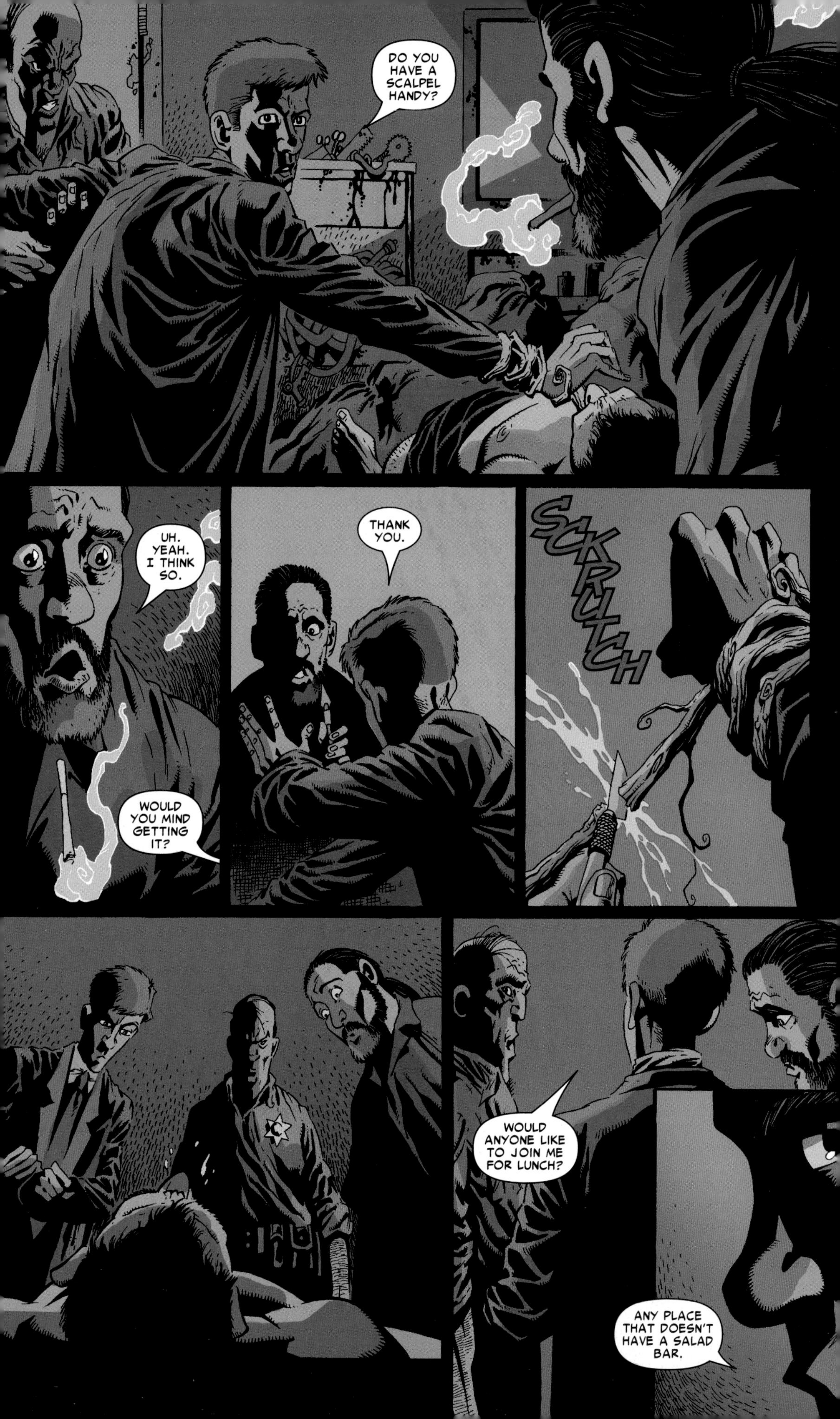
DO YOU HAVE A SCALPEL HANDY?
UH. YEAH. I THINK SO.
WOULD YOU MIND GETTING IT?
THANK YOU.
SCKRUTCH
WOULD ANYONE LIKE TO JOIN ME FOR LUNCH?
ANY PLACE THAT DOESN'T HAVE A SALAD BAR.

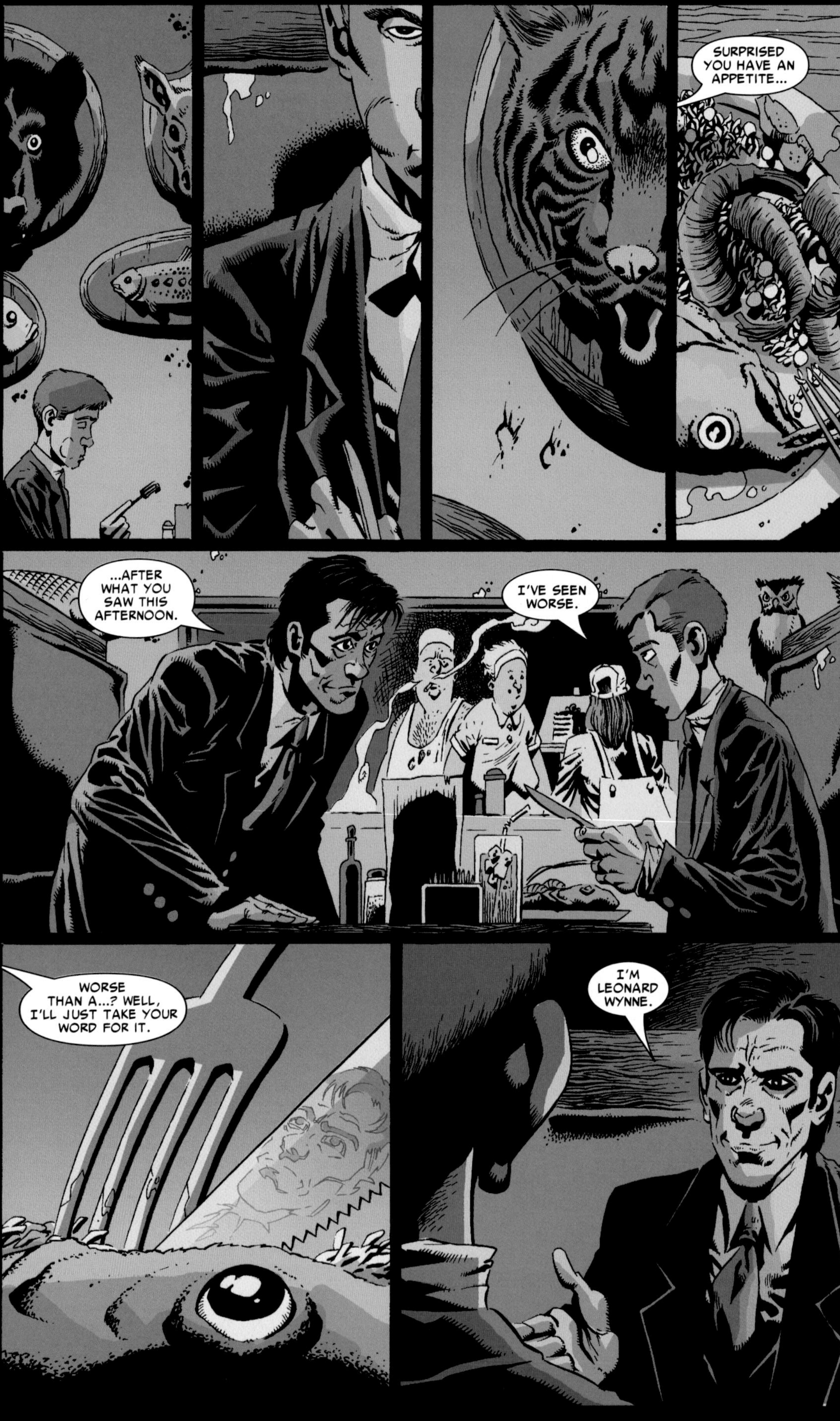
SURPRISED YOU HAVE AN APPETITE...
...AFTER WHAT YOU SAW THIS AFTERNOON.
I'VE SEEN WORSE.
WORSE THAN A...? WELL, I'LL JUST TAKE YOUR WORD FOR IT.
I'M LEONARD WYNNE.

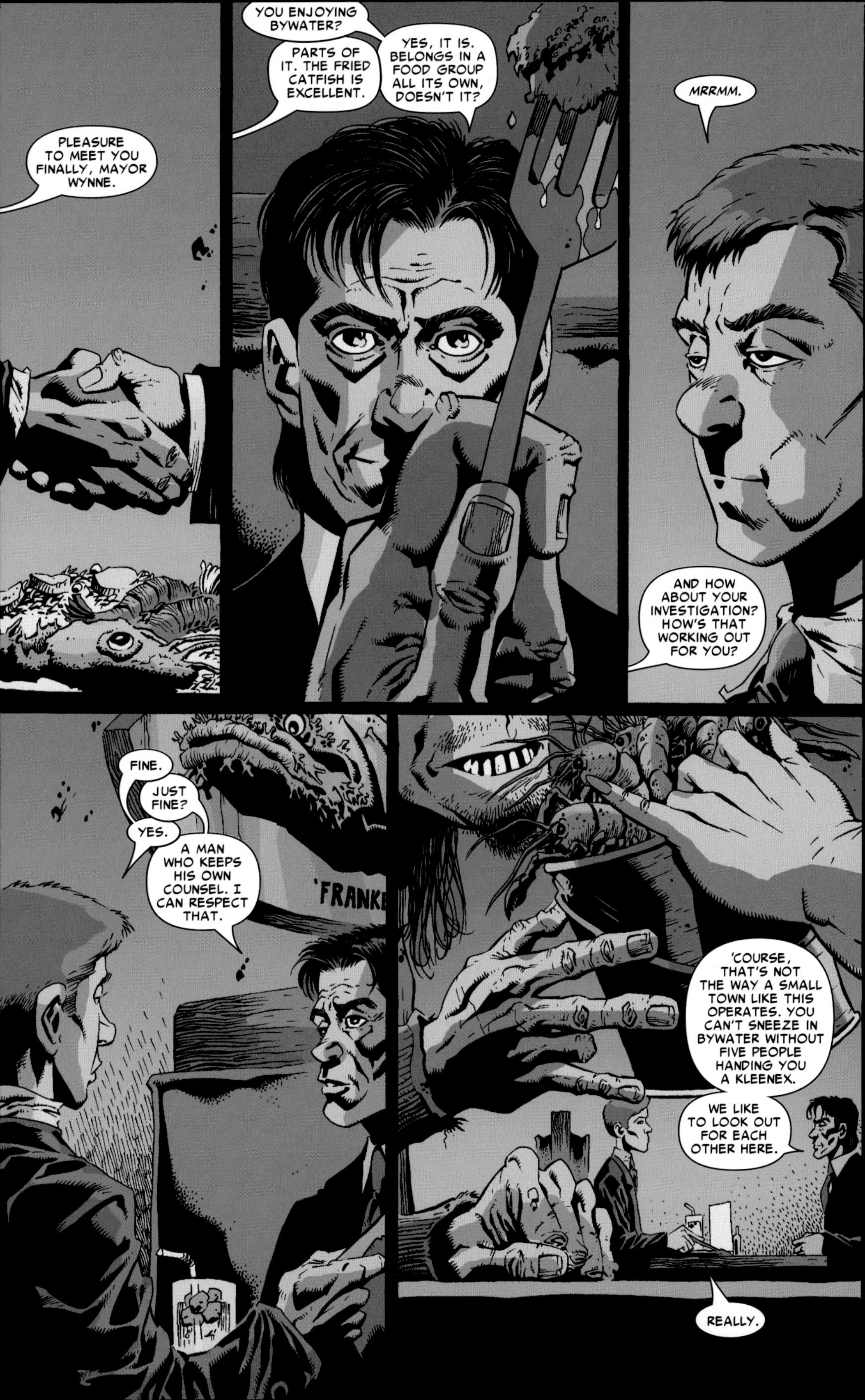
PLEASURE TO MEET YOU FINALLY, MAYOR WYNNE.
YOU ENJOYING BYWATER?
PARTS OF IT. THE FRIED CATFISH IS EXCELLENT.
YES, IT IS. BELONGS IN A FOOD GROUP ALL ITS OWN, DOESN'T IT?
MRRMM.
AND HOW ABOUT YOUR INVESTIGATION? HOW'S THAT WORKING OUT FOR YOU?
FINE.
JUST FINE?
YES.
A MAN WHO KEEPS HIS OWN COUNSEL. I CAN RESPECT THAT.
'FRANKE
'COURSE, THAT'S NOT THE WAY A SMALL TOWN LIKE THIS OPERATES. YOU CAN'T SNEEZE IN BYWATER WITHOUT FIVE PEOPLE HANDING YOU A KLEENEX.
WE LIKE TO LOOK OUT FOR EACH OTHER HERE.
REALLY.

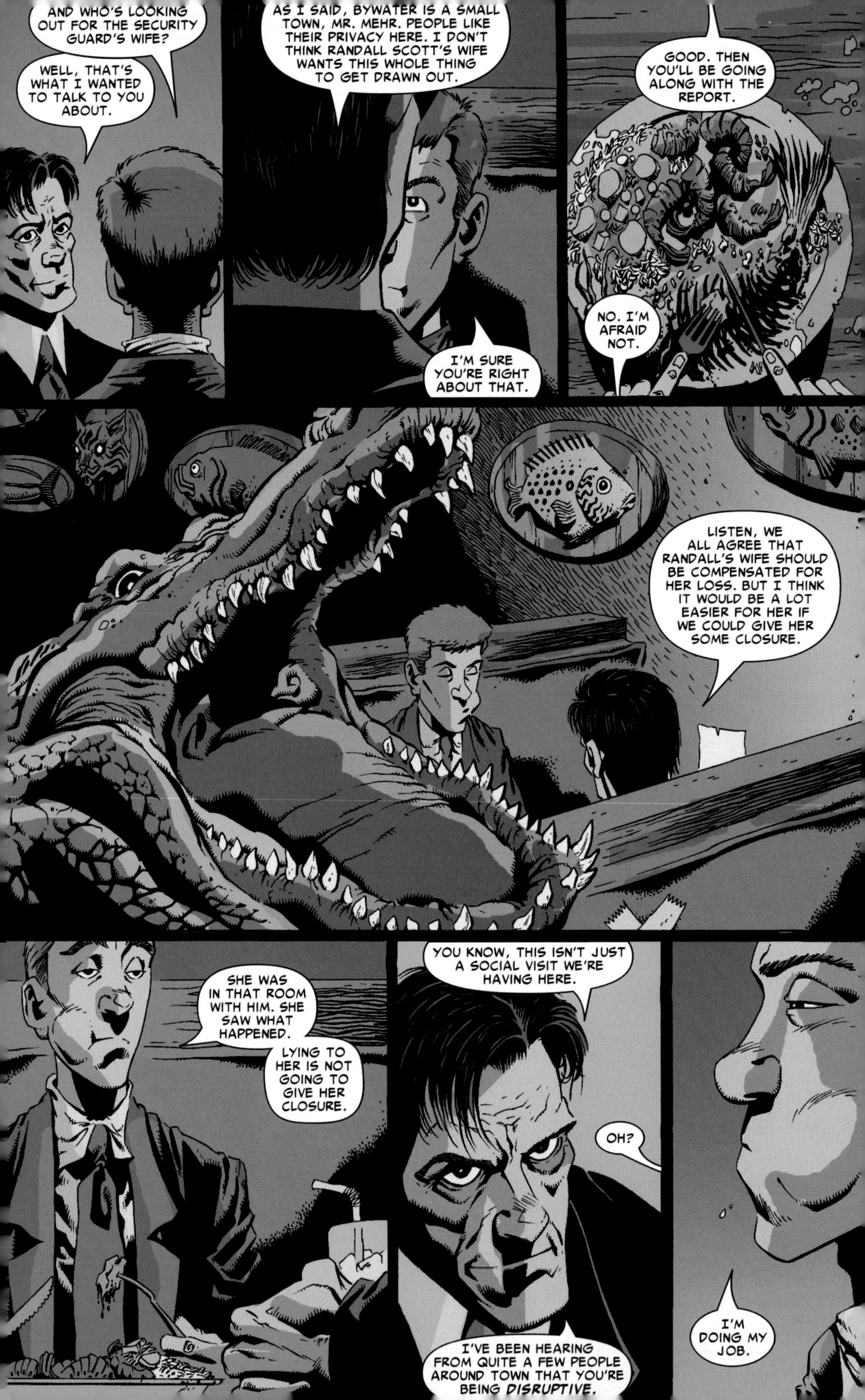
AND WHO'S LOOKING OUT FOR THE SECURITY GUARD'S WIFE?
WELL, THAT'S WHAT I WANTED TO TALK TO YOU ABOUT.
AS I SAID, BYWATER IS A SMALL TOWN, MR. MEHR. PEOPLE LIKE THEIR PRIVACY HERE. I DON'T THINK RANDALL SCOTT'S WIFE WANTS THIS WHOLE THING TO GET DRAWN OUT.
I'M SURE YOU'RE RIGHT ABOUT THAT.
GOOD. THEN YOU'LL BE GOING ALONG WITH THE REPORT.
NO. I'M AFRAID NOT.
LISTEN, WE ALL AGREE THAT RANDALL'S WIFE SHOULD BE COMPENSATED FOR HER LOSS. BUT I THINK IT WOULD BE A LOT EASIER FOR HER IF WE COULD GIVE HER SOME CLOSURE.
SHE WAS IN THAT ROOM WITH HIM. SHE SAW WHAT HAPPENED.
LYING TO HER IS NOT GOING TO GIVE HER CLOSURE.
YOU KNOW, THIS ISN'T JUST A SOCIAL VISIT WE'RE HAVING HERE.
OH?
I'VE BEEN HEARING FROM QUITE A FEW PEOPLE AROUND TOWN THAT YOU'RE BEING *DISRUPTIVE*.
I'M DOING MY JOB.

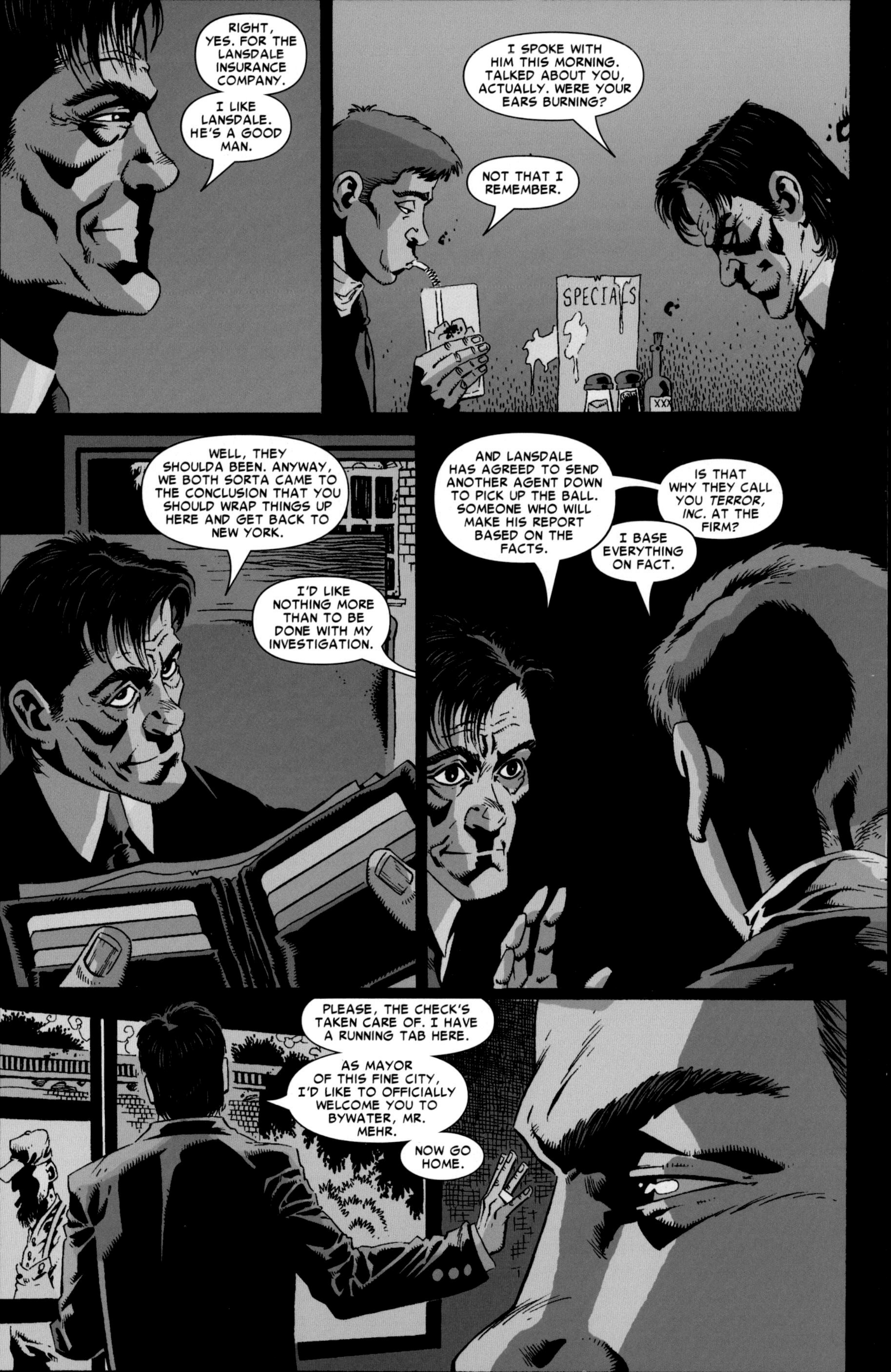
RIGHT, YES. FOR THE LANSDALE INSURANCE COMPANY.
I LIKE LANSDALE. HE'S A GOOD MAN.
I SPOKE WITH HIM THIS MORNING. TALKED ABOUT YOU, ACTUALLY. WERE YOUR EARS BURNING?
NOT THAT I REMEMBER.
SPECIALS
WELL, THEY SHOULDA BEEN. ANYWAY, WE BOTH SORTA CAME TO THE CONCLUSION THAT YOU SHOULD WRAP THINGS UP HERE AND GET BACK TO NEW YORK.
I'D LIKE NOTHING MORE THAN TO BE DONE WITH MY INVESTIGATION.
AND LANSDALE HAS AGREED TO SEND ANOTHER AGENT DOWN TO PICK UP THE BALL. SOMEONE WHO WILL MAKE HIS REPORT BASED ON THE FACTS.
I BASE EVERYTHING ON FACT.
IS THAT WHY THEY CALL YOU *TERROR, INC.* AT THE FIRM?
PLEASE, THE CHECK'S TAKEN CARE OF. I HAVE A RUNNING TAB HERE.
AS MAYOR OF THIS FINE CITY, I'D LIKE TO OFFICIALLY WELCOME YOU TO BYWATER, MR. MEHR.
NOW GO HOME.

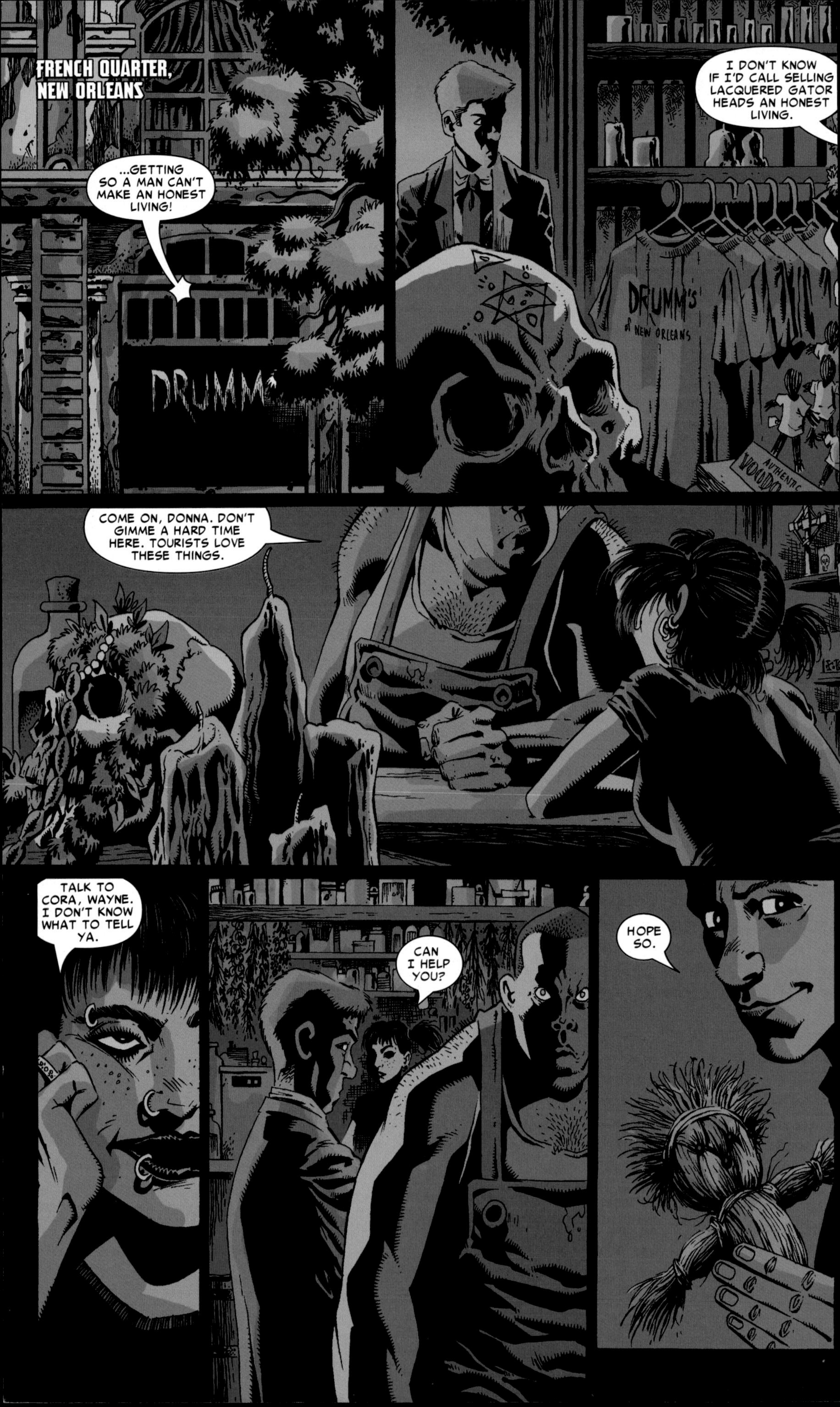
FRENCH QUARTER, NEW ORLEANS
...GETTING SO A MAN CAN'T MAKE AN HONEST LIVING!
DRUMM'S
I DON'T KNOW IF I'D CALL SELLING LACQUERED GATOR HEADS AN HONEST LIVING.
DRUMM'S of NEW ORLEANS
AUTHENTIC VOODOO
COME ON, DONNA. DON'T GIMME A HARD TIME HERE. TOURISTS LOVE THESE THINGS.
TALK TO CORA, WAYNE. I DON'T KNOW WHAT TO TELL YA.
CAN I HELP YOU?
HOPE SO.

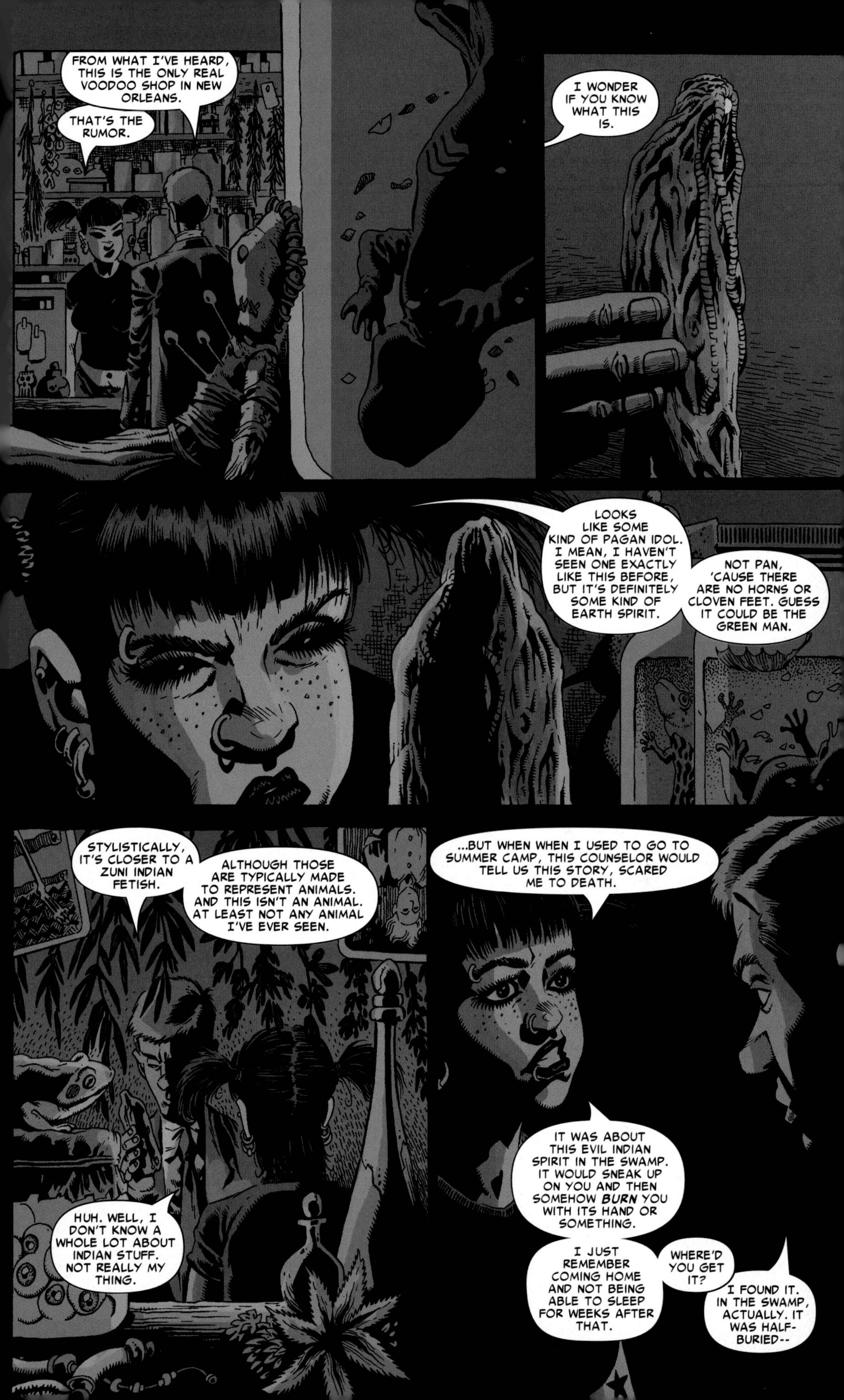
FROM WHAT I'VE HEARD, THIS IS THE ONLY REAL VOODOO SHOP IN NEW ORLEANS.
THAT'S THE RUMOR.
I WONDER IF YOU KNOW WHAT THIS IS.
LOOKS LIKE SOME KIND OF PAGAN IDOL. I MEAN, I HAVEN'T SEEN ONE EXACTLY LIKE THIS BEFORE, BUT IT'S DEFINITELY SOME KIND OF EARTH SPIRIT.
NOT PAN, 'CAUSE THERE ARE NO HORNS OR CLOVEN FEET. GUESS IT COULD BE THE GREEN MAN.
STYLISTICALLY, IT'S CLOSER TO A ZUNI INDIAN FETISH.
ALTHOUGH THOSE ARE TYPICALLY MADE TO REPRESENT ANIMALS. AND THIS ISN'T AN ANIMAL. AT LEAST NOT ANY ANIMAL I'VE EVER SEEN.
HUH. WELL, I DON'T KNOW A WHOLE LOT ABOUT INDIAN STUFF. NOT REALLY MY THING.
...BUT WHEN WHEN I USED TO GO TO SUMMER CAMP, THIS COUNSELOR WOULD TELL US THIS STORY, SCARED ME TO DEATH.
IT WAS ABOUT THIS EVIL INDIAN SPIRIT IN THE SWAMP. IT WOULD SNEAK UP ON YOU AND THEN SOMEHOW *BURN* YOU WITH ITS HAND OR SOMETHING.
I JUST REMEMBER COMING HOME AND NOT BEING ABLE TO SLEEP FOR WEEKS AFTER THAT.
WHERE'D YOU GET IT?
I FOUND IT. IN THE SWAMP, ACTUALLY. IT WAS HALF-BURIED--

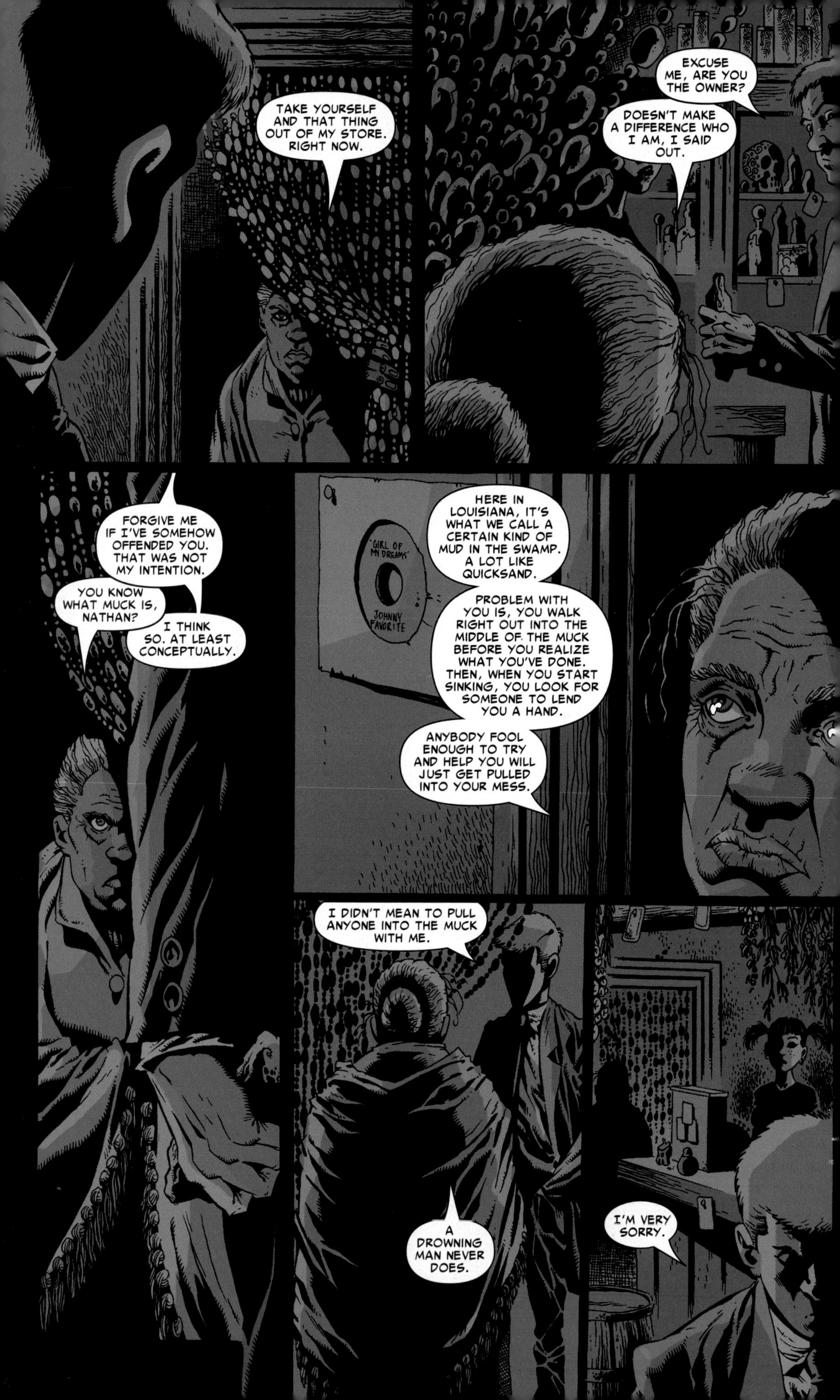
TAKE YOURSELF AND THAT THING OUT OF MY STORE. RIGHT NOW.
EXCUSE ME, ARE YOU THE OWNER?
DOESN'T MAKE A DIFFERENCE WHO I AM, I SAID OUT.
FORGIVE ME IF I'VE SOMEHOW OFFENDED YOU. THAT WAS NOT MY INTENTION.
YOU KNOW WHAT MUCK IS, NATHAN?
I THINK SO. AT LEAST CONCEPTUALLY.
'GIRL OF MY DREAMS'
JOHNNY FAVORITE
HERE IN LOUISIANA, IT'S WHAT WE CALL A CERTAIN KIND OF MUD IN THE SWAMP. A LOT LIKE QUICKSAND.
PROBLEM WITH YOU IS, YOU WALK RIGHT OUT INTO THE MIDDLE OF THE MUCK BEFORE YOU REALIZE WHAT YOU'VE DONE. THEN, WHEN YOU START SINKING, YOU LOOK FOR SOMEONE TO LEND YOU A HAND.
ANYBODY FOOL ENOUGH TO TRY AND HELP YOU WILL JUST GET PULLED INTO YOUR MESS.
I DIDN'T MEAN TO PULL ANYONE INTO THE MUCK WITH ME.
A DROWNING MAN NEVER DOES.
I'M VERY SORRY.

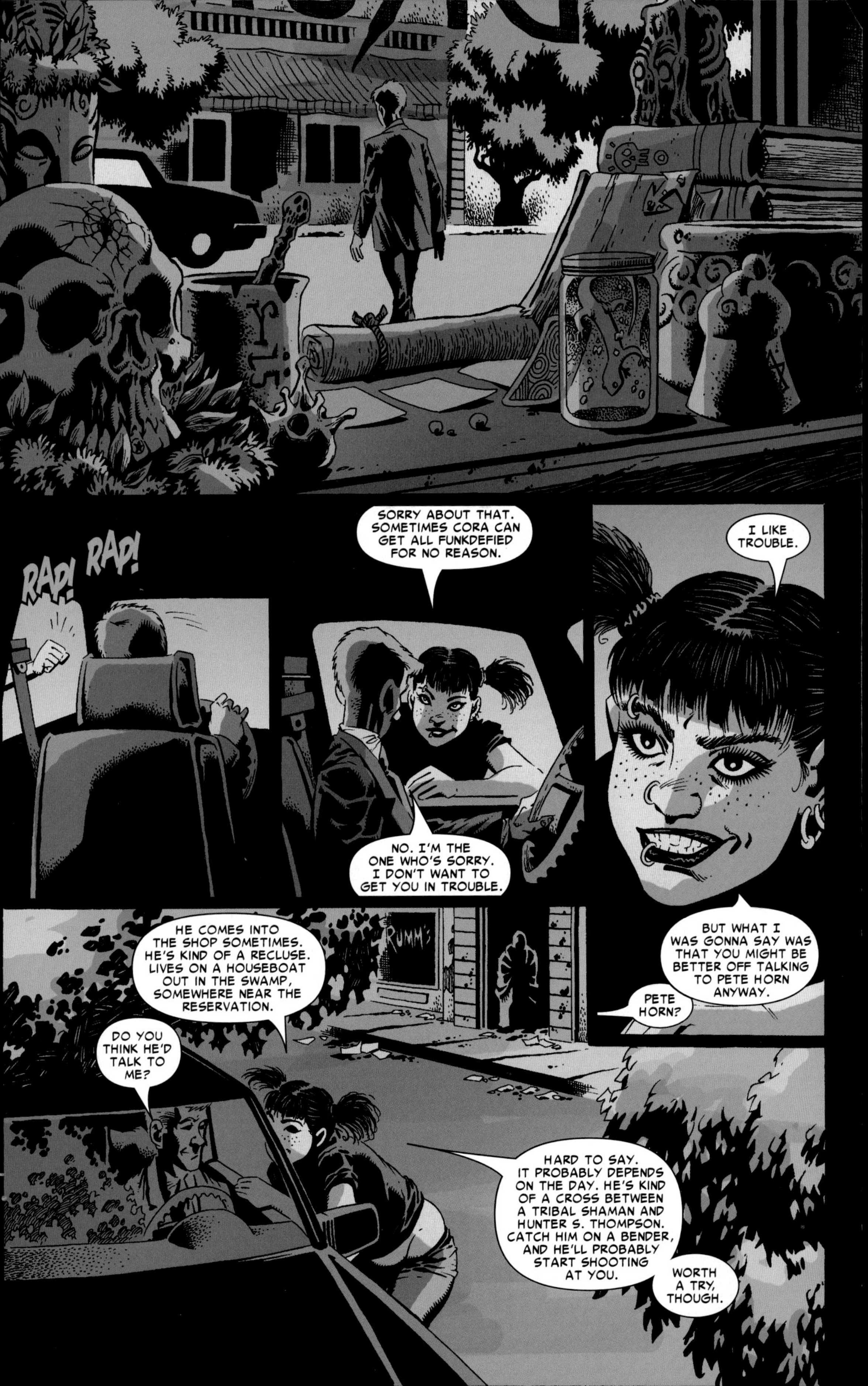
RAP! RAP!
SORRY ABOUT THAT. SOMETIMES CORA CAN GET ALL FUNKDEFIED FOR NO REASON.
NO. I'M THE ONE WHO'S SORRY. I DON'T WANT TO GET YOU IN TROUBLE.
I LIKE TROUBLE.
BUT WHAT I WAS GONNA SAY WAS THAT YOU MIGHT BE BETTER OFF TALKING TO PETE HORN ANYWAY.
PETE HORN?
HE COMES INTO THE SHOP SOMETIMES. HE'S KIND OF A RECLUSE. LIVES ON A HOUSEBOAT OUT IN THE SWAMP, SOMEWHERE NEAR THE RESERVATION.
DO YOU THINK HE'D TALK TO ME?
HARD TO SAY. IT PROBABLY DEPENDS ON THE DAY. HE'S KIND OF A CROSS BETWEEN A TRIBAL SHAMAN AND HUNTER S. THOMPSON. CATCH HIM ON A BENDER, AND HE'LL PROBABLY START SHOOTING AT YOU.
WORTH A TRY, THOUGH.

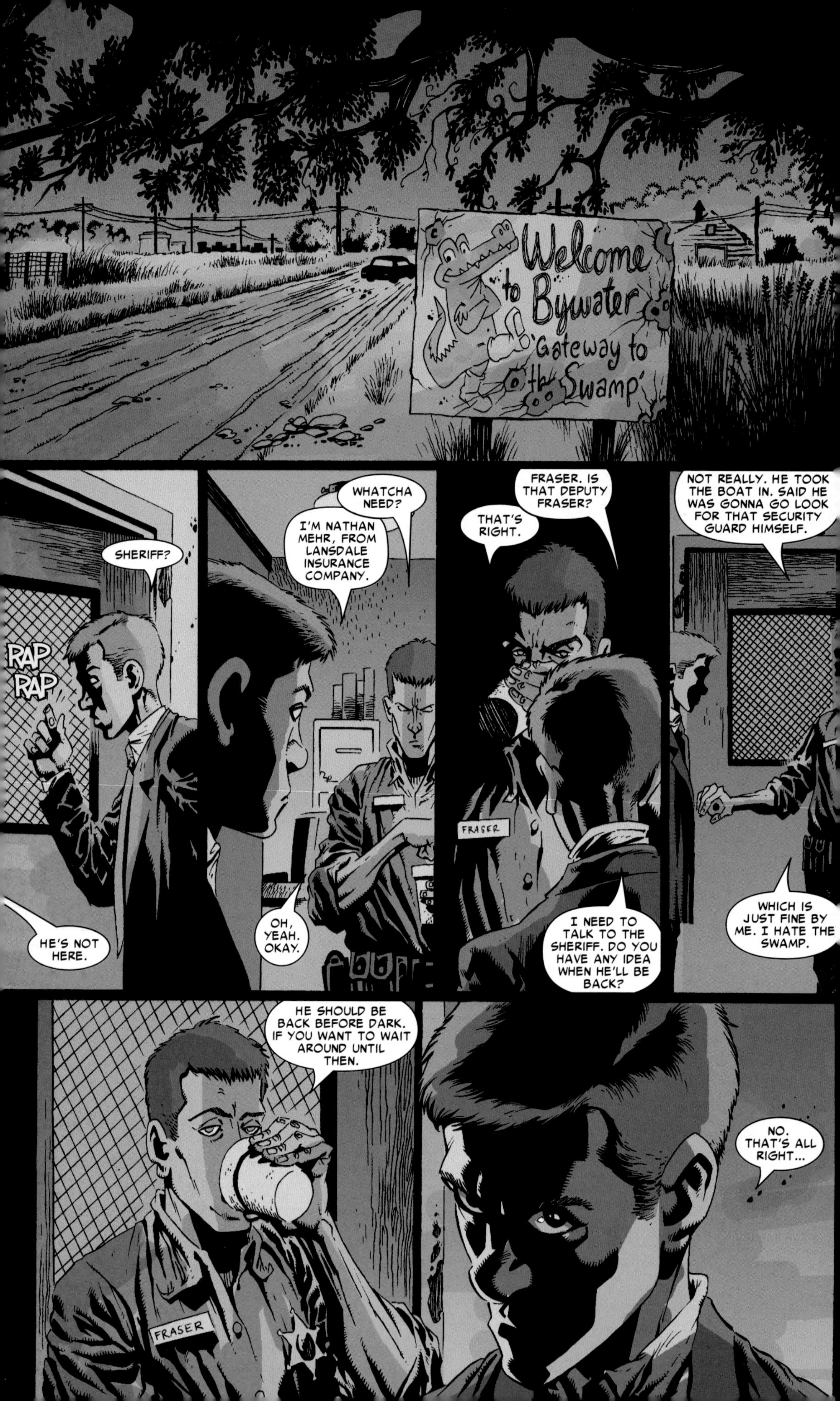
Welcome to Bywater 'Gateway to the Swamp'
SHERIFF?
RAP RAP
HE'S NOT HERE.
WHATCHA NEED?
I'M NATHAN MEHR, FROM LANSDALE INSURANCE COMPANY.
OH, YEAH. OKAY.
FRASER. IS THAT DEPUTY FRASER?
THAT'S RIGHT.
FRASER
I NEED TO TALK TO THE SHERIFF. DO YOU HAVE ANY IDEA WHEN HE'LL BE BACK?
NOT REALLY. HE TOOK THE BOAT IN. SAID HE WAS GONNA GO LOOK FOR THAT SECURITY GUARD HIMSELF.
WHICH IS JUST FINE BY ME. I HATE THE SWAMP.
HE SHOULD BE BACK BEFORE DARK. IF YOU WANT TO WAIT AROUND UNTIL THEN.
FRASER
NO. THAT'S ALL RIGHT...

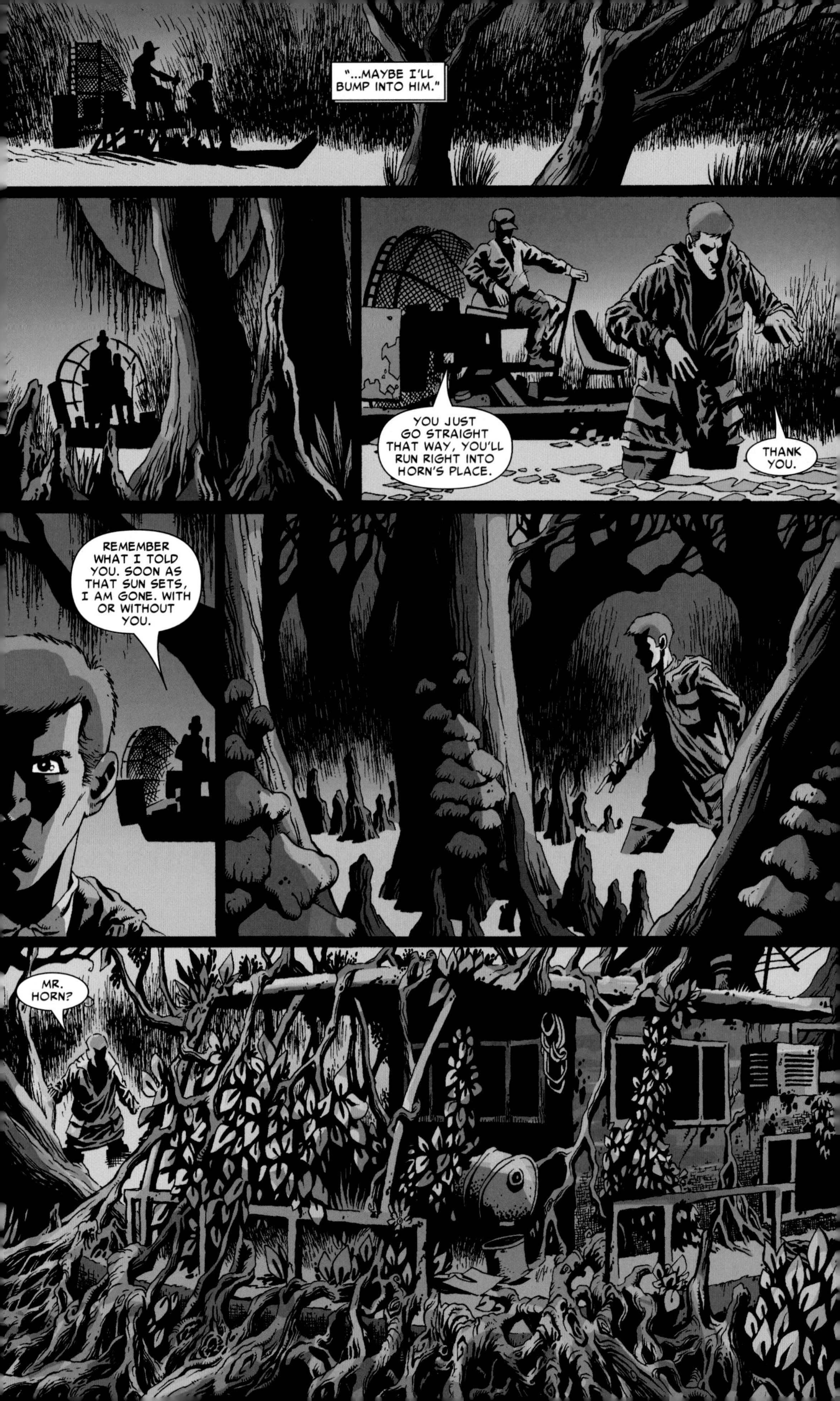
"...MAYBE I'LL BUMP INTO HIM."
YOU JUST GO STRAIGHT THAT WAY, YOU'LL RUN RIGHT INTO HORN'S PLACE.
THANK YOU.
REMEMBER WHAT I TOLD YOU. SOON AS THAT SUN SETS, I AM GONE. WITH OR WITHOUT YOU.
MR. HORN?

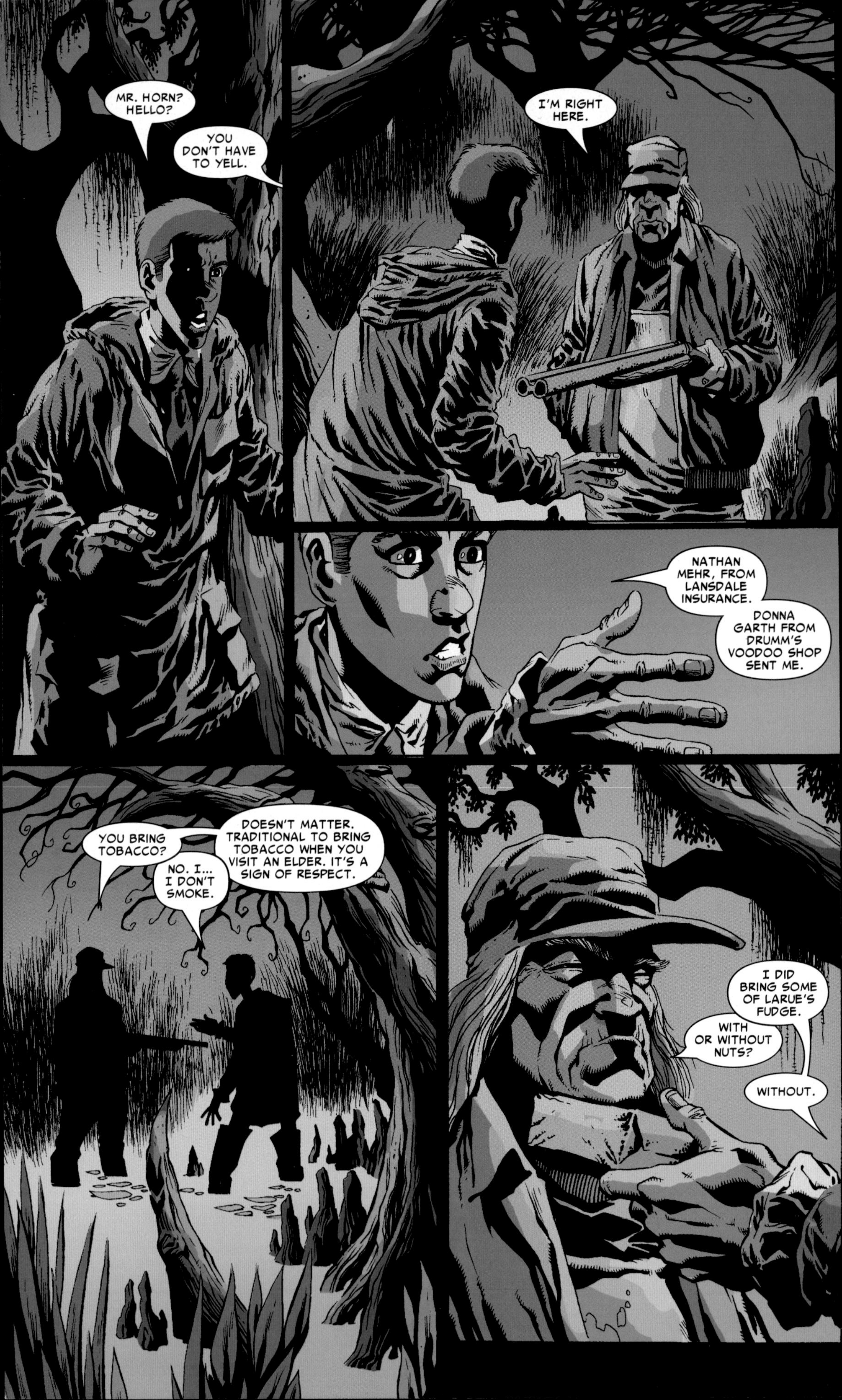
MR. HORN? HELLO?
YOU DON'T HAVE TO YELL.
I'M RIGHT HERE.
NATHAN MEHR, FROM LANSDALE INSURANCE.
DONNA GARTH FROM DRUMM'S VOODOO SHOP SENT ME.
YOU BRING TOBACCO?
NO. I... I DON'T SMOKE.
DOESN'T MATTER. TRADITIONAL TO BRING TOBACCO WHEN YOU VISIT AN ELDER. IT'S A SIGN OF RESPECT.
I DID BRING SOME OF LARUE'S FUDGE.
WITH OR WITHOUT NUTS?
WITHOUT.

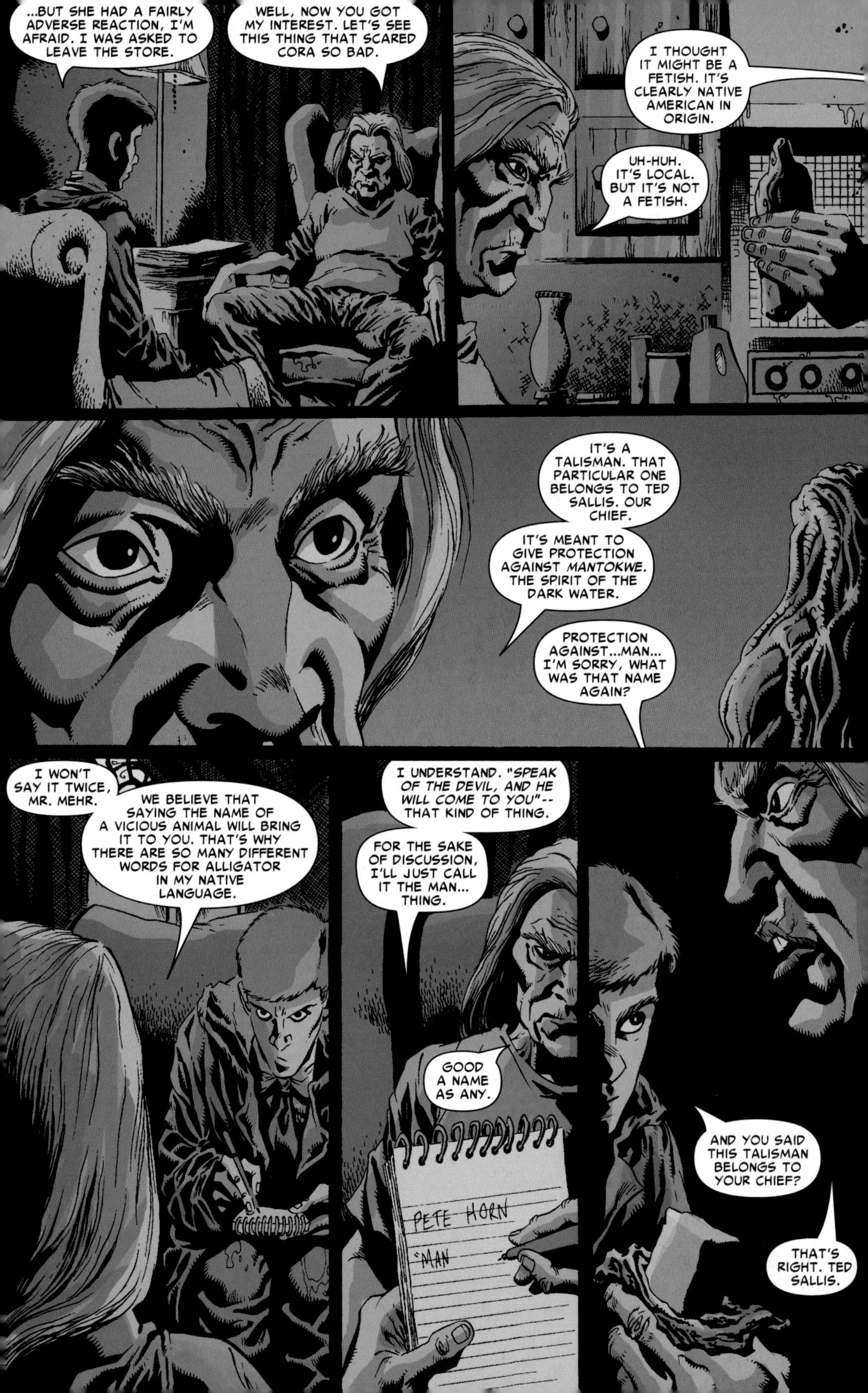
...BUT SHE HAD A FAIRLY ADVERSE REACTION, I'M AFRAID. I WAS ASKED TO LEAVE THE STORE.
WELL, NOW YOU GOT MY INTEREST. LET'S SEE THIS THING THAT SCARED CORA SO BAD.
I THOUGHT IT MIGHT BE A FETISH. IT'S CLEARLY NATIVE AMERICAN IN ORIGIN.
UH-HUH. IT'S LOCAL. BUT IT'S NOT A FETISH.
IT'S A TALISMAN. THAT PARTICULAR ONE BELONGS TO TED SALLIS. OUR CHIEF.
IT'S MEANT TO GIVE PROTECTION AGAINST *MANTOKWE*. THE SPIRIT OF THE DARK WATER.
PROTECTION AGAINST...MAN... I'M SORRY, WHAT WAS THAT NAME AGAIN?
I WON'T SAY IT TWICE, MR. MEHR.
WE BELIEVE THAT SAYING THE NAME OF A VICIOUS ANIMAL WILL BRING IT TO YOU. THAT'S WHY THERE ARE SO MANY DIFFERENT WORDS FOR ALLIGATOR IN MY NATIVE LANGUAGE.
I UNDERSTAND. *"SPEAK OF THE DEVIL, AND HE WILL COME TO YOU"*-- THAT KIND OF THING.
FOR THE SAKE OF DISCUSSION, I'LL JUST CALL IT THE MAN... THING.
GOOD A NAME AS ANY.
PETE HORN
MAN
AND YOU SAID THIS TALISMAN BELONGS TO YOUR CHIEF?
THAT'S RIGHT. TED SALLIS.

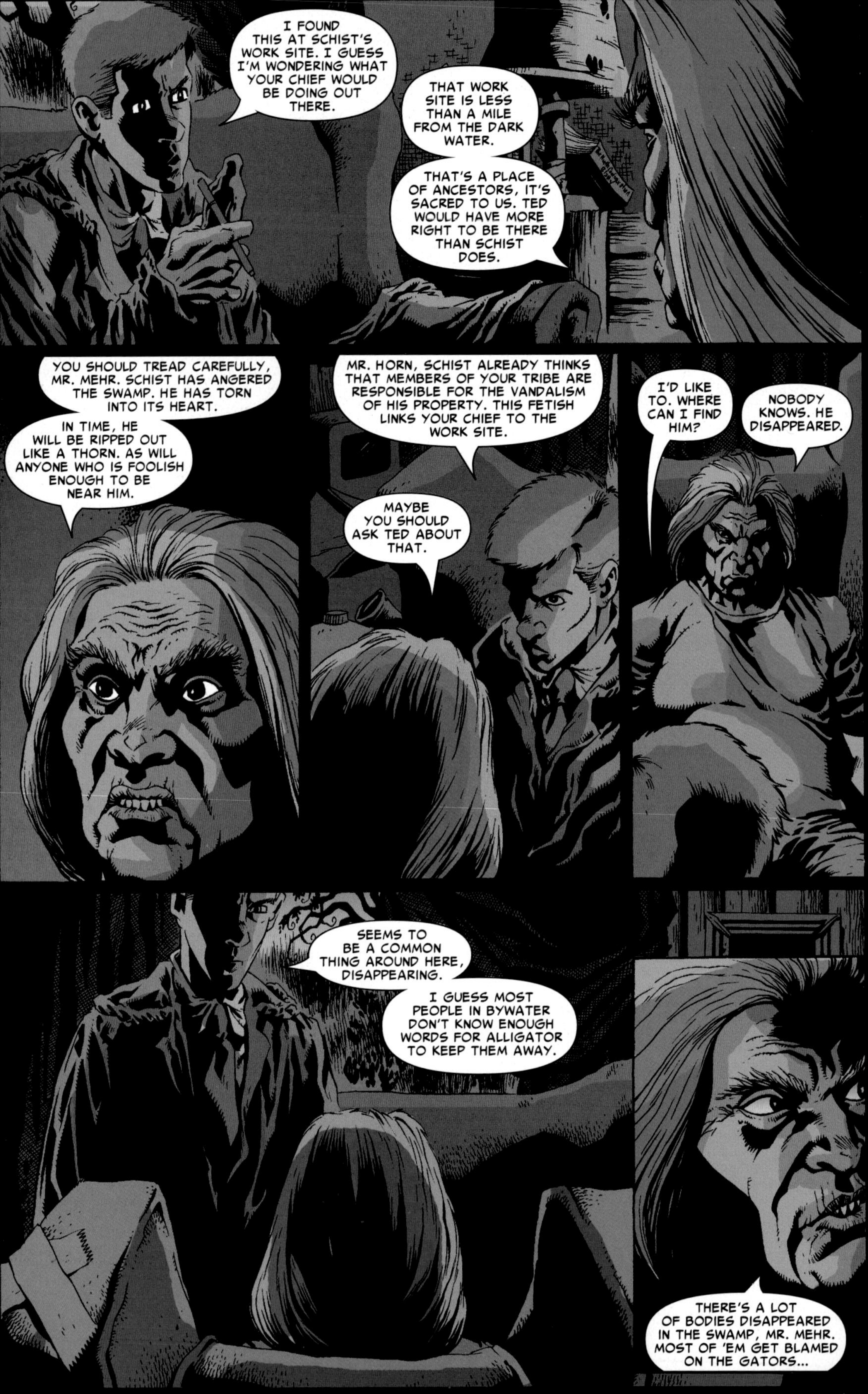
I FOUND THIS AT SCHIST'S WORK SITE. I GUESS I'M WONDERING WHAT YOUR CHIEF WOULD BE DOING OUT THERE.
THAT WORK SITE IS LESS THAN A MILE FROM THE DARK WATER.
THAT'S A PLACE OF ANCESTORS, IT'S SACRED TO US. TED WOULD HAVE MORE RIGHT TO BE THERE THAN SCHIST DOES.
YOU SHOULD TREAD CAREFULLY, MR. MEHR. SCHIST HAS ANGERED THE SWAMP. HE HAS TORN INTO ITS HEART.
IN TIME, HE WILL BE RIPPED OUT LIKE A THORN. AS WILL ANYONE WHO IS FOOLISH ENOUGH TO BE NEAR HIM.
MR. HORN, SCHIST ALREADY THINKS THAT MEMBERS OF YOUR TRIBE ARE RESPONSIBLE FOR THE VANDALISM OF HIS PROPERTY. THIS FETISH LINKS YOUR CHIEF TO THE WORK SITE.
MAYBE YOU SHOULD ASK TED ABOUT THAT.
I'D LIKE TO. WHERE CAN I FIND HIM?
NOBODY KNOWS. HE DISAPPEARED.
SEEMS TO BE A COMMON THING AROUND HERE, DISAPPEARING.
I GUESS MOST PEOPLE IN BYWATER DON'T KNOW ENOUGH WORDS FOR ALLIGATOR TO KEEP THEM AWAY.
THERE'S A LOT OF BODIES DISAPPEARED IN THE SWAMP, MR. MEHR. MOST OF 'EM GET BLAMED ON THE GATORS...

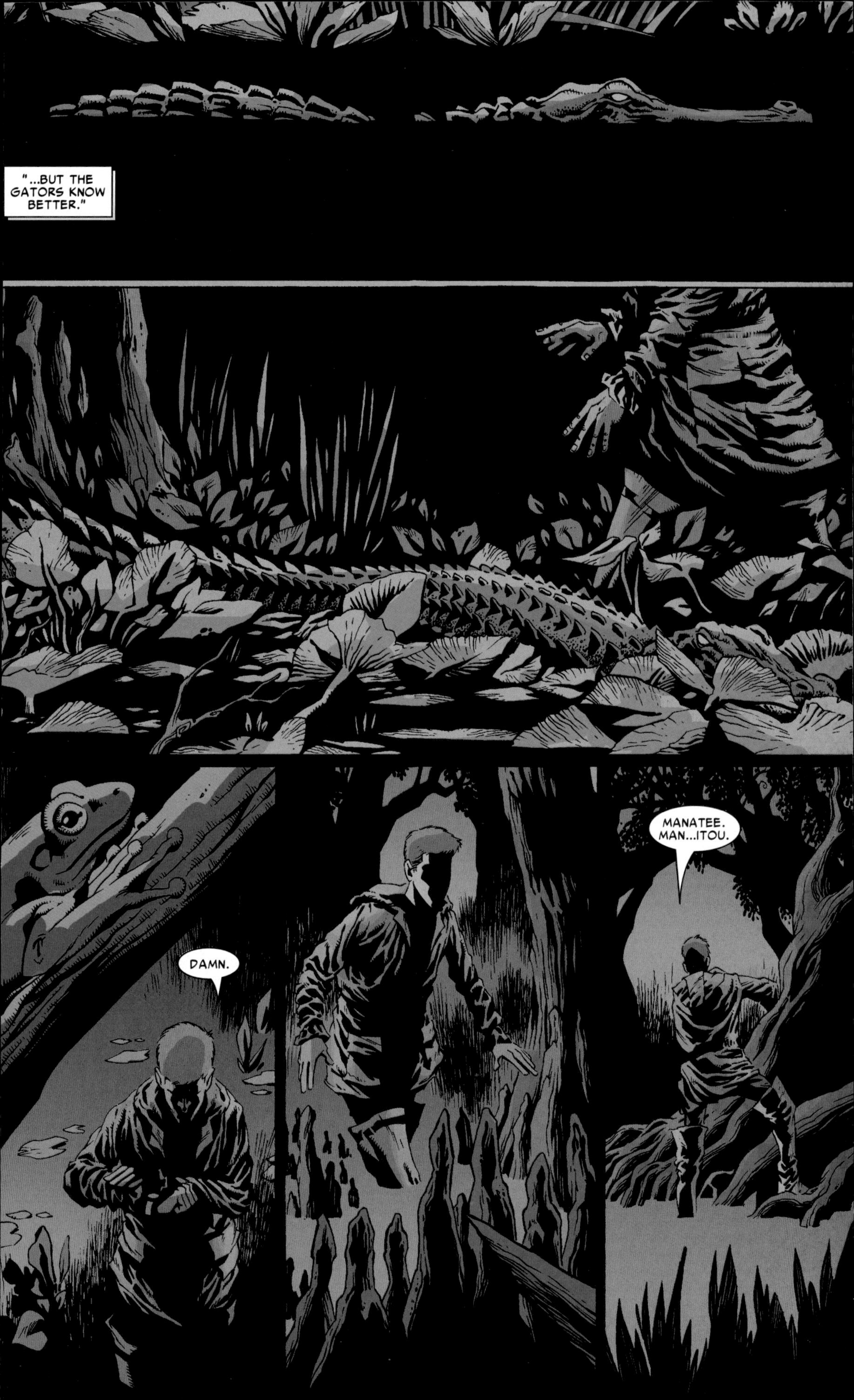
"...BUT THE GATORS KNOW BETTER."
DAMN.
MANATEE. MAN...ITOU.

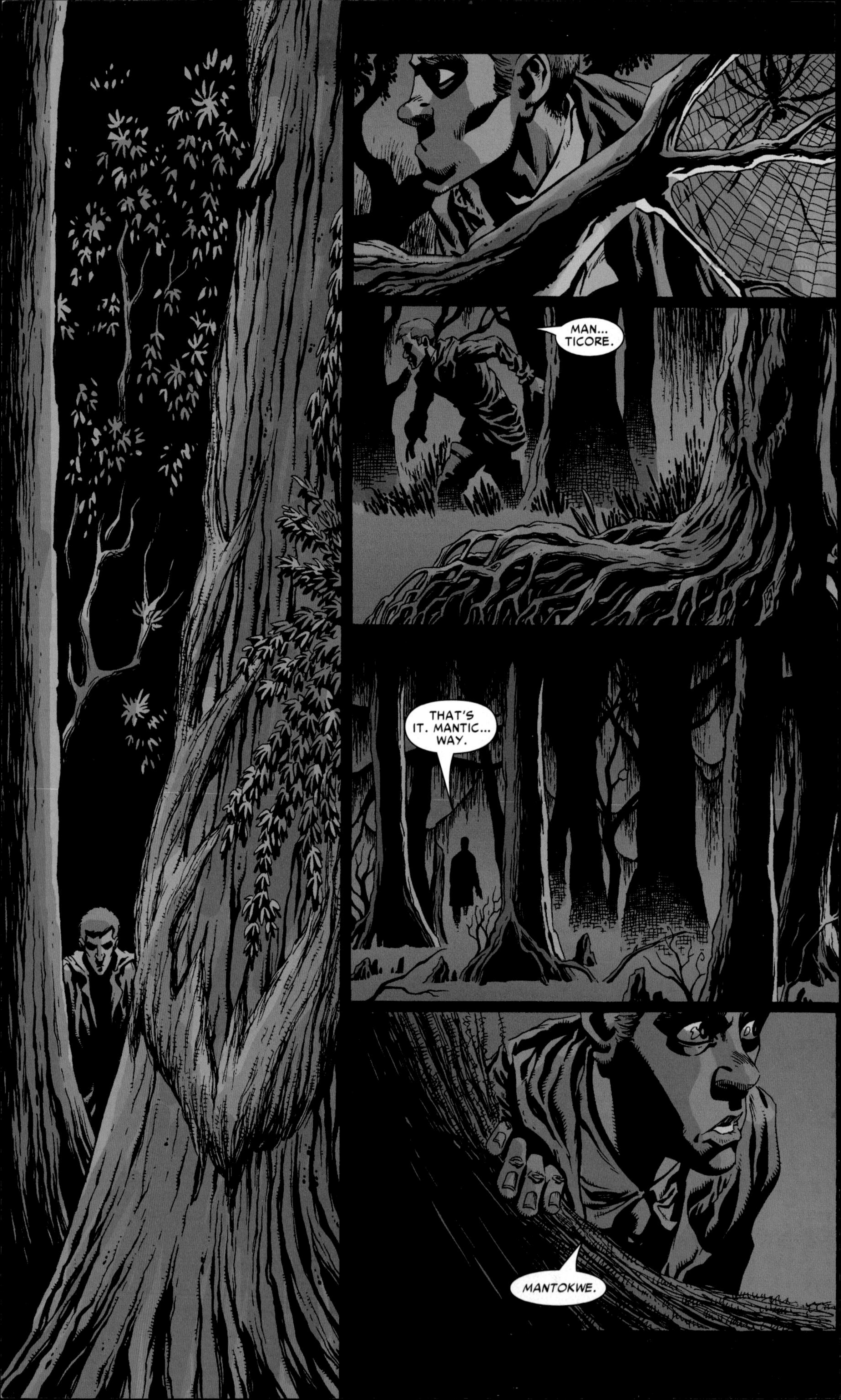
MAN... TICORE.
THAT'S IT. MANTIC... WAY.
MANTOKWE.

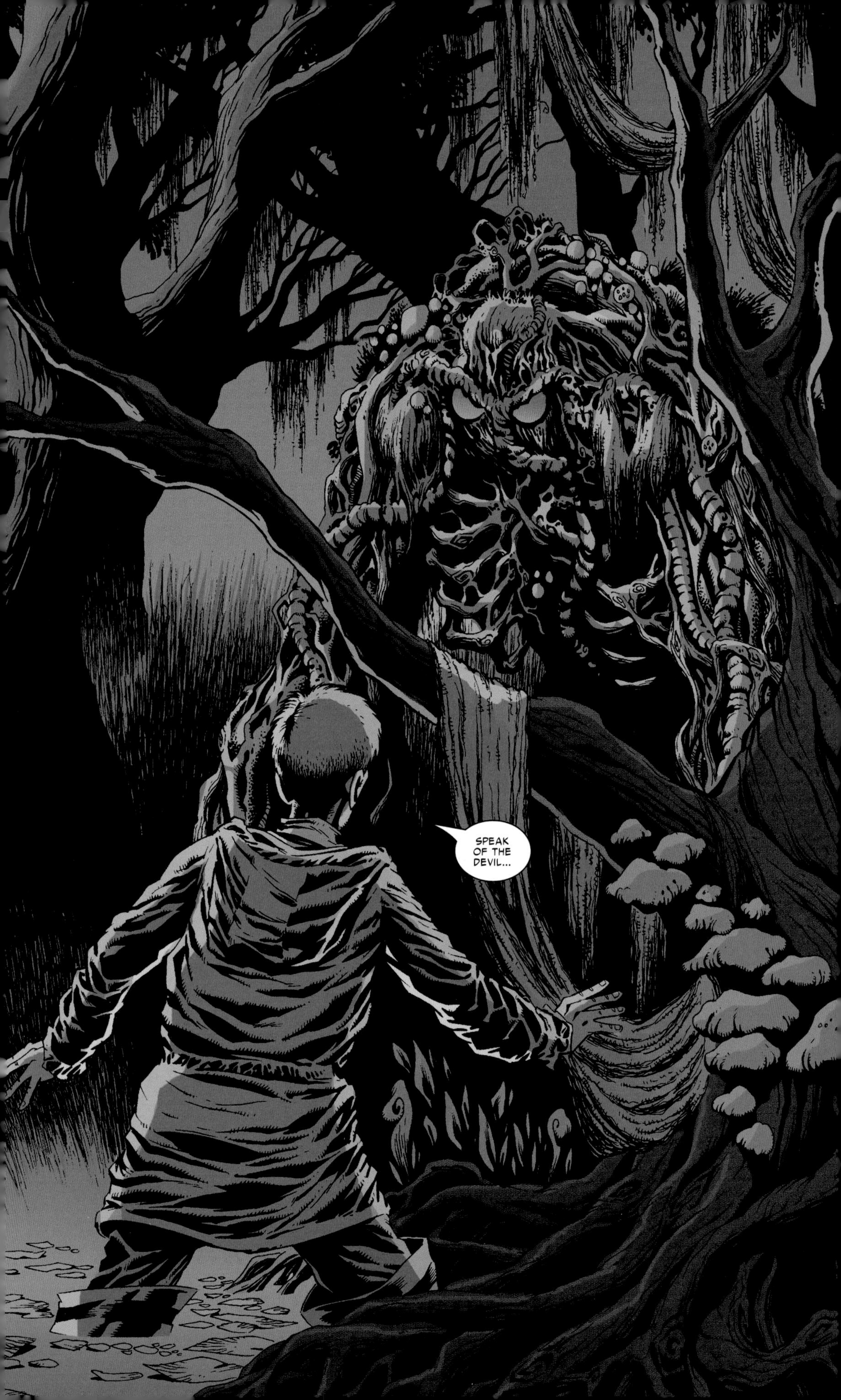
SPEAK OF THE DEVIL...

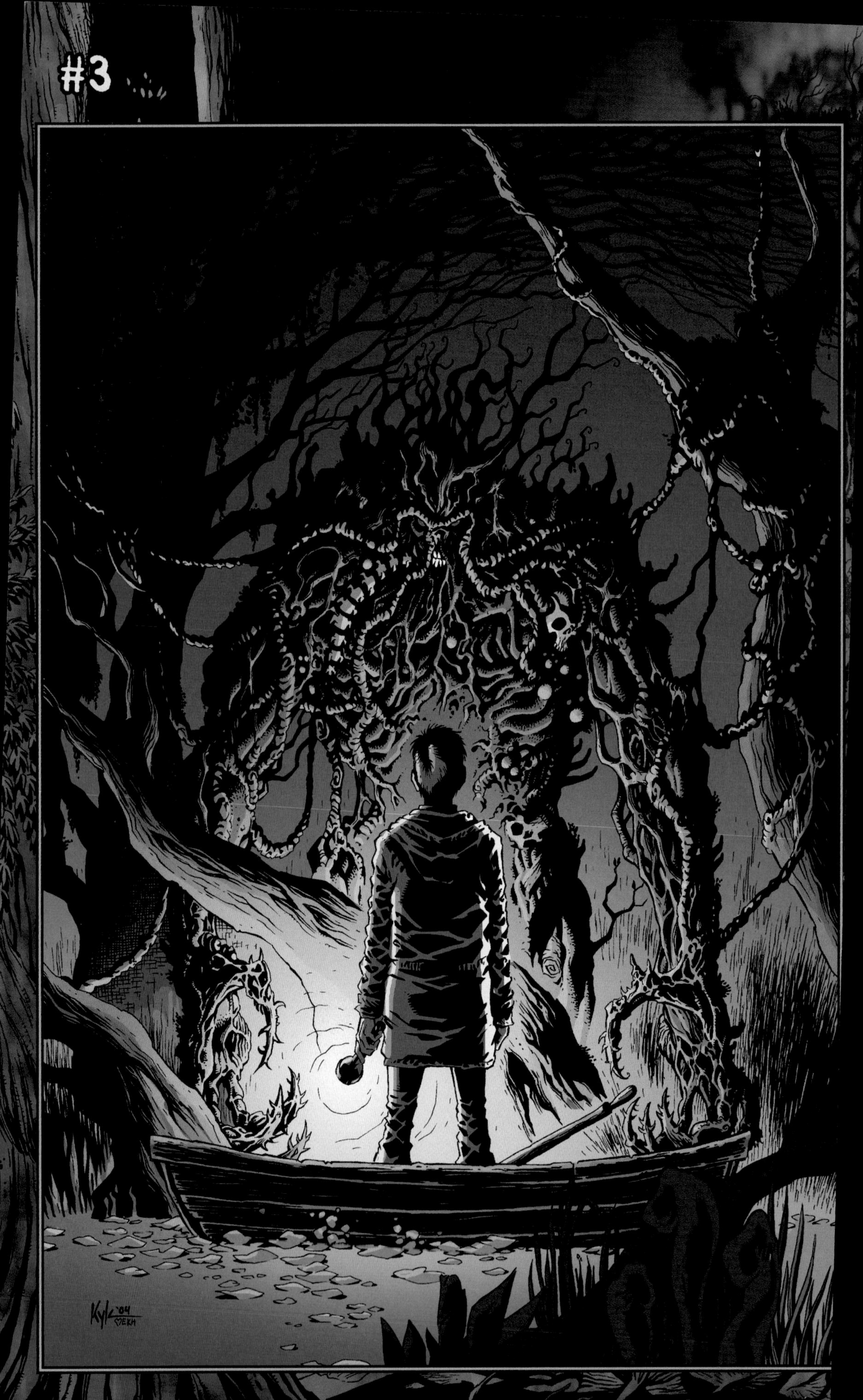
#3

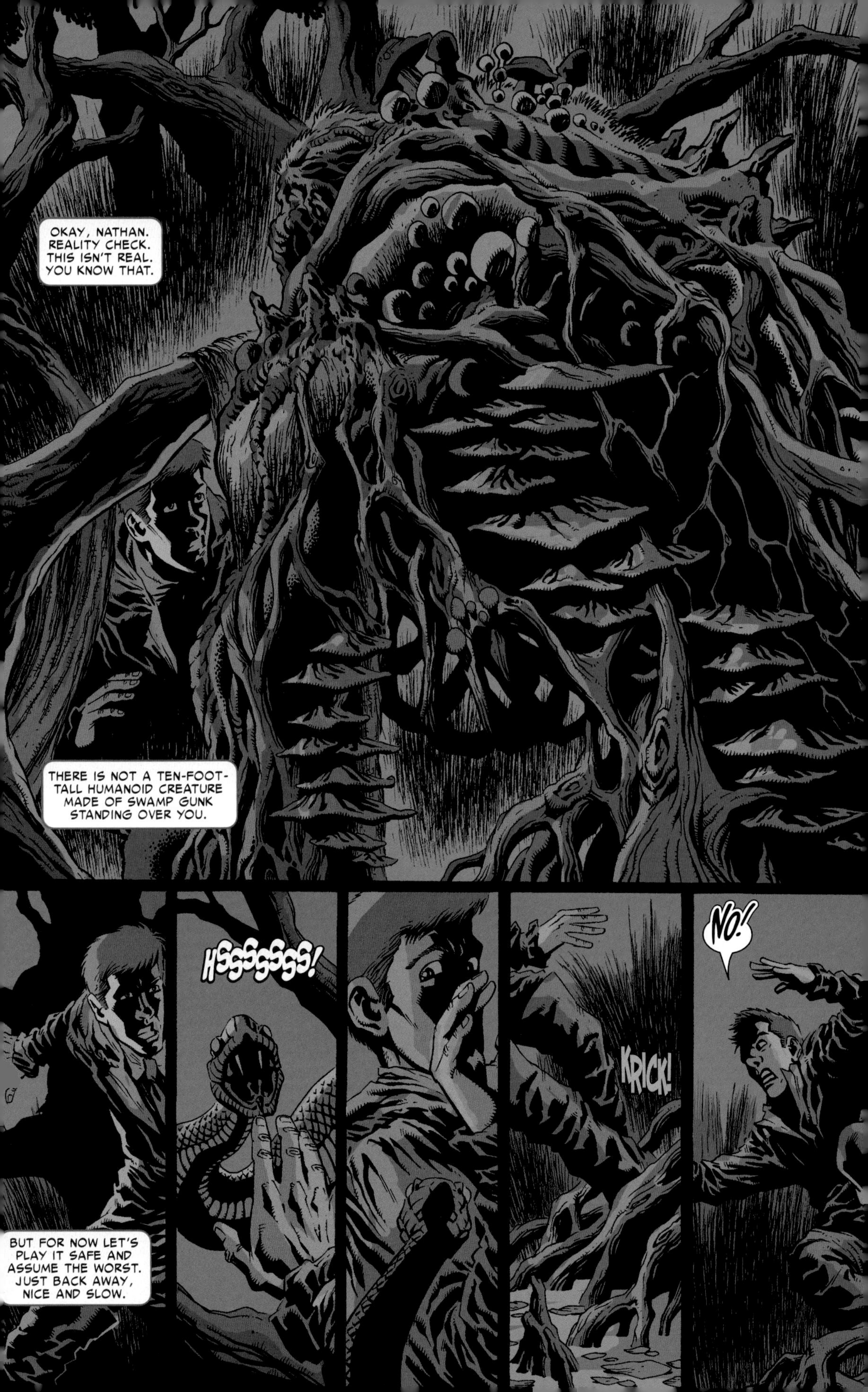
OKAY, NATHAN. REALITY CHECK. THIS ISN'T REAL. YOU KNOW THAT.
THERE IS NOT A TEN-FOOT-TALL HUMANOID CREATURE MADE OF SWAMP GUNK STANDING OVER YOU.
BUT FOR NOW LET'S PLAY IT SAFE AND ASSUME THE WORST. JUST BACK AWAY, NICE AND SLOW.
HSSSSSSS!
KRICK!
NO!

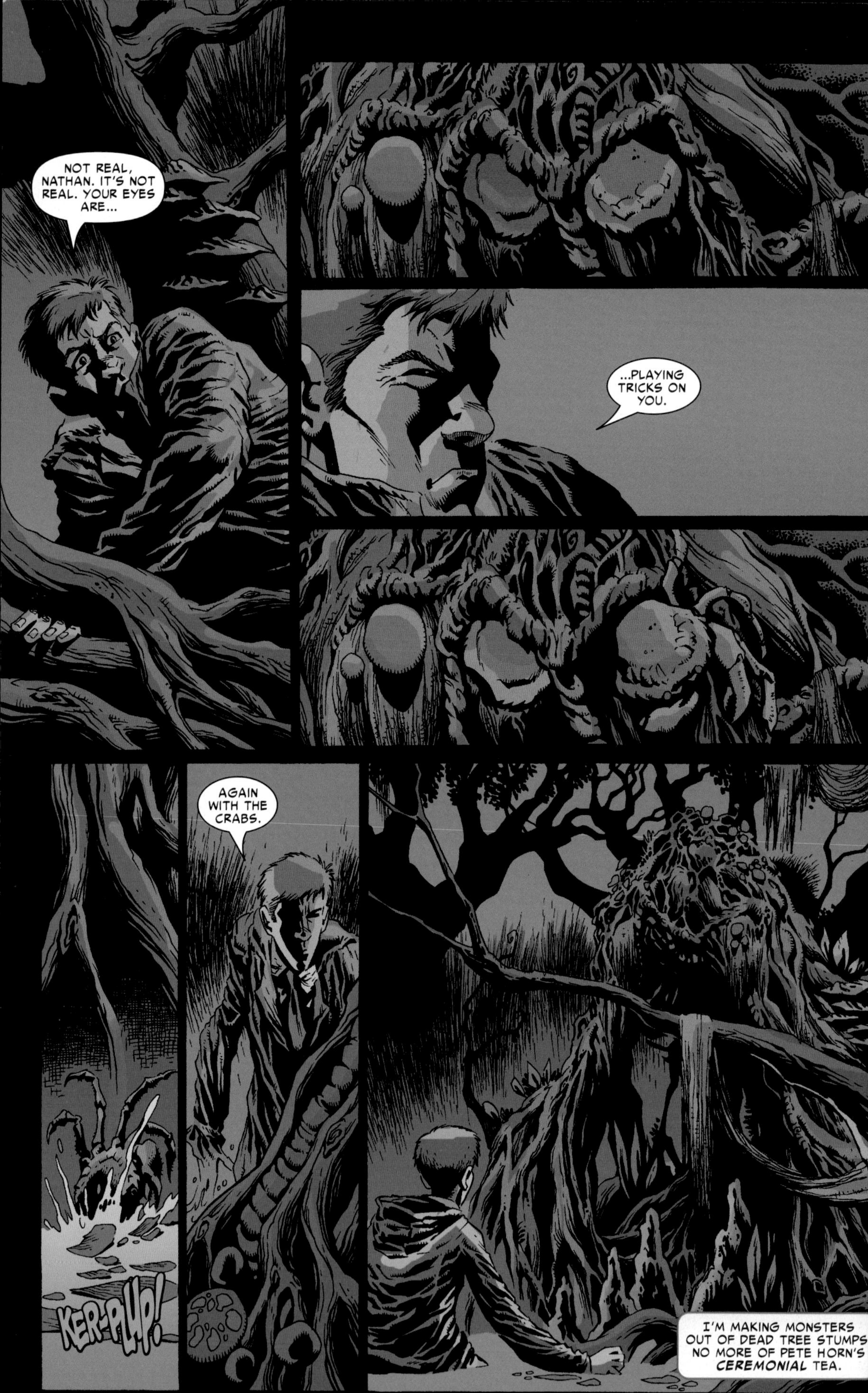
NOT REAL, NATHAN. IT'S NOT REAL. YOUR EYES ARE...
...PLAYING TRICKS ON YOU.
KER-PLUP!
AGAIN WITH THE CRABS.
I'M MAKING MONSTERS OUT OF DEAD TREE STUMPS. NO MORE OF PETE HORN'S CEREMONIAL TEA.

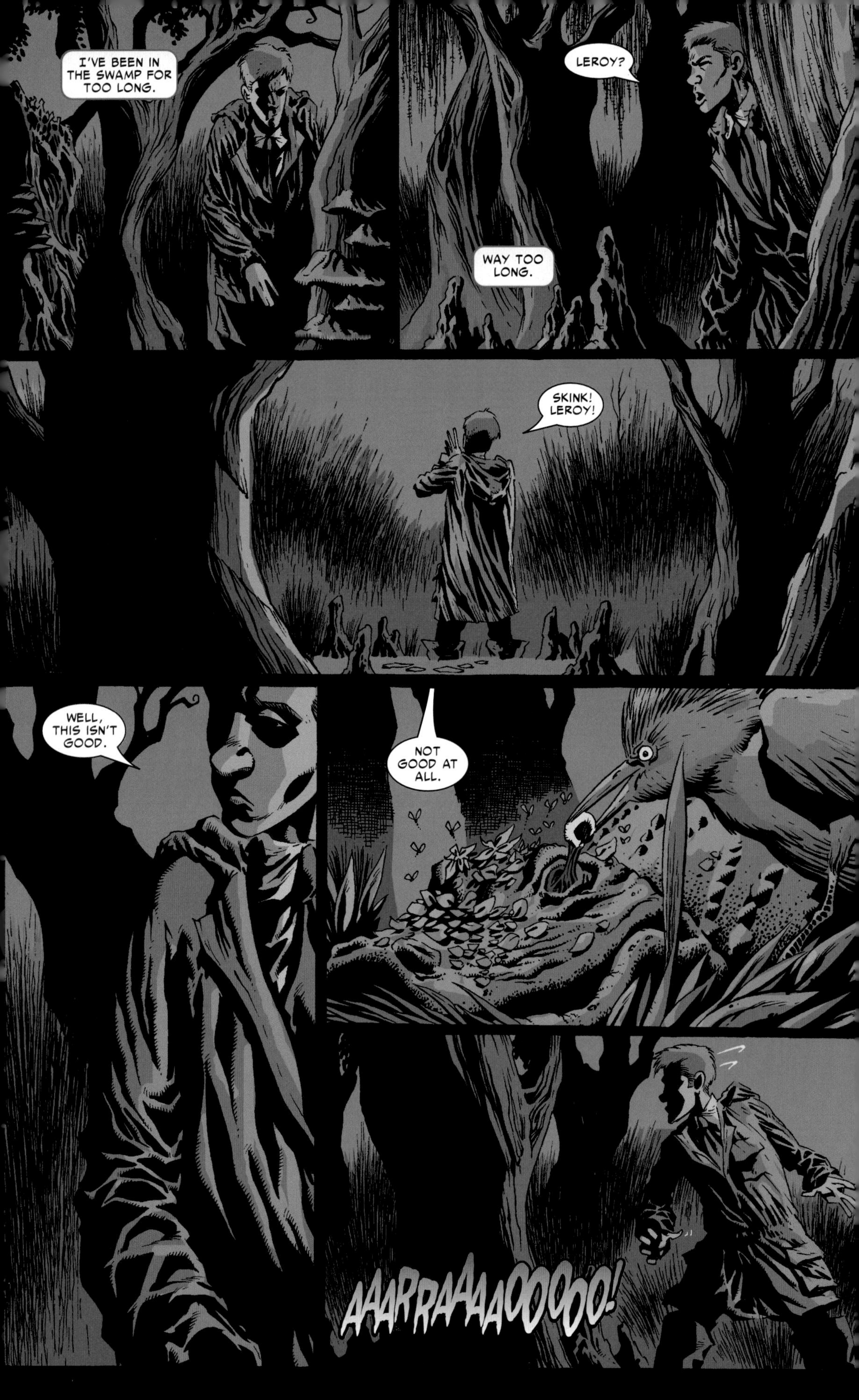
I'VE BEEN IN THE SWAMP FOR TOO LONG.
LEROY?
WAY TOO LONG.
SKINK! LEROY!
WELL, THIS ISN'T GOOD.
NOT GOOD AT ALL.
AAARRAAAAOOOOOO!

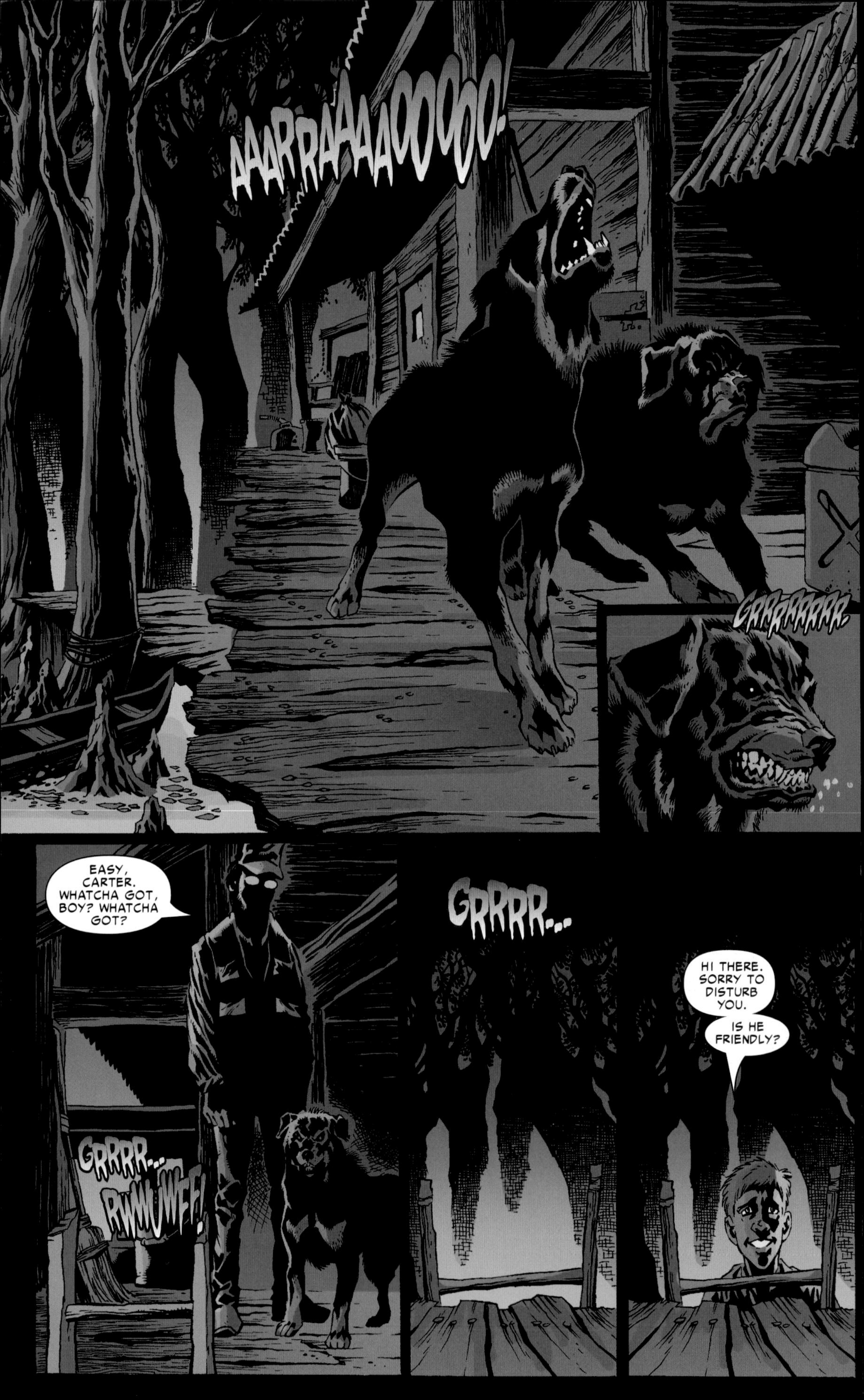
AAARRAAAAOOOOO!
GRRRRRRRR
EASY, CARTER. WHATCHA GOT, BOY? WHATCHA GOT?
GRRRR... RWMUWFF!
GRRRR...
HI THERE. SORRY TO DISTURB YOU.
IS HE FRIENDLY?

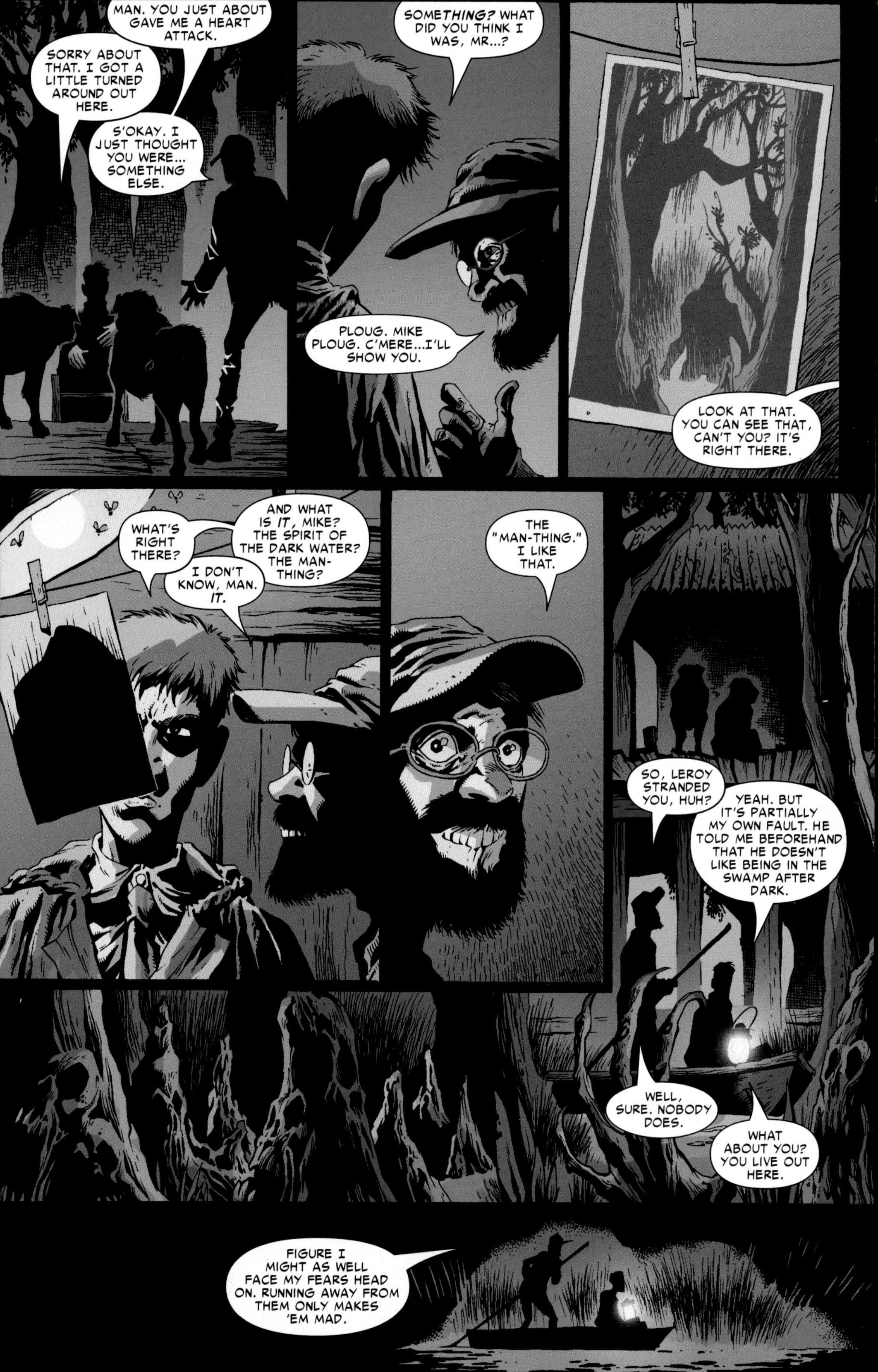

MAN. YOU JUST ABOUT GAVE ME A HEART ATTACK.
SORRY ABOUT THAT. I GOT A LITTLE TURNED AROUND OUT HERE.
S'OKAY. I JUST THOUGHT YOU WERE... SOMETHING ELSE.
SOMETHING? WHAT DID YOU THINK I WAS, MR...?
PLOUG. MIKE PLOUG. C'MERE...I'LL SHOW YOU.
LOOK AT THAT. YOU CAN SEE THAT, CAN'T YOU? IT'S RIGHT THERE.
WHAT'S RIGHT THERE?
I DON'T KNOW, MAN. IT.
AND WHAT IS IT, MIKE? THE SPIRIT OF THE DARK WATER? THE MAN-THING?
THE "MAN-THING." I LIKE THAT.
SO, LEROY STRANDED YOU, HUH?
YEAH. BUT IT'S PARTIALLY MY OWN FAULT. HE TOLD ME BEFOREHAND THAT HE DOESN'T LIKE BEING IN THE SWAMP AFTER DARK.
WELL, SURE. NOBODY DOES.
WHAT ABOUT YOU? YOU LIVE OUT HERE.
FIGURE I MIGHT AS WELL FACE MY FEARS HEAD ON. RUNNING AWAY FROM THEM ONLY MAKES 'EM MAD.

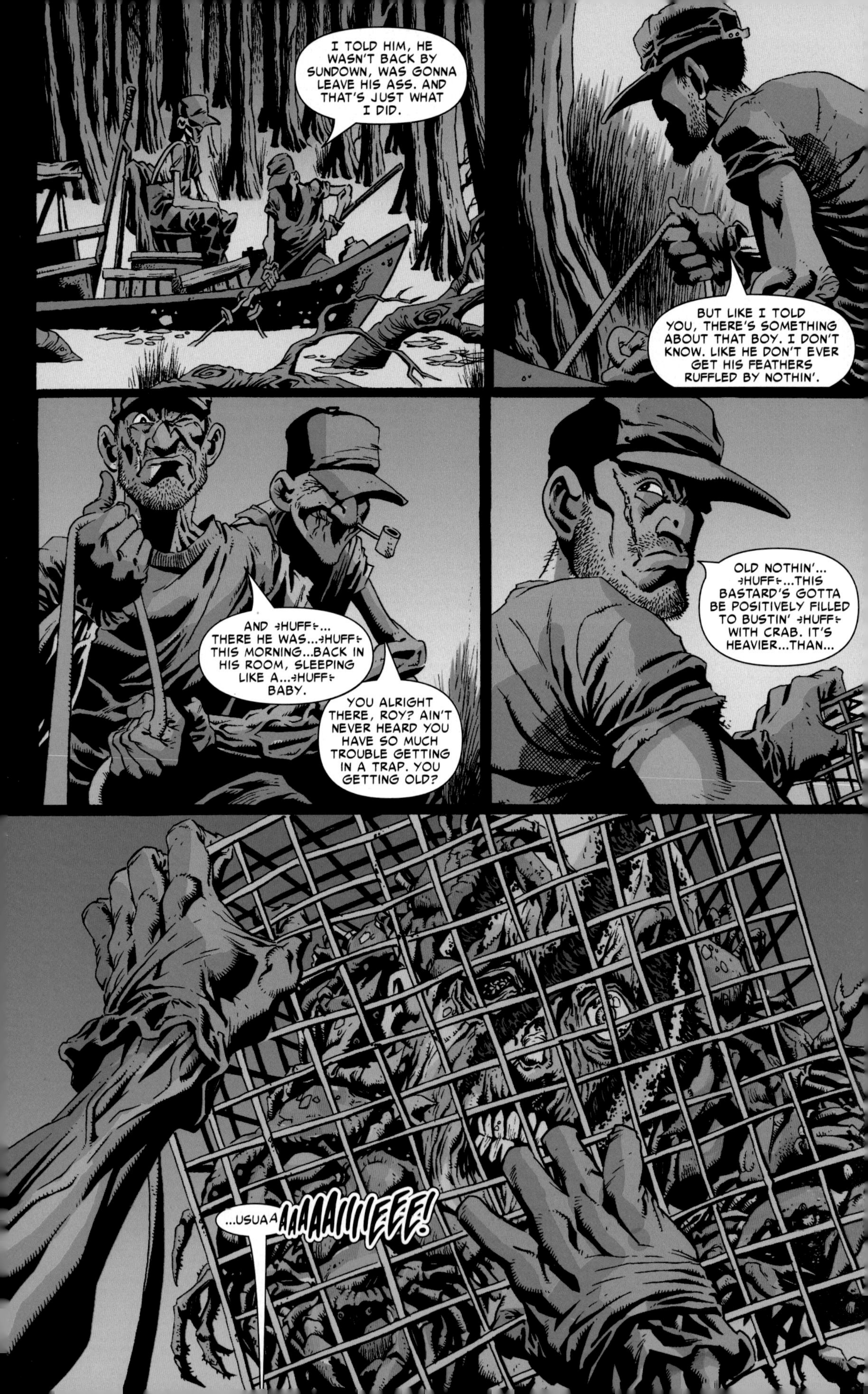
I TOLD HIM, HE WASN'T BACK BY SUNDOWN, WAS GONNA LEAVE HIS ASS. AND THAT'S JUST WHAT I DID.
BUT LIKE I TOLD YOU, THERE'S SOMETHING ABOUT THAT BOY. I DON'T KNOW. LIKE HE DON'T EVER GET HIS FEATHERS RUFFLED BY NOTHIN'.
AND ⫶HUFF⫶... THERE HE WAS...⫶HUFF⫶ THIS MORNING...BACK IN HIS ROOM, SLEEPING LIKE A...⫶HUFF⫶ BABY.
YOU ALRIGHT THERE, ROY? AIN'T NEVER HEARD YOU HAVE SO MUCH TROUBLE GETTING IN A TRAP. YOU GETTING OLD?
OLD NOTHIN'... ⫶HUFF⫶...THIS BASTARD'S GOTTA BE POSITIVELY FILLED TO BUSTIN' ⫶HUFF⫶ WITH CRAB. IT'S HEAVIER...THAN...
...USUAAAAAAIIIIEEE!

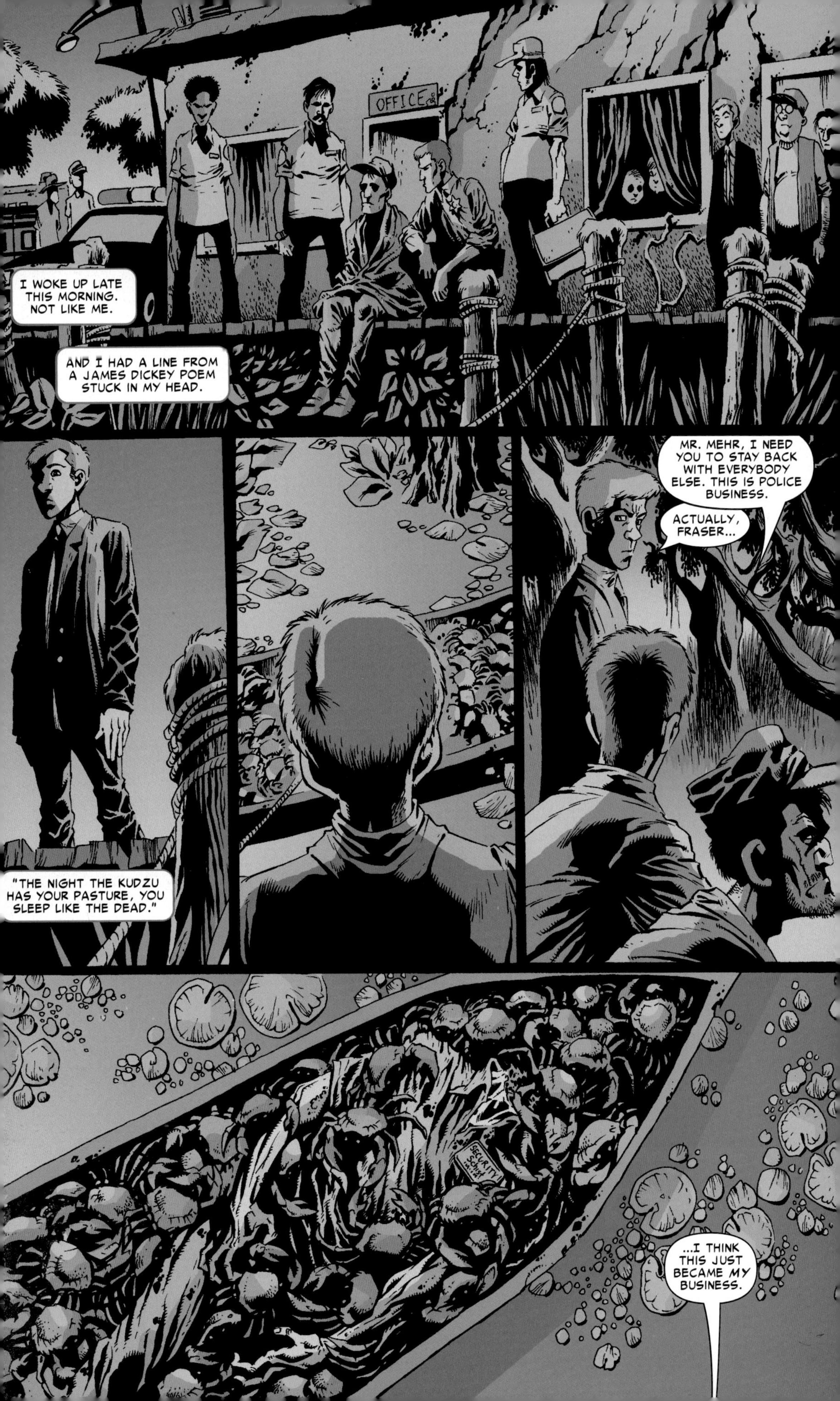
OFFICE
I WOKE UP LATE THIS MORNING. NOT LIKE ME.
AND I HAD A LINE FROM A JAMES DICKEY POEM STUCK IN MY HEAD.
"THE NIGHT THE KUDZU HAS YOUR PASTURE, YOU SLEEP LIKE THE DEAD."
MR. MEHR, I NEED YOU TO STAY BACK WITH EVERYBODY ELSE. THIS IS POLICE BUSINESS.
ACTUALLY, FRASER...
...I THINK THIS JUST BECAME *MY* BUSINESS.

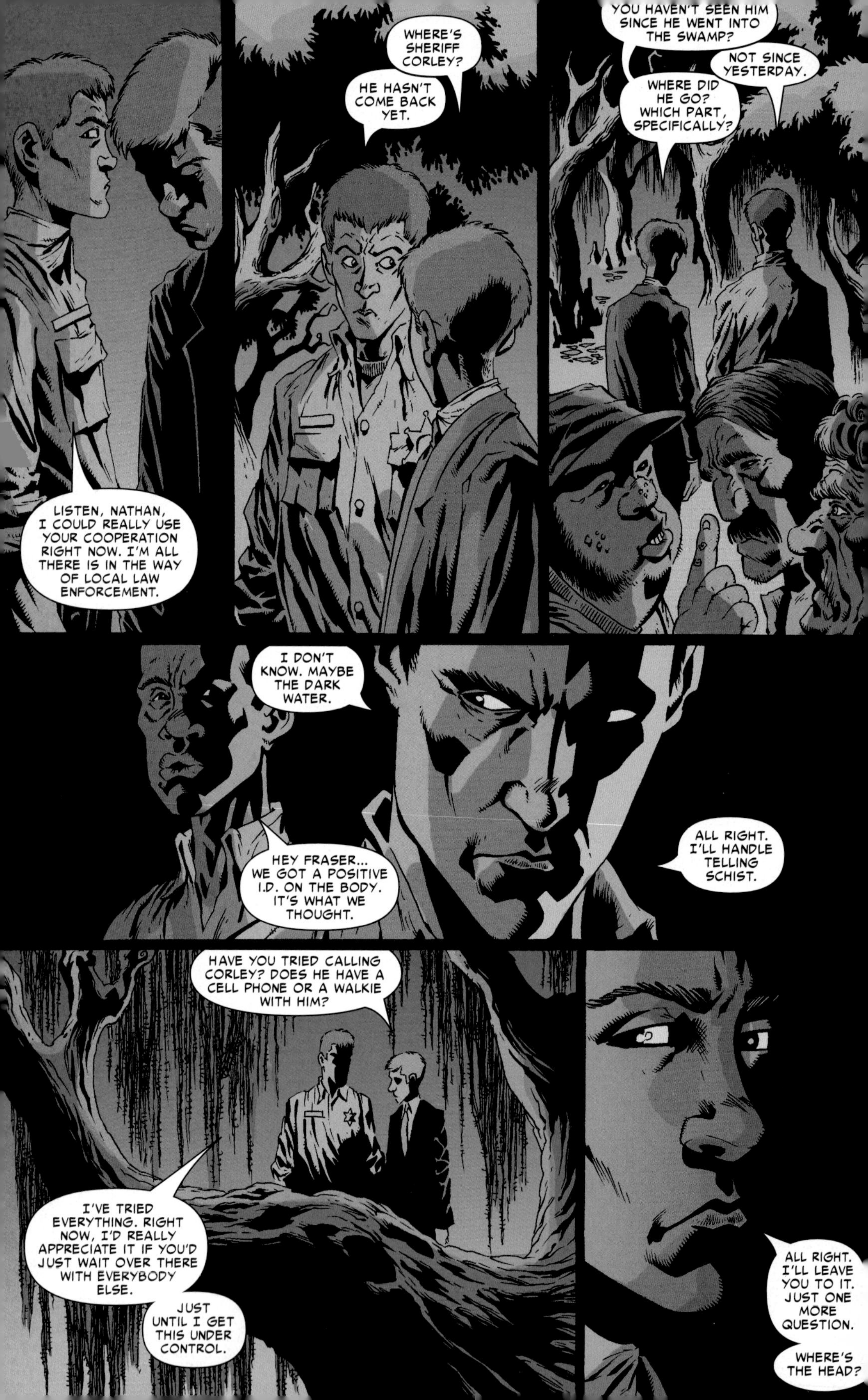
LISTEN, NATHAN, I COULD REALLY USE YOUR COOPERATION RIGHT NOW. I'M ALL THERE IS IN THE WAY OF LOCAL LAW ENFORCEMENT.
WHERE'S SHERIFF CORLEY?
HE HASN'T COME BACK YET.
YOU HAVEN'T SEEN HIM SINCE HE WENT INTO THE SWAMP?
NOT SINCE YESTERDAY.
WHERE DID HE GO? WHICH PART, SPECIFICALLY?
I DON'T KNOW. MAYBE THE DARK WATER.
HEY FRASER... WE GOT A POSITIVE I.D. ON THE BODY. IT'S WHAT WE THOUGHT.
ALL RIGHT. I'LL HANDLE TELLING SCHIST.
HAVE YOU TRIED CALLING CORLEY? DOES HE HAVE A CELL PHONE OR A WALKIE WITH HIM?
I'VE TRIED EVERYTHING. RIGHT NOW, I'D REALLY APPRECIATE IT IF YOU'D JUST WAIT OVER THERE WITH EVERYBODY ELSE.
JUST UNTIL I GET THIS UNDER CONTROL.
ALL RIGHT. I'LL LEAVE YOU TO IT. JUST ONE MORE QUESTION.
WHERE'S THE HEAD?

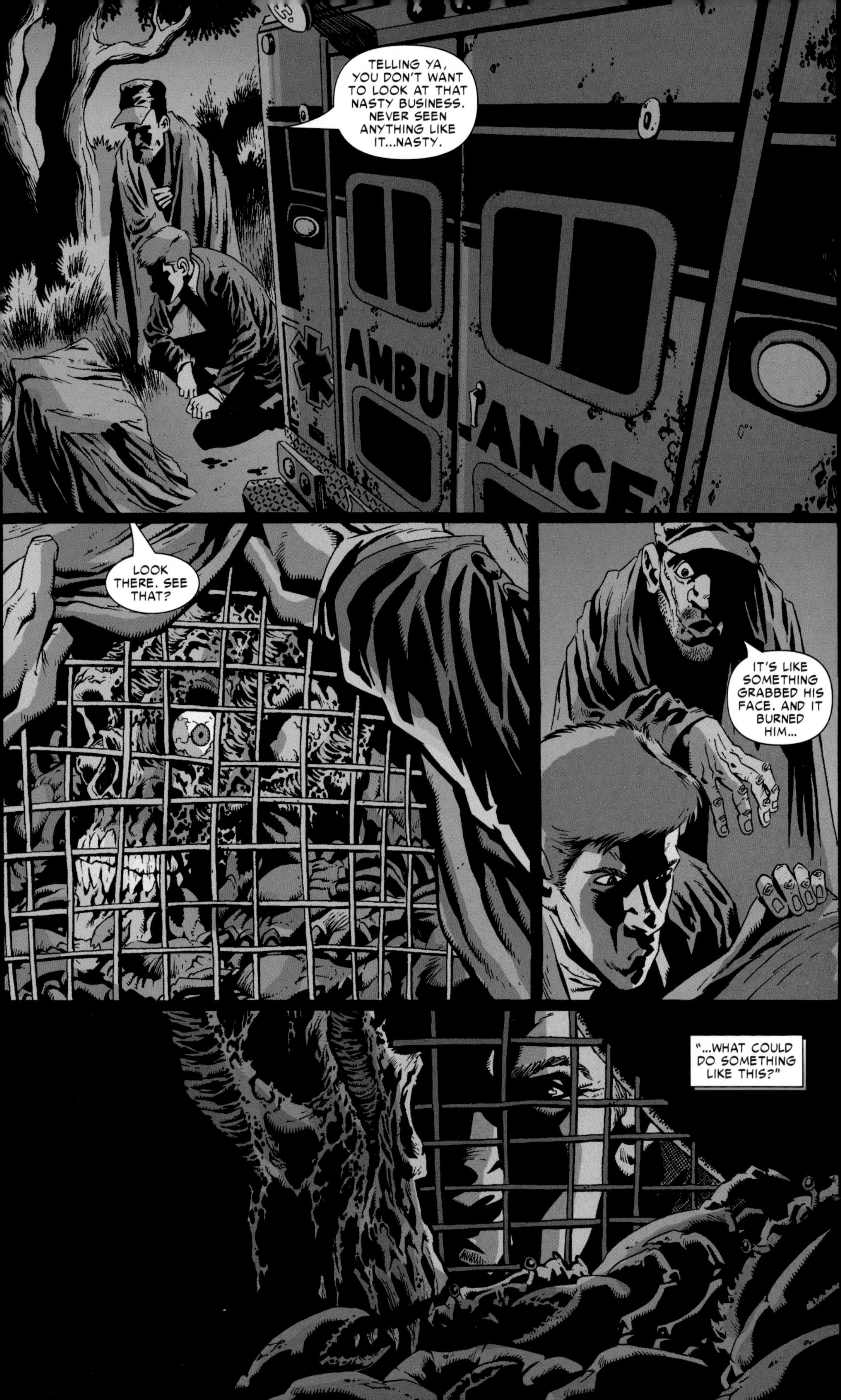
TELLING YA, YOU DON'T WANT TO LOOK AT THAT NASTY BUSINESS. NEVER SEEN ANYTHING LIKE IT...NASTY.
AMBULANCE
LOOK THERE. SEE THAT?
IT'S LIKE SOMETHING GRABBED HIS FACE. AND IT BURNED HIM...
"...WHAT COULD DO SOMETHING LIKE THIS?"

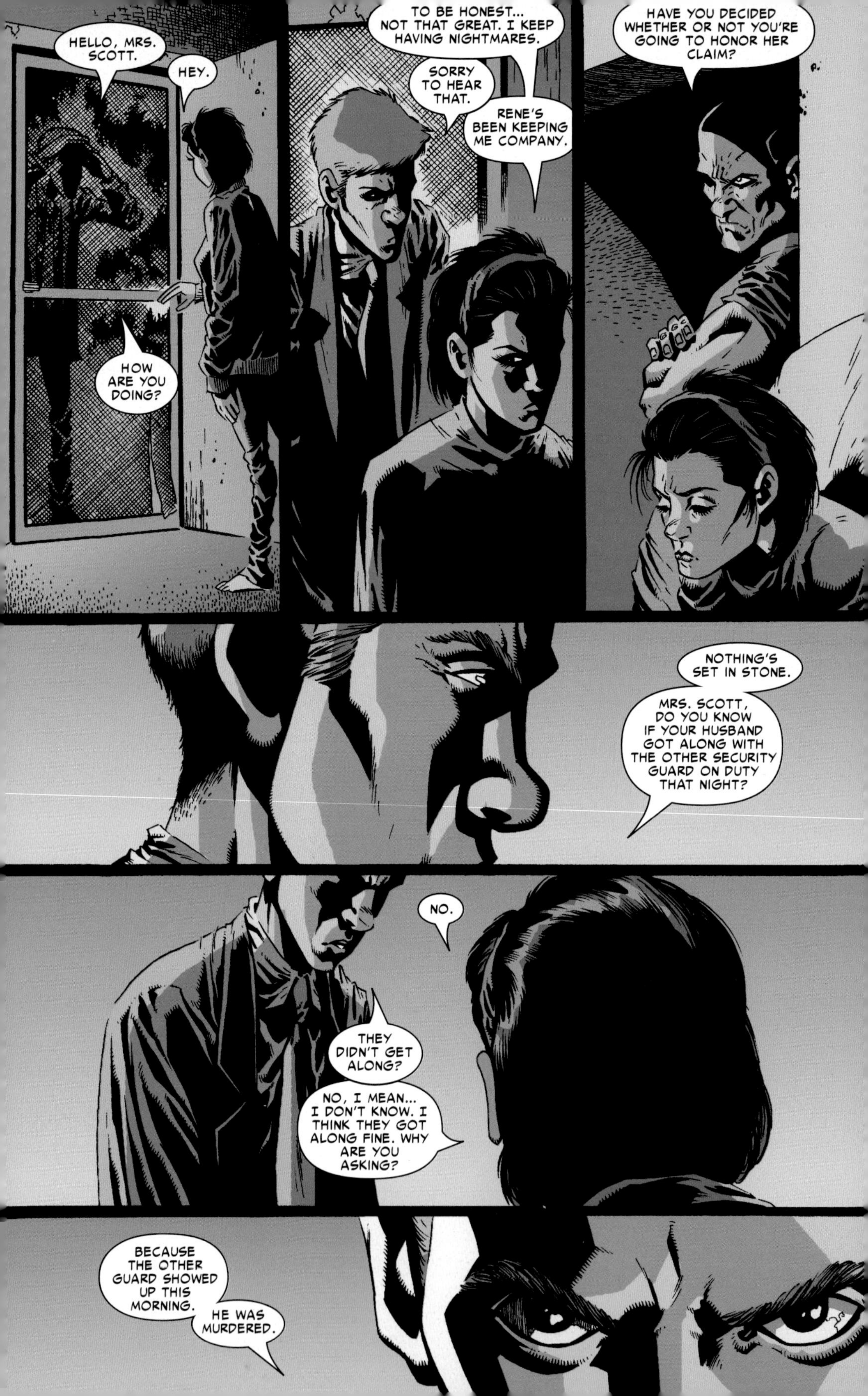
HELLO, MRS. SCOTT.
HEY.
HOW ARE YOU DOING?
TO BE HONEST... NOT THAT GREAT. I KEEP HAVING NIGHTMARES.
SORRY TO HEAR THAT.
RENE'S BEEN KEEPING ME COMPANY.
HAVE YOU DECIDED WHETHER OR NOT YOU'RE GOING TO HONOR HER CLAIM?
NOTHING'S SET IN STONE.
MRS. SCOTT, DO YOU KNOW IF YOUR HUSBAND GOT ALONG WITH THE OTHER SECURITY GUARD ON DUTY THAT NIGHT?
NO.
THEY DIDN'T GET ALONG?
NO, I MEAN... I DON'T KNOW. I THINK THEY GOT ALONG FINE. WHY ARE YOU ASKING?
BECAUSE THE OTHER GUARD SHOWED UP THIS MORNING.
HE WAS MURDERED.

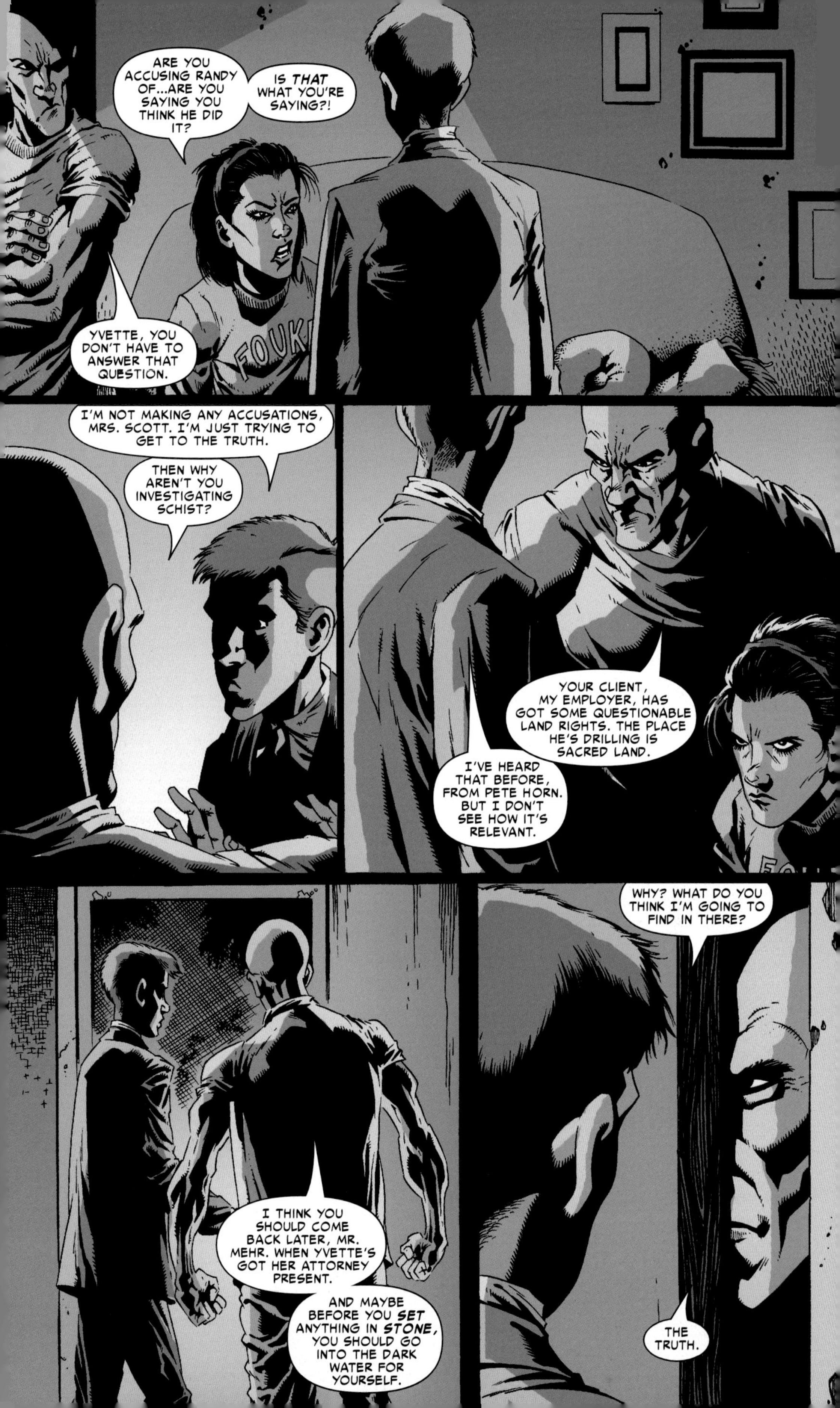
ARE YOU ACCUSING RANDY OF...ARE YOU SAYING YOU THINK HE DID IT?
IS *THAT* WHAT YOU'RE SAYING?!
YVETTE, YOU DON'T HAVE TO ANSWER THAT QUESTION.
FOUK
I'M NOT MAKING ANY ACCUSATIONS, MRS. SCOTT. I'M JUST TRYING TO GET TO THE TRUTH.
THEN WHY AREN'T YOU INVESTIGATING SCHIST?
YOUR CLIENT, MY EMPLOYER, HAS GOT SOME QUESTIONABLE LAND RIGHTS. THE PLACE HE'S DRILLING IS SACRED LAND.
I'VE HEARD THAT BEFORE, FROM PETE HORN. BUT I DON'T SEE HOW IT'S RELEVANT.
I THINK YOU SHOULD COME BACK LATER, MR. MEHR. WHEN YVETTE'S GOT HER ATTORNEY PRESENT.
AND MAYBE BEFORE YOU *SET* ANYTHING IN *STONE*, YOU SHOULD GO INTO THE DARK WATER FOR YOURSELF.
WHY? WHAT DO YOU THINK I'M GOING TO FIND IN THERE?
THE TRUTH.

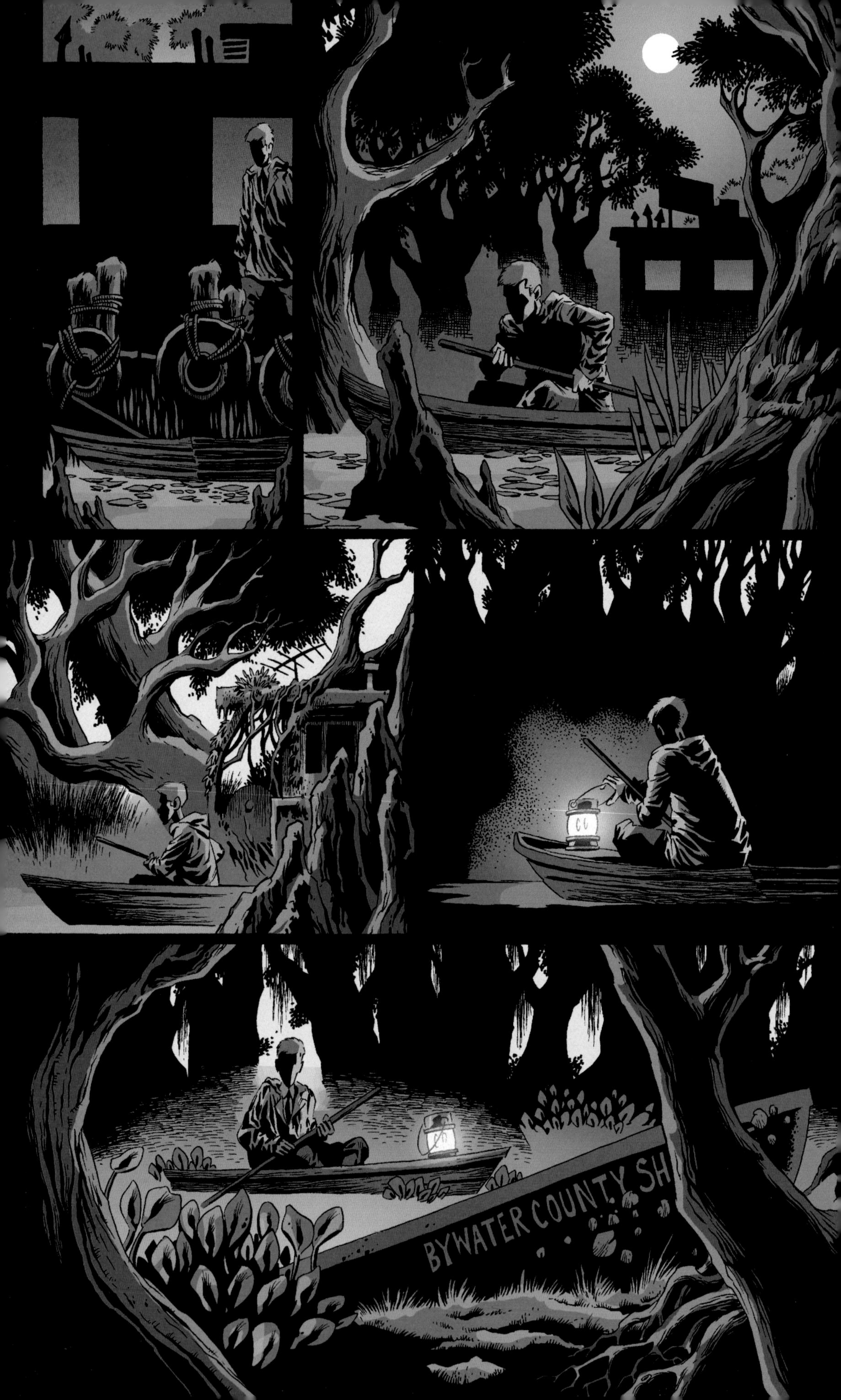
BYWATER COUNTY SH

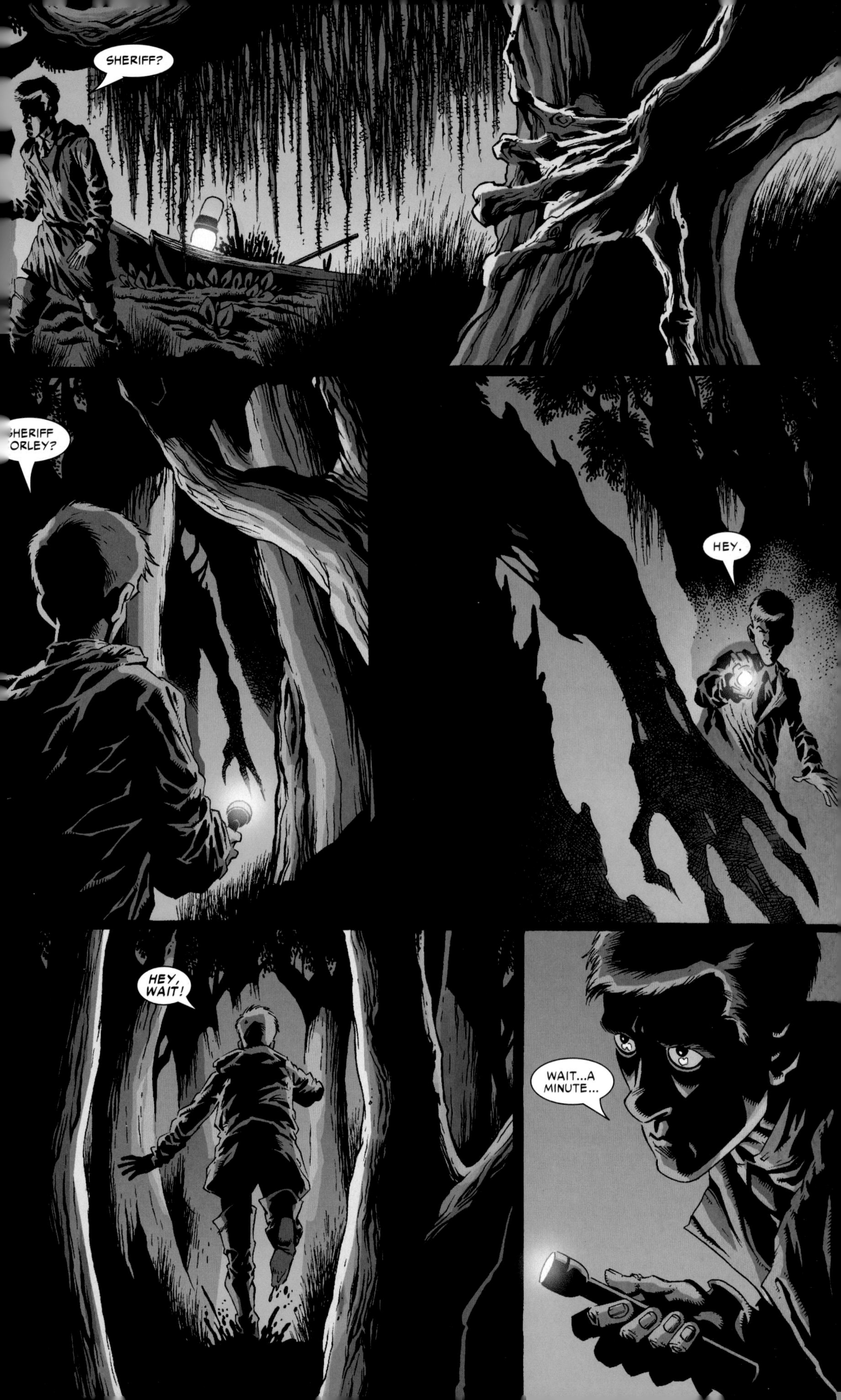
SHERIFF?
SHERIFF ORLEY?
HEY.
HEY, WAIT!
WAIT...A MINUTE...

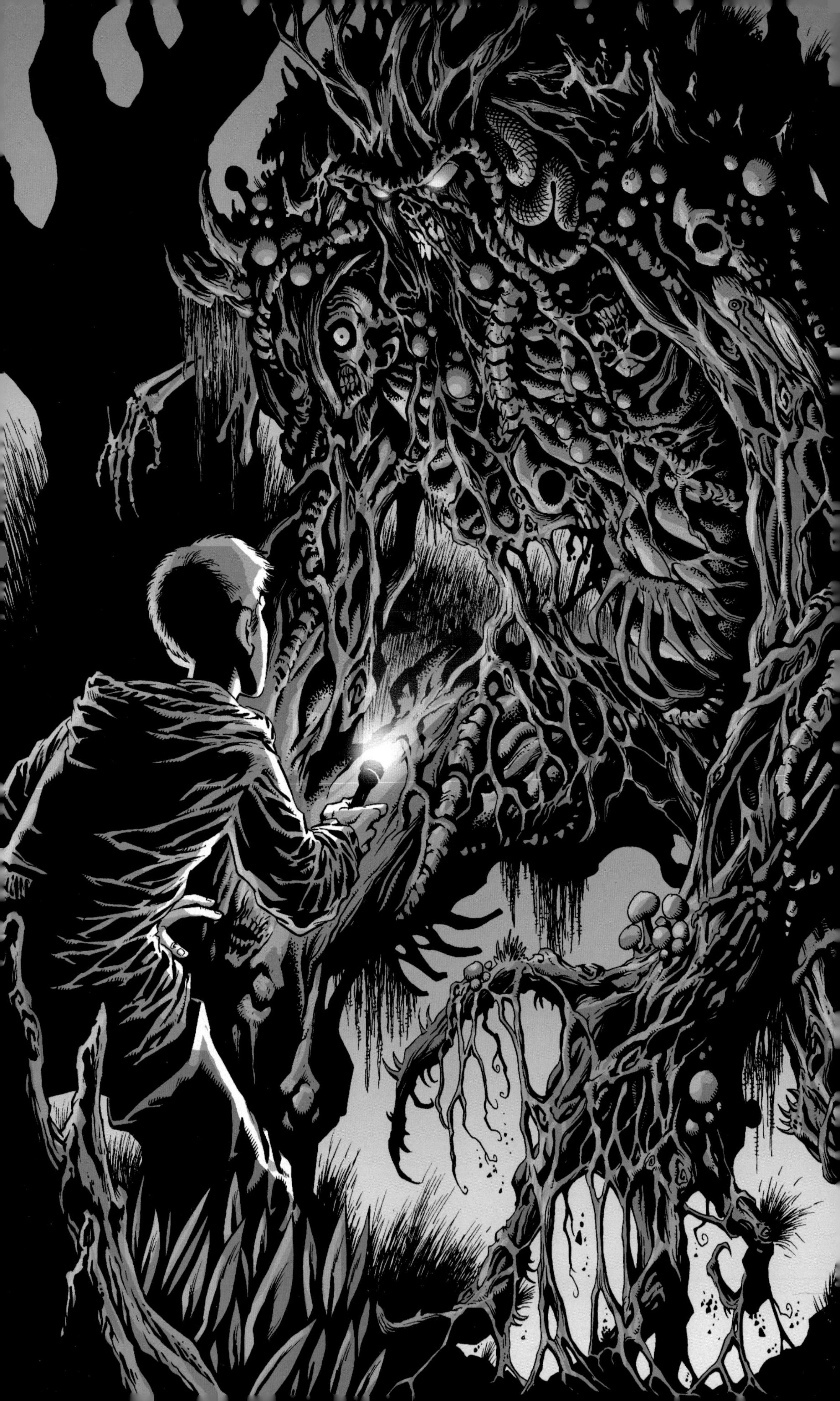

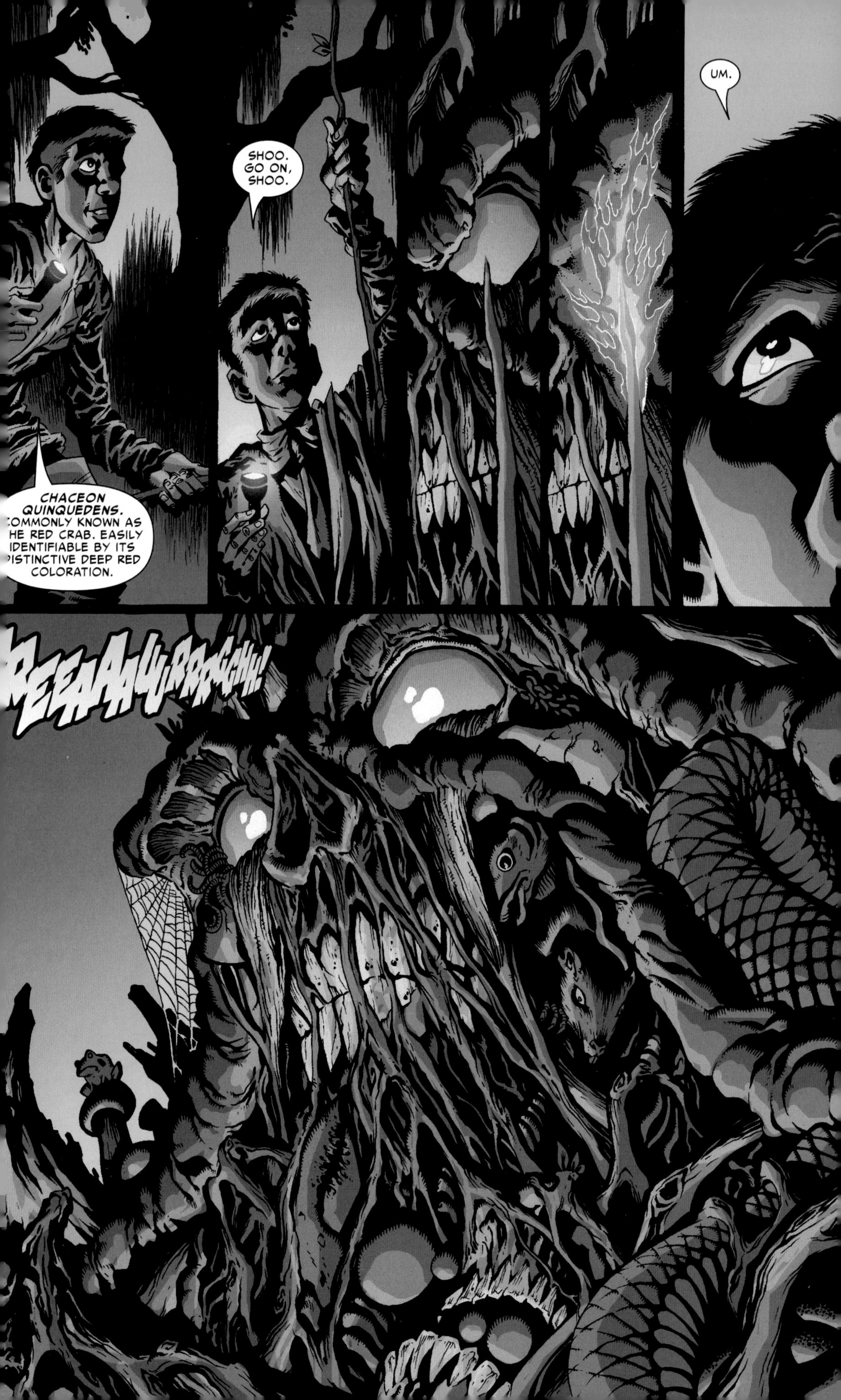
CHACEON QUINQUEDENS. OMMONLY KNOWN AS HE RED CRAB. EASILY IDENTIFIABLE BY ITS ISTINCTIVE DEEP RED COLORATION.
SHOO. GO ON, SHOO.
UM.
REEAAUURRRGHH!

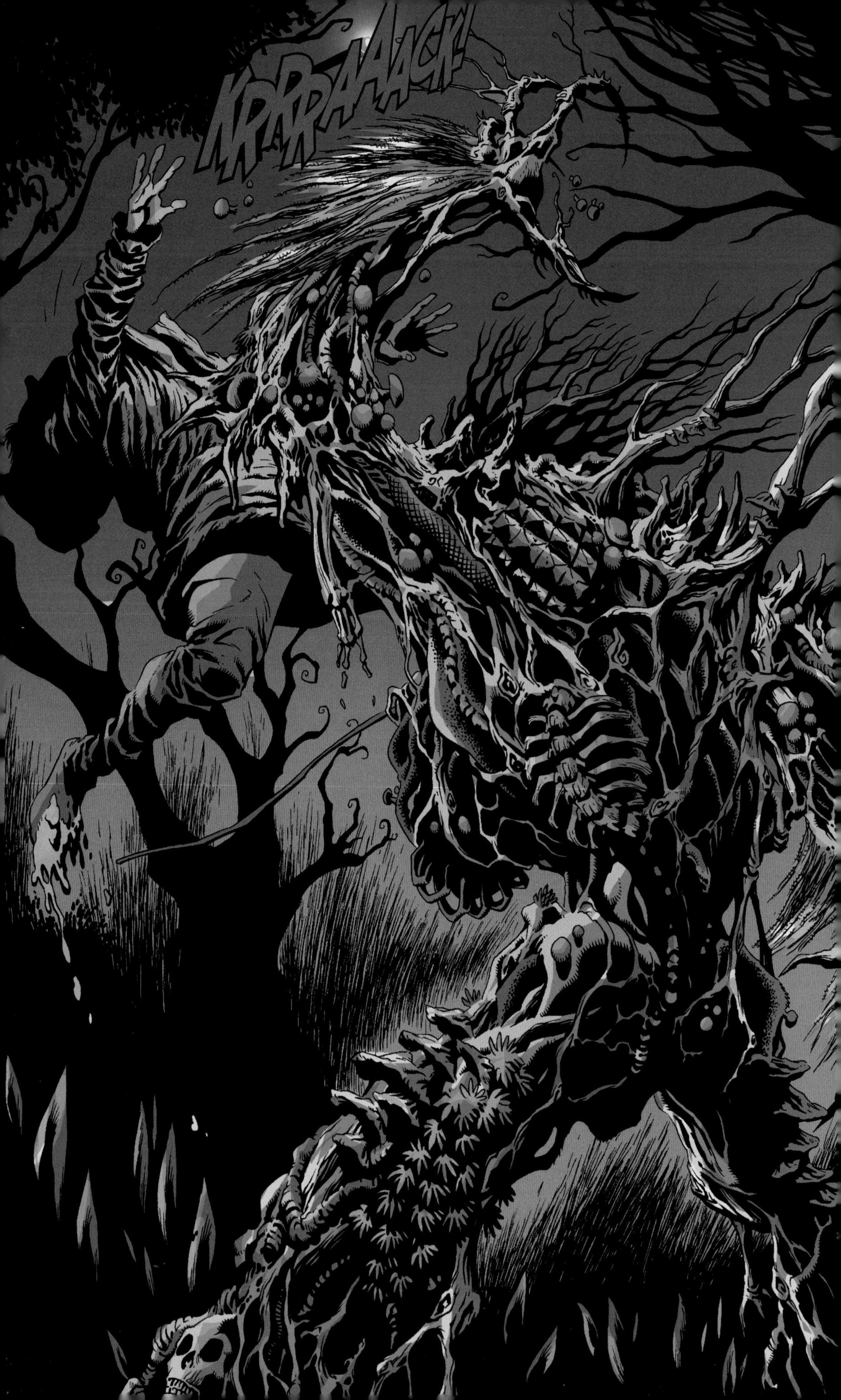
KRRRAAAACK!

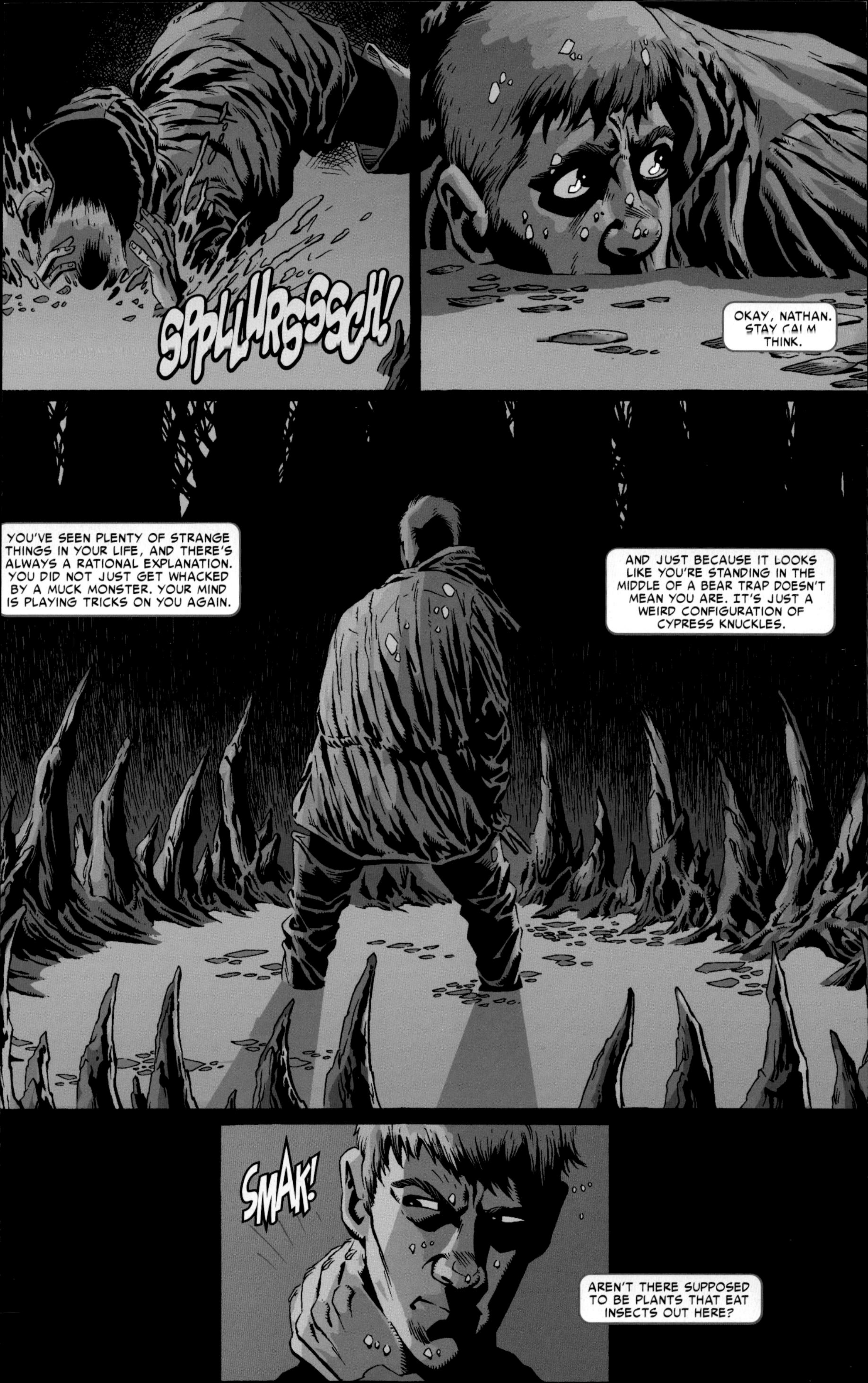
SPPLLURSSSCH!
OKAY, NATHAN. STAY CALM THINK.
YOU'VE SEEN PLENTY OF STRANGE THINGS IN YOUR LIFE, AND THERE'S ALWAYS A RATIONAL EXPLANATION. YOU DID NOT JUST GET WHACKED BY A MUCK MONSTER. YOUR MIND IS PLAYING TRICKS ON YOU AGAIN.
AND JUST BECAUSE IT LOOKS LIKE YOU'RE STANDING IN THE MIDDLE OF A BEAR TRAP DOESN'T MEAN YOU ARE. IT'S JUST A WEIRD CONFIGURATION OF CYPRESS KNUCKLES.
SMAK!
AREN'T THERE SUPPOSED TO BE PLANTS THAT EAT INSECTS OUT HERE?

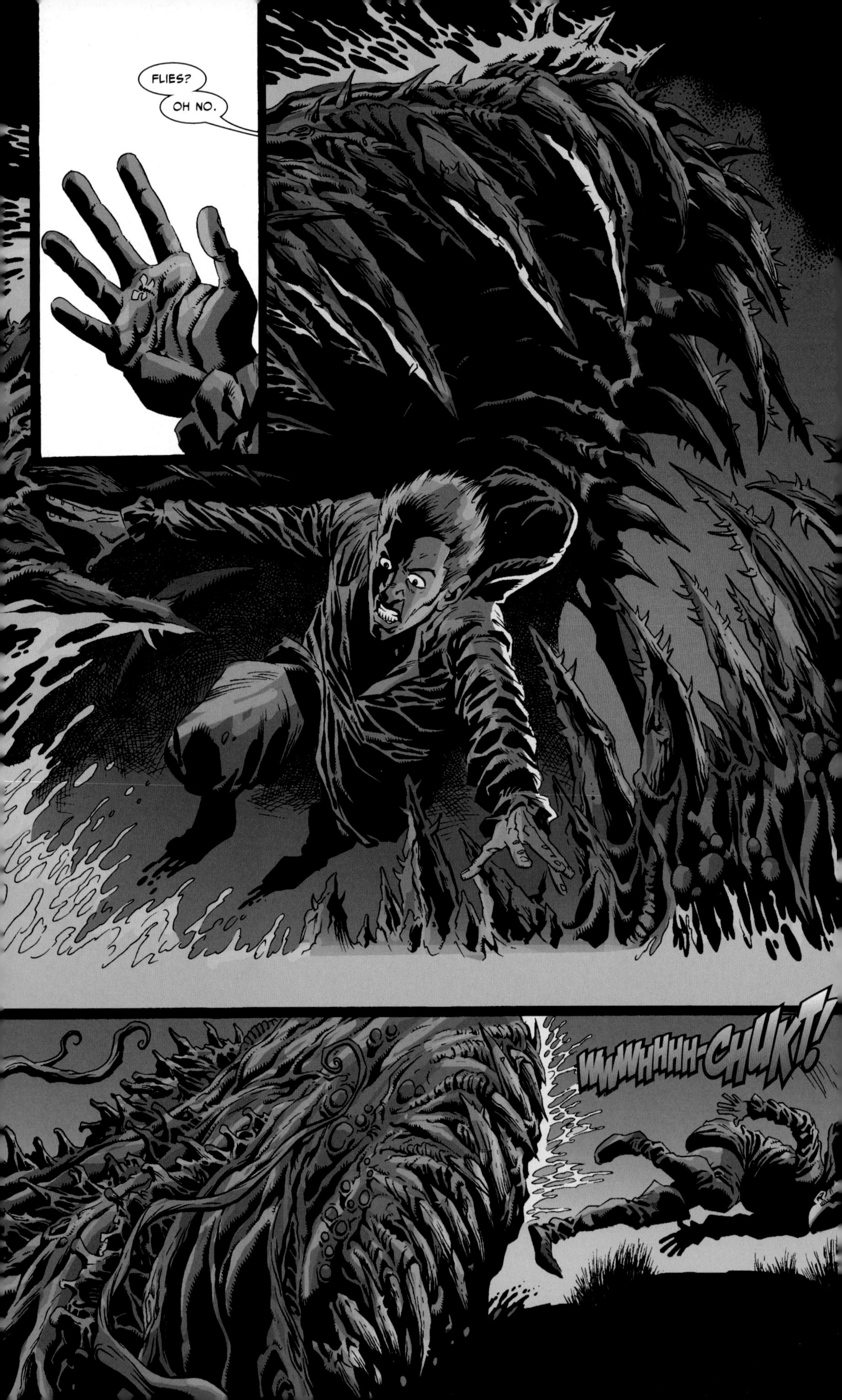
FLIES?
OH NO.
WWWHHHH-CHUKT!

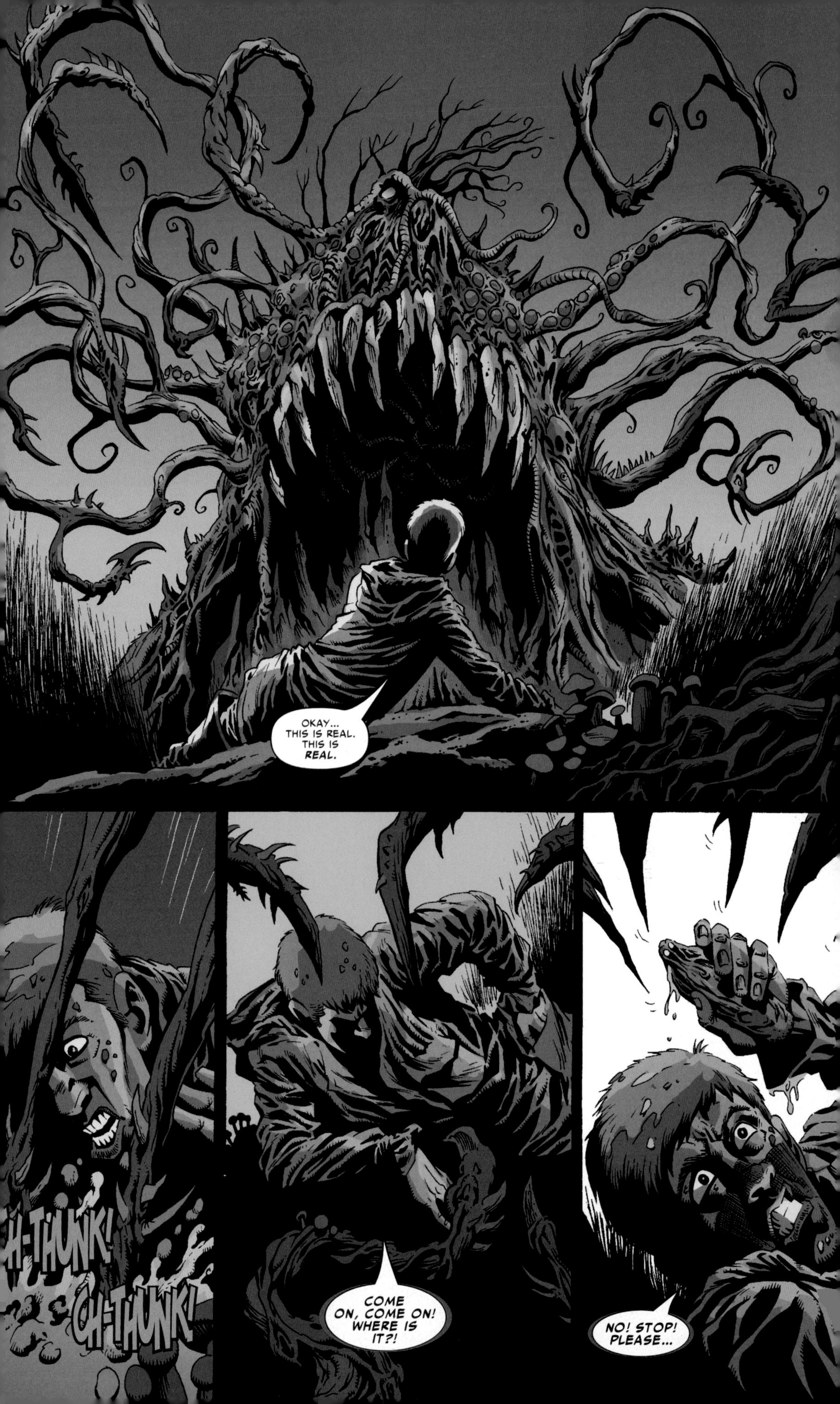
OKAY... THIS IS REAL. THIS IS REAL.
H-THUNK!
CH-THUNK!
COME ON, COME ON! WHERE IS IT?!
NO! STOP! PLEASE...

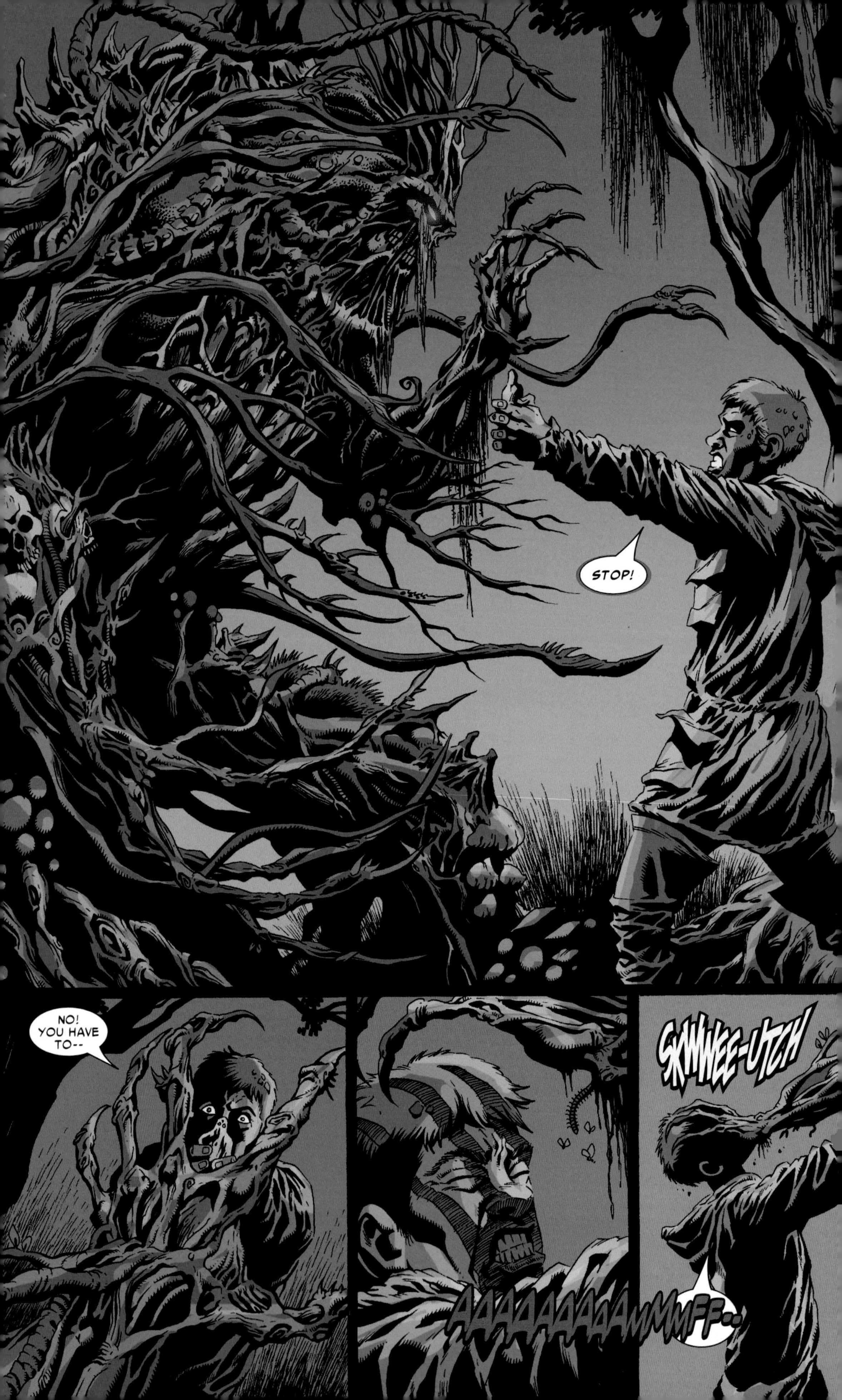
STOP!
NO! YOU HAVE TO--
SKWWEE-UTCH
AAAAAAAAAMMFF..

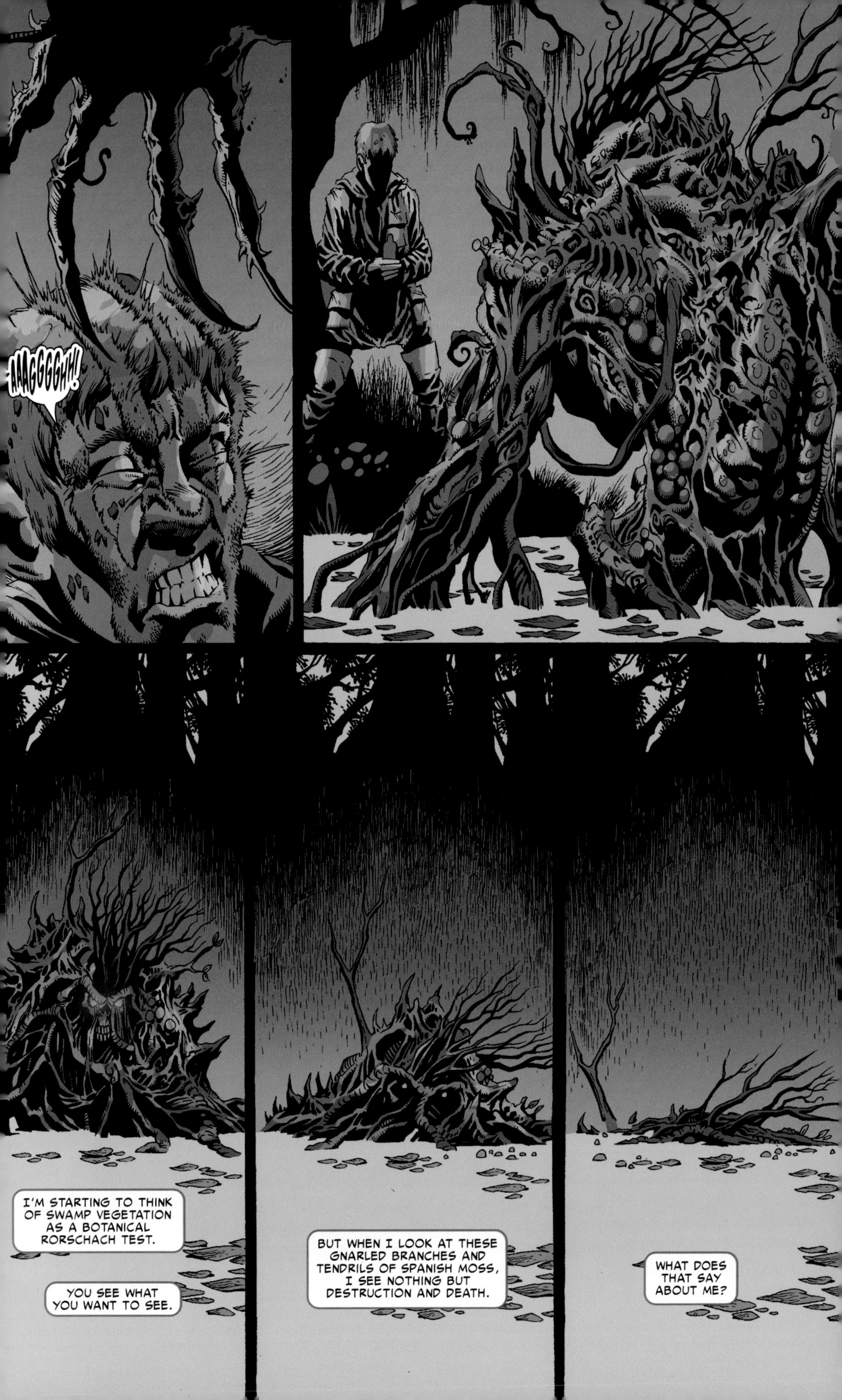
AAAGGGGHH!
I'M STARTING TO THINK OF SWAMP VEGETATION AS A BOTANICAL RORSCHACH TEST.
YOU SEE WHAT YOU WANT TO SEE.
BUT WHEN I LOOK AT THESE GNARLED BRANCHES AND TENDRILS OF SPANISH MOSS, I SEE NOTHING BUT DESTRUCTION AND DEATH.
WHAT DOES THAT SAY ABOUT ME?

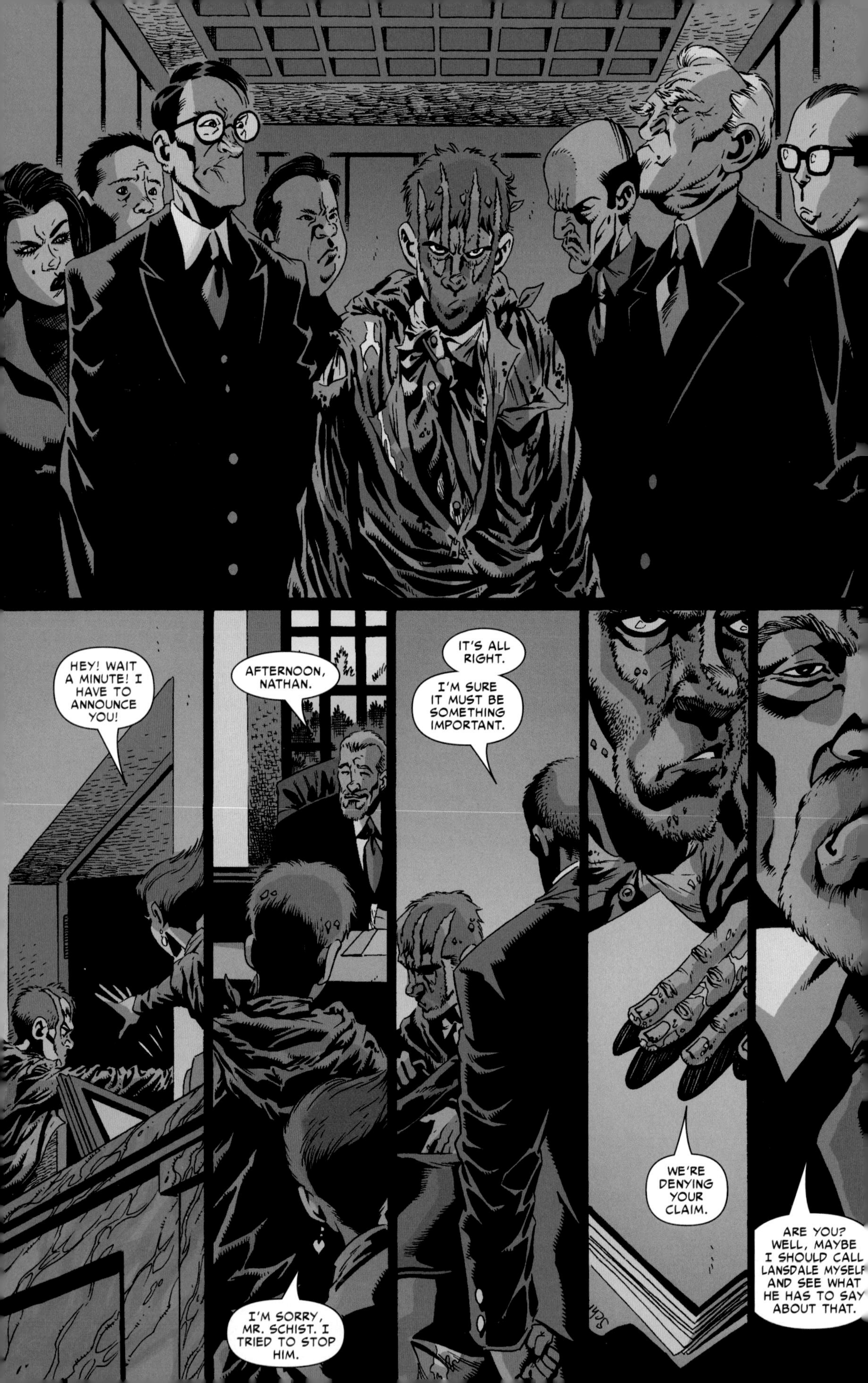
HEY! WAIT A MINUTE! I HAVE TO ANNOUNCE YOU!
AFTERNOON, NATHAN.
I'M SORRY, MR. SCHIST. I TRIED TO STOP HIM.
IT'S ALL RIGHT.
I'M SURE IT MUST BE SOMETHING IMPORTANT.
WE'RE DENYING YOUR CLAIM.
ARE YOU? WELL, MAYBE I SHOULD CALL LANSDALE MYSELF AND SEE WHAT HE HAS TO SAY ABOUT THAT.

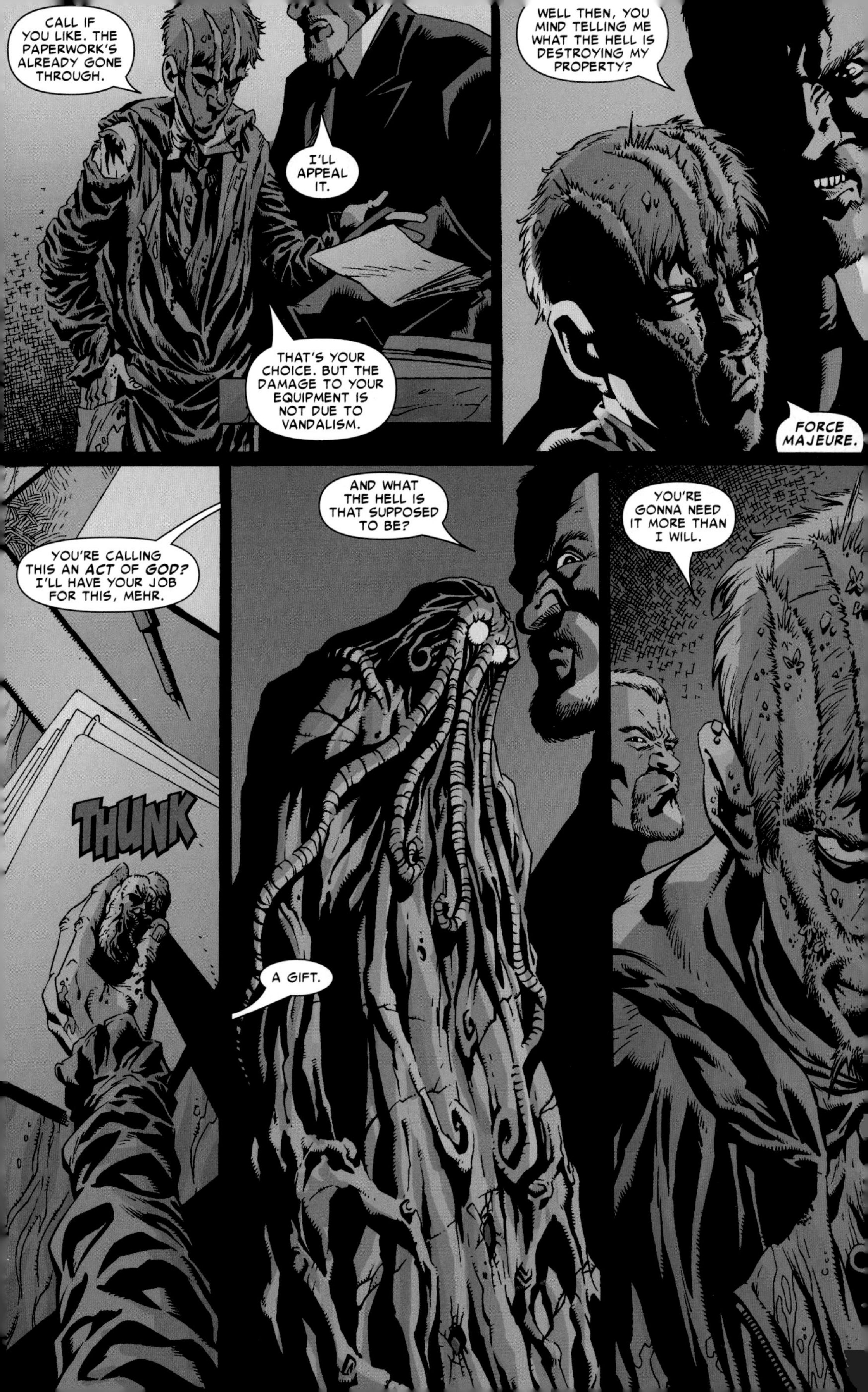
CALL IF YOU LIKE. THE PAPERWORK'S ALREADY GONE THROUGH.
I'LL APPEAL IT.
THAT'S YOUR CHOICE. BUT THE DAMAGE TO YOUR EQUIPMENT IS NOT DUE TO VANDALISM.
WELL THEN, YOU MIND TELLING ME WHAT THE HELL IS DESTROYING MY PROPERTY?
FORCE MAJEURE.
YOU'RE CALLING THIS AN *ACT* OF *GOD?* I'LL HAVE YOUR JOB FOR THIS, MEHR.
THUNK
AND WHAT THE HELL IS THAT SUPPOSED TO BE?
A GIFT.
YOU'RE GONNA NEED IT MORE THAN I WILL.

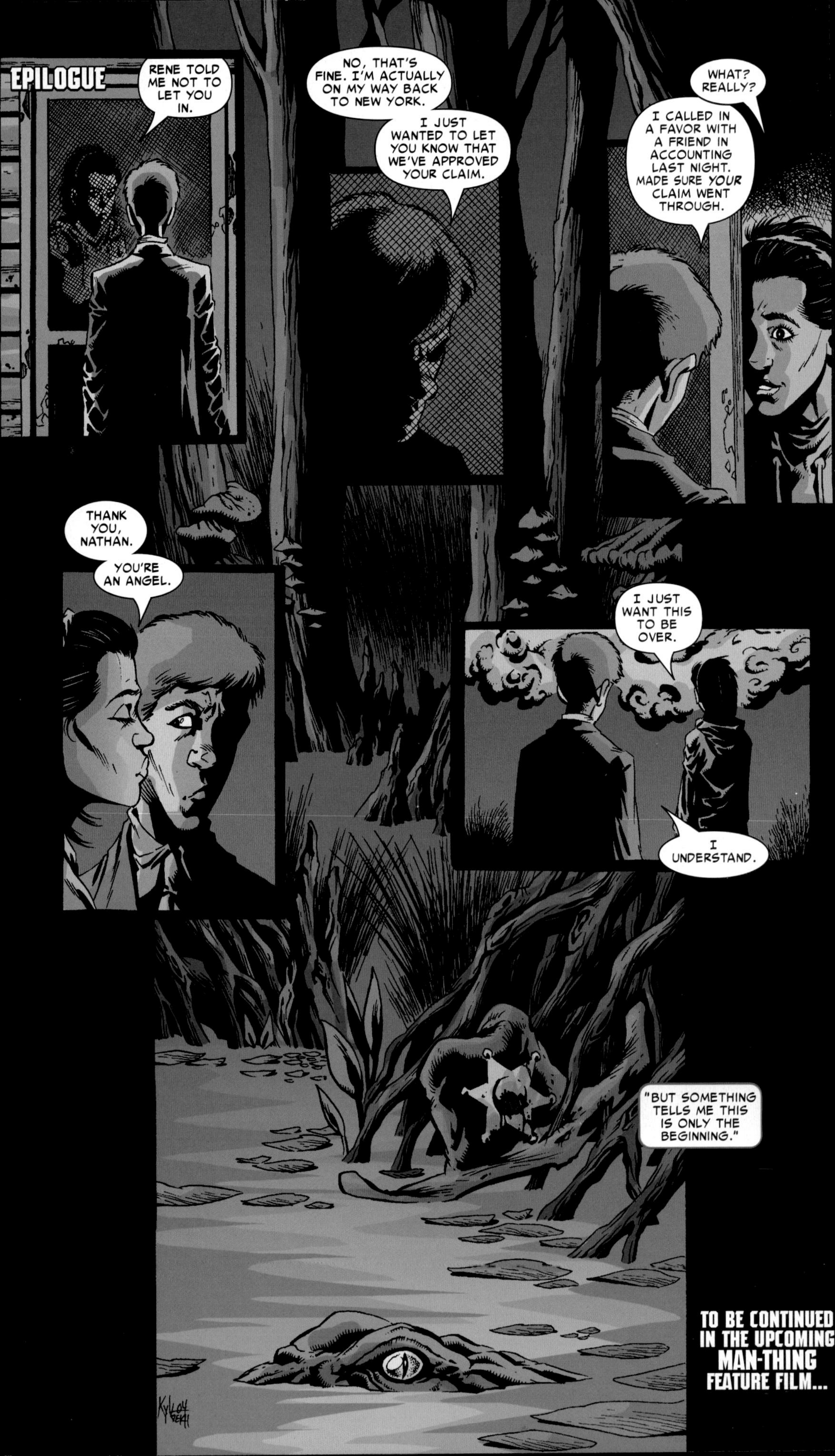
EPILOGUE
RENE TOLD ME NOT TO LET YOU IN.
NO, THAT'S FINE. I'M ACTUALLY ON MY WAY BACK TO NEW YORK.
I JUST WANTED TO LET YOU KNOW THAT WE'VE APPROVED YOUR CLAIM.
WHAT? REALLY?
I CALLED IN A FAVOR WITH A FRIEND IN ACCOUNTING LAST NIGHT. MADE SURE YOUR CLAIM WENT THROUGH.
THANK YOU, NATHAN.
YOU'RE AN ANGEL.
I JUST WANT THIS TO BE OVER.
I UNDERSTAND.
"BUT SOMETHING TELLS ME THIS IS ONLY THE BEGINNING."
TO BE CONTINUED IN THE UPCOMING MAN-THING FEATURE FILM...

Savage Tales #1 (1971)

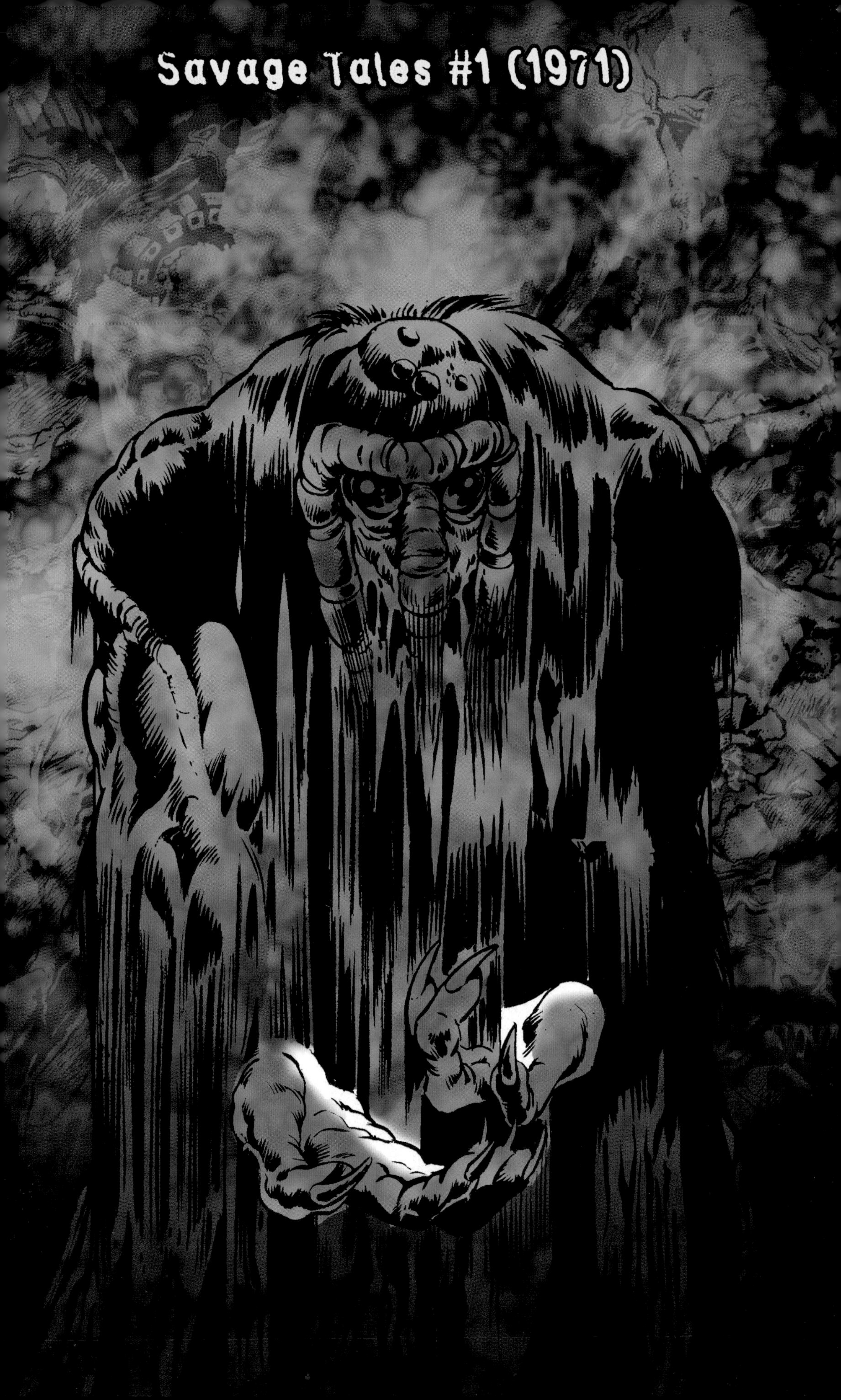

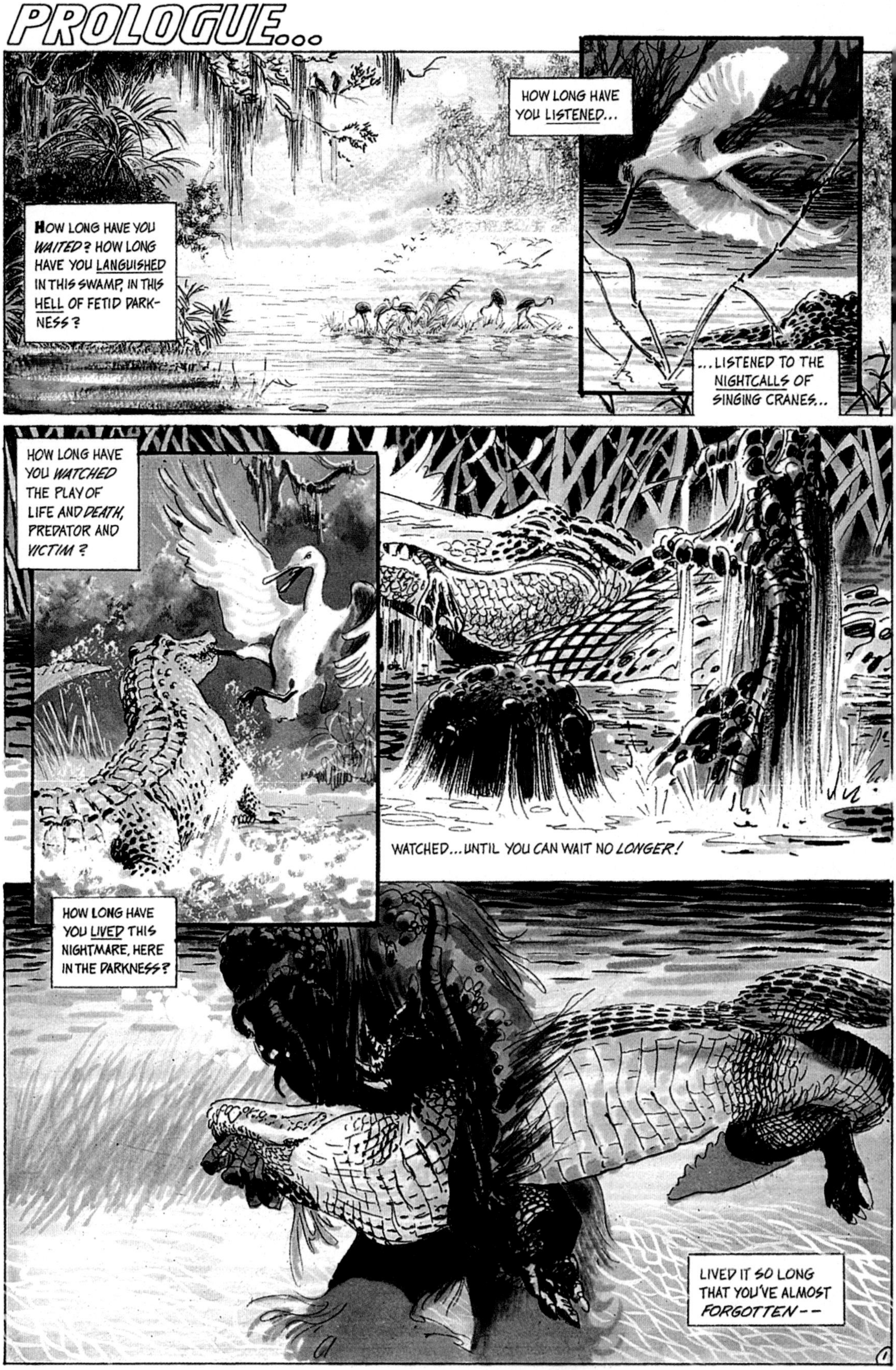
PROLOGUE...
HOW LONG HAVE YOU WAITED? HOW LONG HAVE YOU LANGUISHED IN THIS SWAMP, IN THIS HELL OF FETID DARKNESS?
HOW LONG HAVE YOU LISTENED...
...LISTENED TO THE NIGHTCALLS OF SINGING CRANES...
HOW LONG HAVE YOU WATCHED THE PLAY OF LIFE AND DEATH, PREDATOR AND VICTIM?
WATCHED...UNTIL YOU CAN WAIT NO LONGER!
HOW LONG HAVE YOU LIVED THIS NIGHTMARE, HERE IN THE DARKNESS?
LIVED IT SO LONG THAT YOU'VE ALMOST FORGOTTEN--
1

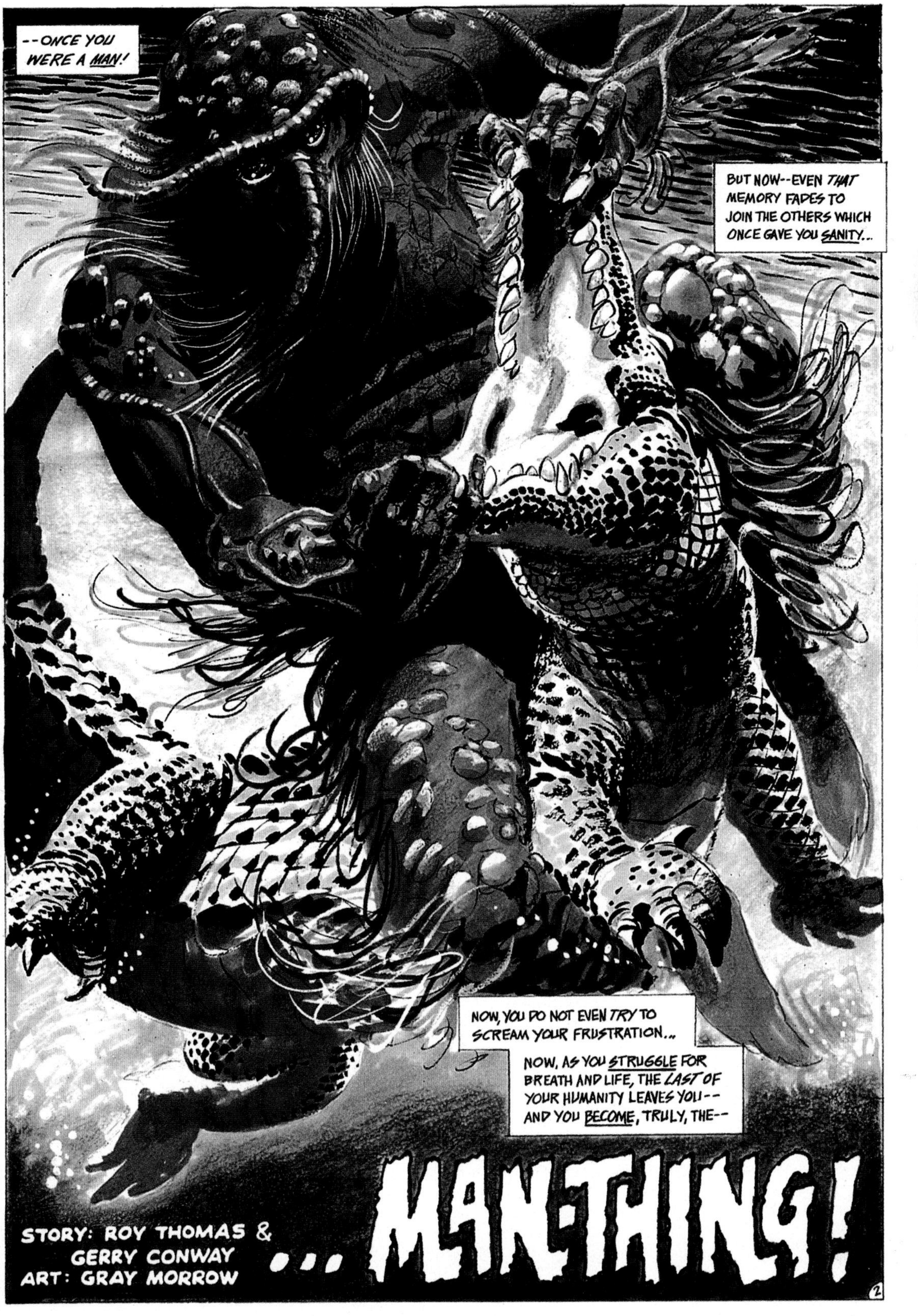
--ONCE YOU WERE A MAN!
BUT NOW--EVEN THAT MEMORY FADES TO JOIN THE OTHERS WHICH ONCE GAVE YOU SANITY...
NOW, YOU DO NOT EVEN TRY TO SCREAM YOUR FRUSTRATION...
NOW, AS YOU STRUGGLE FOR BREATH AND LIFE, THE LAST OF YOUR HUMANITY LEAVES YOU--AND YOU BECOME, TRULY, THE--
...MAN-THING!
STORY: ROY THOMAS & GERRY CONWAY
ART: GRAY MORROW
2

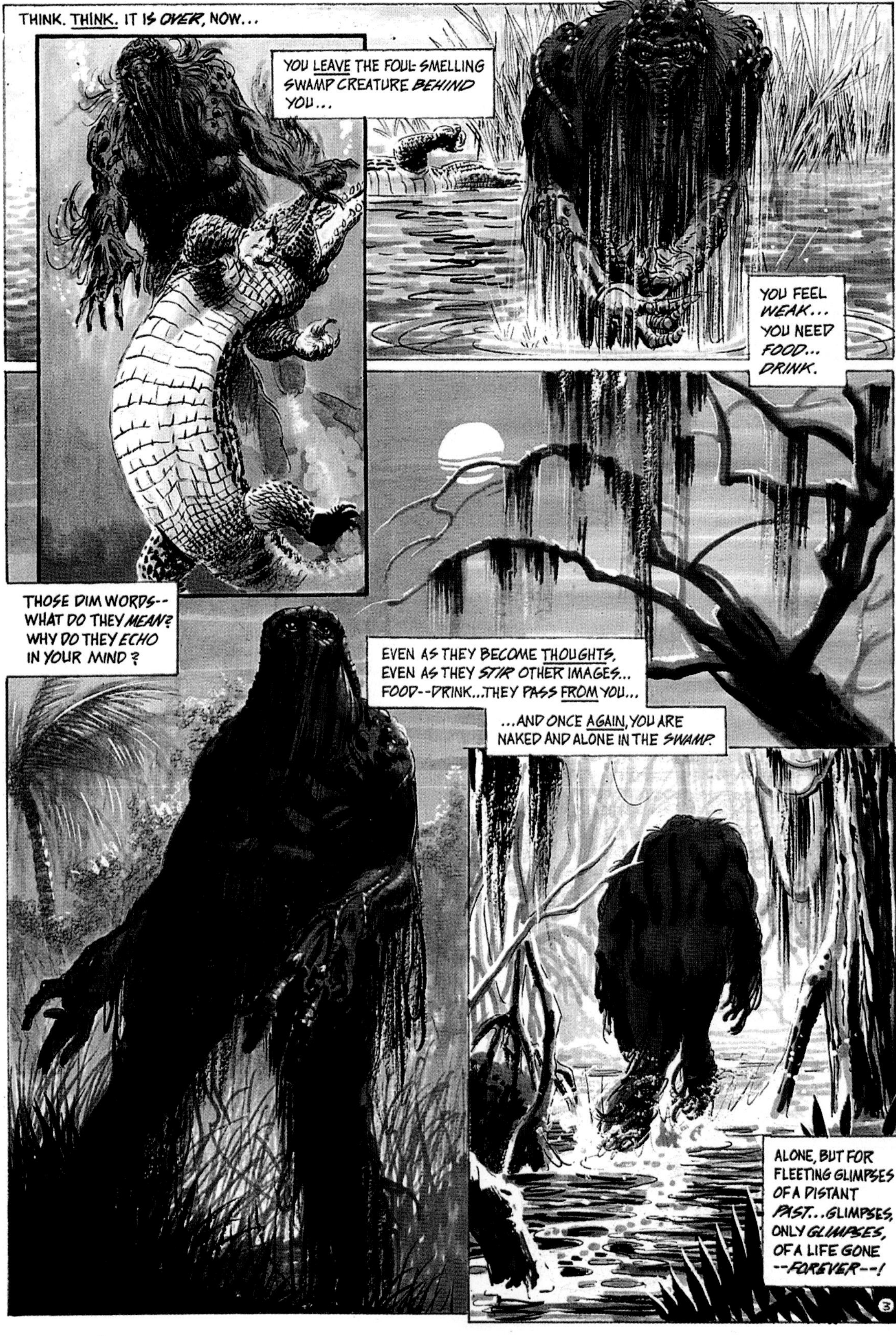

THINK. THINK. IT IS OVER, NOW...
YOU LEAVE THE FOUL-SMELLING SWAMP CREATURE BEHIND YOU...
YOU FEEL WEAK... YOU NEED FOOD... DRINK.
THOSE DIM WORDS-- WHAT DO THEY MEAN? WHY DO THEY ECHO IN YOUR MIND?
EVEN AS THEY BECOME THOUGHTS, EVEN AS THEY STIR OTHER IMAGES... FOOD--DRINK...THEY PASS FROM YOU...
...AND ONCE AGAIN, YOU ARE NAKED AND ALONE IN THE SWAMP.
ALONE, BUT FOR FLEETING GLIMPSES OF A DISTANT PAST...GLIMPSES, ONLY GLIMPSES, OF A LIFE GONE --FOREVER--!

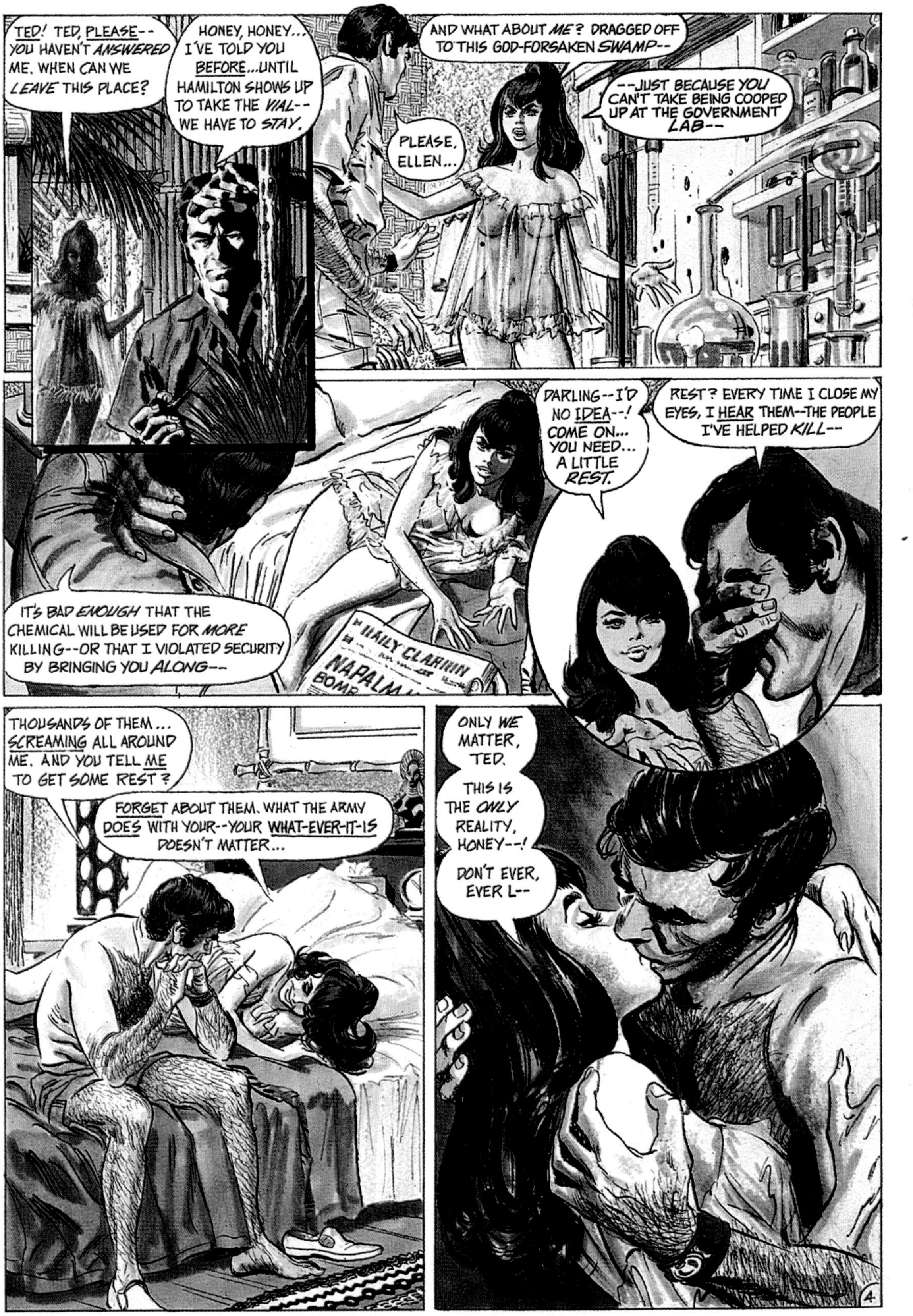
TED! TED, PLEASE-- YOU HAVEN'T ANSWERED ME. WHEN CAN WE LEAVE THIS PLACE?
HONEY, HONEY... I'VE TOLD YOU BEFORE...UNTIL HAMILTON SHOWS UP TO TAKE THE VIAL-- WE HAVE TO STAY.
AND WHAT ABOUT ME? DRAGGED OFF TO THIS GOD-FORSAKEN SWAMP--
--JUST BECAUSE YOU CAN'T TAKE BEING COOPED UP AT THE GOVERNMENT LAB--
PLEASE, ELLEN...
IT'S BAD ENOUGH THAT THE CHEMICAL WILL BE USED FOR MORE KILLING--OR THAT I VIOLATED SECURITY BY BRINGING YOU ALONG--
DAILY CLARION
NAPALM BOMB
DARLING--I'D NO IDEA--! COME ON... YOU NEED... A LITTLE REST.
REST? EVERY TIME I CLOSE MY EYES, I HEAR THEM--THE PEOPLE I'VE HELPED KILL--
THOUSANDS OF THEM... SCREAMING ALL AROUND ME. AND YOU TELL ME TO GET SOME REST?
FORGET ABOUT THEM. WHAT THE ARMY DOES WITH YOUR--YOUR WHAT-EVER-IT-IS DOESN'T MATTER...
ONLY WE MATTER, TED.
THIS IS THE ONLY REALITY, HONEY--!
DON'T EVER, EVER L--
4

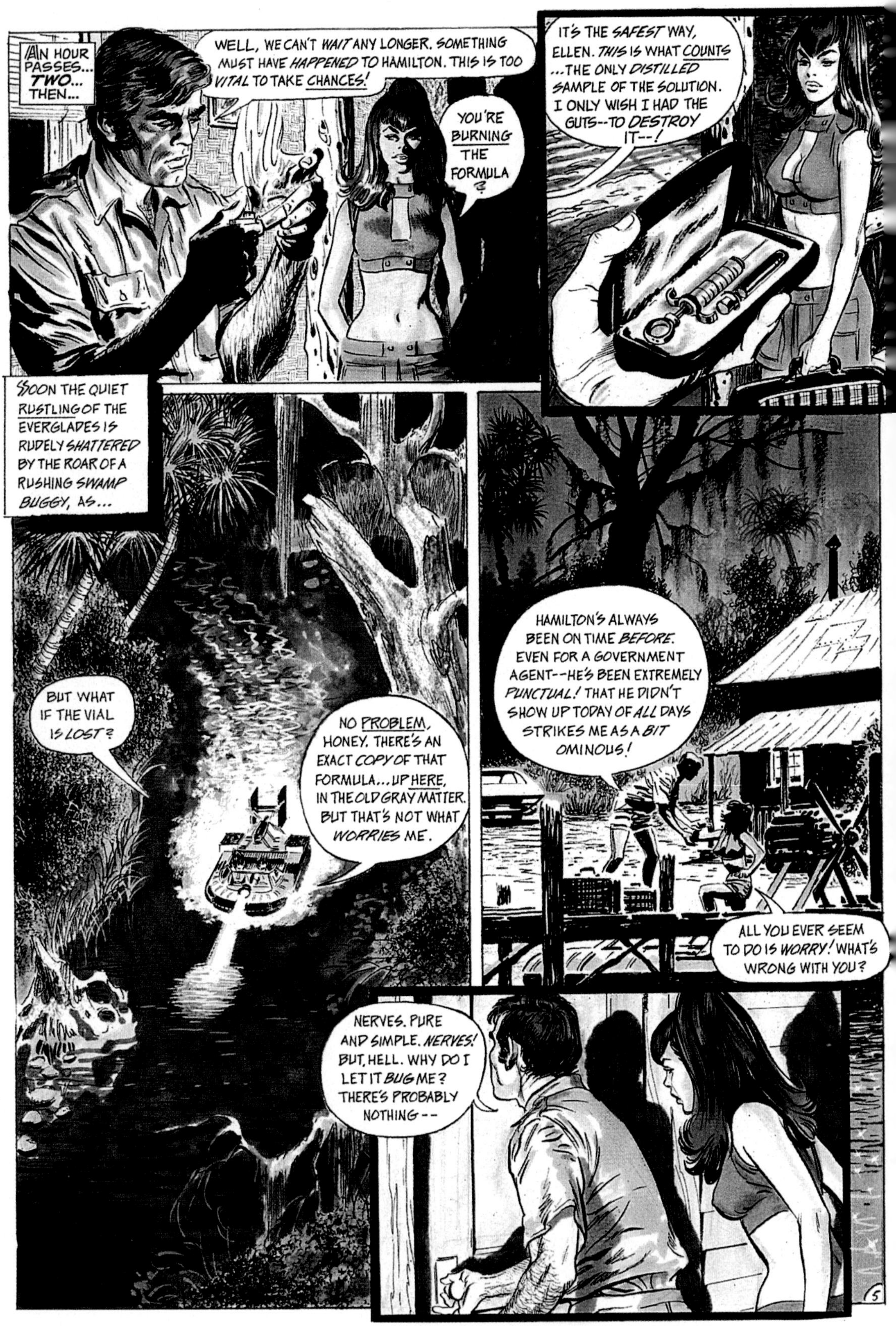
AN HOUR PASSES... TWO... THEN...
WELL, WE CAN'T WAIT ANY LONGER. SOMETHING MUST HAVE HAPPENED TO HAMILTON. THIS IS TOO VITAL TO TAKE CHANCES!
YOU'RE BURNING THE FORMULA?
IT'S THE SAFEST WAY, ELLEN. THIS IS WHAT COUNTS ...THE ONLY DISTILLED SAMPLE OF THE SOLUTION. I ONLY WISH I HAD THE GUTS--TO DESTROY IT--!
SOON THE QUIET RUSTLING OF THE EVERGLADES IS RUDELY SHATTERED BY THE ROAR OF A RUSHING SWAMP BUGGY, AS...
BUT WHAT IF THE VIAL IS LOST?
NO PROBLEM, HONEY. THERE'S AN EXACT COPY OF THAT FORMULA... UP HERE, IN THE OLD GRAY MATTER. BUT THAT'S NOT WHAT WORRIES ME.
HAMILTON'S ALWAYS BEEN ON TIME BEFORE. EVEN FOR A GOVERNMENT AGENT--HE'S BEEN EXTREMELY PUNCTUAL! THAT HE DIDN'T SHOW UP TODAY OF ALL DAYS STRIKES ME AS A BIT OMINOUS!
ALL YOU EVER SEEM TO DO IS WORRY! WHAT'S WRONG WITH YOU?
NERVES. PURE AND SIMPLE. NERVES! BUT, HELL. WHY DO I LET IT BUG ME? THERE'S PROBABLY NOTHING--
5

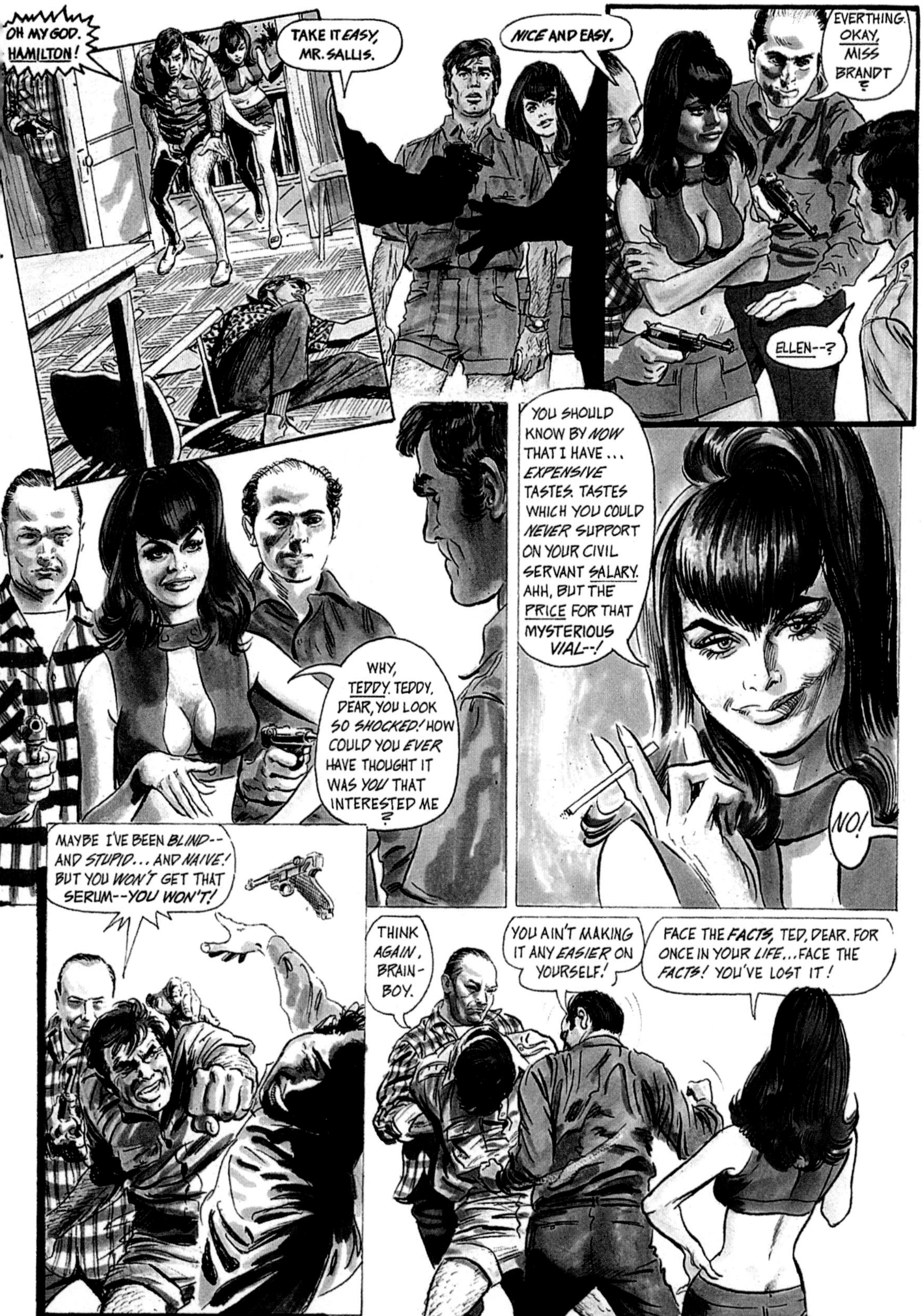

OH MY GOD. HAMILTON!
TAKE IT EASY, MR. SALLIS.
NICE AND EASY.
EVERTHING OKAY, MISS BRANDT?
ELLEN--?
WHY, TEDDY. TEDDY, DEAR, YOU LOOK SO SHOCKED! HOW COULD YOU EVER HAVE THOUGHT IT WAS YOU THAT INTERESTED ME?
YOU SHOULD KNOW BY NOW THAT I HAVE... EXPENSIVE TASTES. TASTES WHICH YOU COULD NEVER SUPPORT ON YOUR CIVIL SERVANT SALARY. AHH, BUT THE PRICE FOR THAT MYSTERIOUS VIAL--!
NO!
MAYBE I'VE BEEN BLIND-- AND STUPID... AND NAIVE! BUT YOU WON'T GET THAT SERUM--YOU WON'T!
THINK AGAIN, BRAIN-BOY.
YOU AIN'T MAKING IT ANY EASIER ON YOURSELF!
FACE THE FACTS, TED, DEAR. FOR ONCE IN YOUR LIFE... FACE THE FACTS! YOU'VE LOST IT!

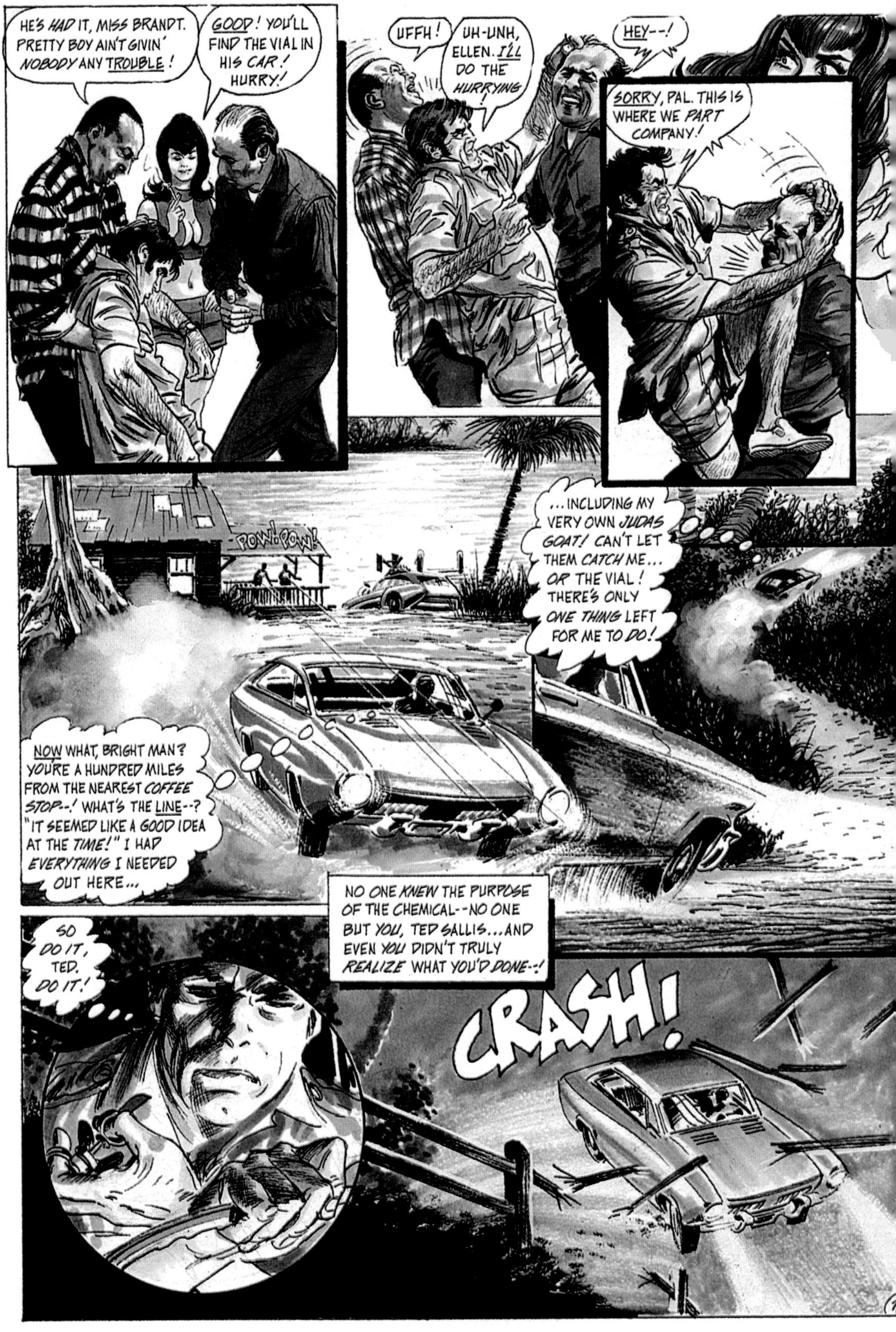
HE'S HAD IT, MISS BRANDT. PRETTY BOY AIN'T GIVIN' NOBODY ANY TROUBLE!
GOOD! YOU'LL FIND THE VIAL IN HIS CAR! HURRY!
UFFH!
UH-UNH, ELLEN. I'LL DO THE HURRYING!
HEY--!
SORRY, PAL. THIS IS WHERE WE PART COMPANY!
POW! POW!
...INCLUDING MY VERY OWN JUDAS GOAT! CAN'T LET THEM CATCH ME... OR THE VIAL! THERE'S ONLY ONE THING LEFT FOR ME TO DO!
NOW WHAT, BRIGHT MAN? YOU'RE A HUNDRED MILES FROM THE NEAREST COFFEE STOP--! WHAT'S THE LINE--? "IT SEEMED LIKE A GOOD IDEA AT THE TIME!" I HAD EVERYTHING I NEEDED OUT HERE...
NO ONE KNEW THE PURPOSE OF THE CHEMICAL--NO ONE BUT YOU, TED SALLIS...AND EVEN YOU DIDN'T TRULY REALIZE WHAT YOU'D DONE--!
SO DO IT, TED. DO IT!
CRASH!

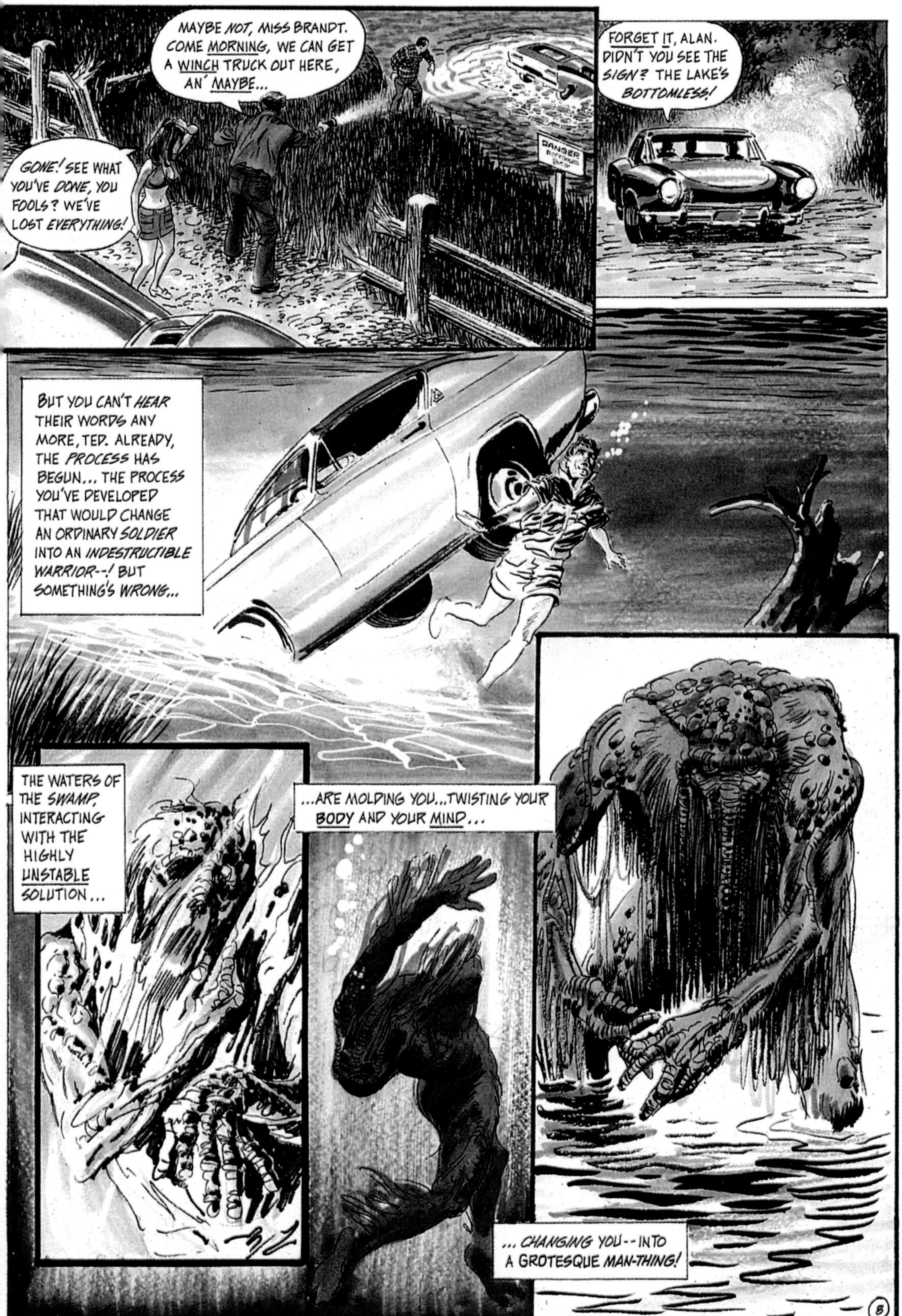

MAYBE NOT, MISS BRANDT. COME MORNING, WE CAN GET A WINCH TRUCK OUT HERE, AN' MAYBE...
GONE! SEE WHAT YOU'VE DONE, YOU FOOLS? WE'VE LOST EVERYTHING!
DANGER
FORGET IT, ALAN. DIDN'T YOU SEE THE SIGN? THE LAKE'S BOTTOMLESS!
BUT YOU CAN'T HEAR THEIR WORDS ANY MORE, TED. ALREADY, THE PROCESS HAS BEGUN... THE PROCESS YOU'VE DEVELOPED THAT WOULD CHANGE AN ORDINARY SOLDIER INTO AN INDESTRUCTIBLE WARRIOR--! BUT SOMETHING'S WRONG...
THE WATERS OF THE SWAMP, INTERACTING WITH THE HIGHLY UNSTABLE SOLUTION...
...ARE MOLDING YOU...TWISTING YOUR BODY AND YOUR MIND...
...CHANGING YOU--INTO A GROTESQUE MAN-THING!

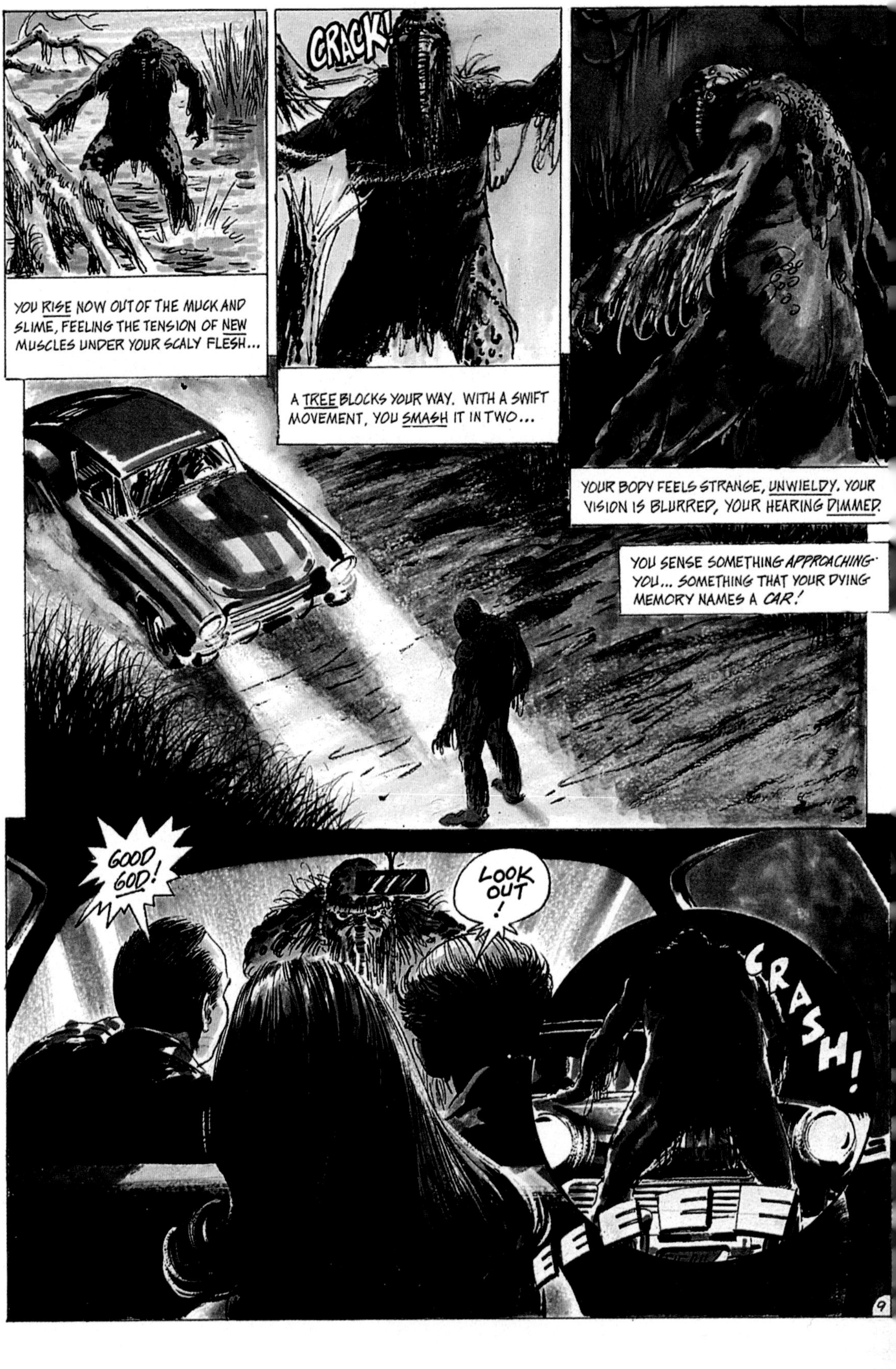

YOU RISE NOW OUT OF THE MUCK AND SLIME, FEELING THE TENSION OF NEW MUSCLES UNDER YOUR SCALY FLESH...
CRACK!
A TREE BLOCKS YOUR WAY. WITH A SWIFT MOVEMENT, YOU SMASH IT IN TWO...
YOUR BODY FEELS STRANGE, UNWIELDY. YOUR VISION IS BLURRED, YOUR HEARING DIMMED.
YOU SENSE SOMETHING APPROACHING YOU... SOMETHING THAT YOUR DYING MEMORY NAMES A CAR!
GOOD GOD!
LOOK OUT!
CRASH!
EEEEEEE

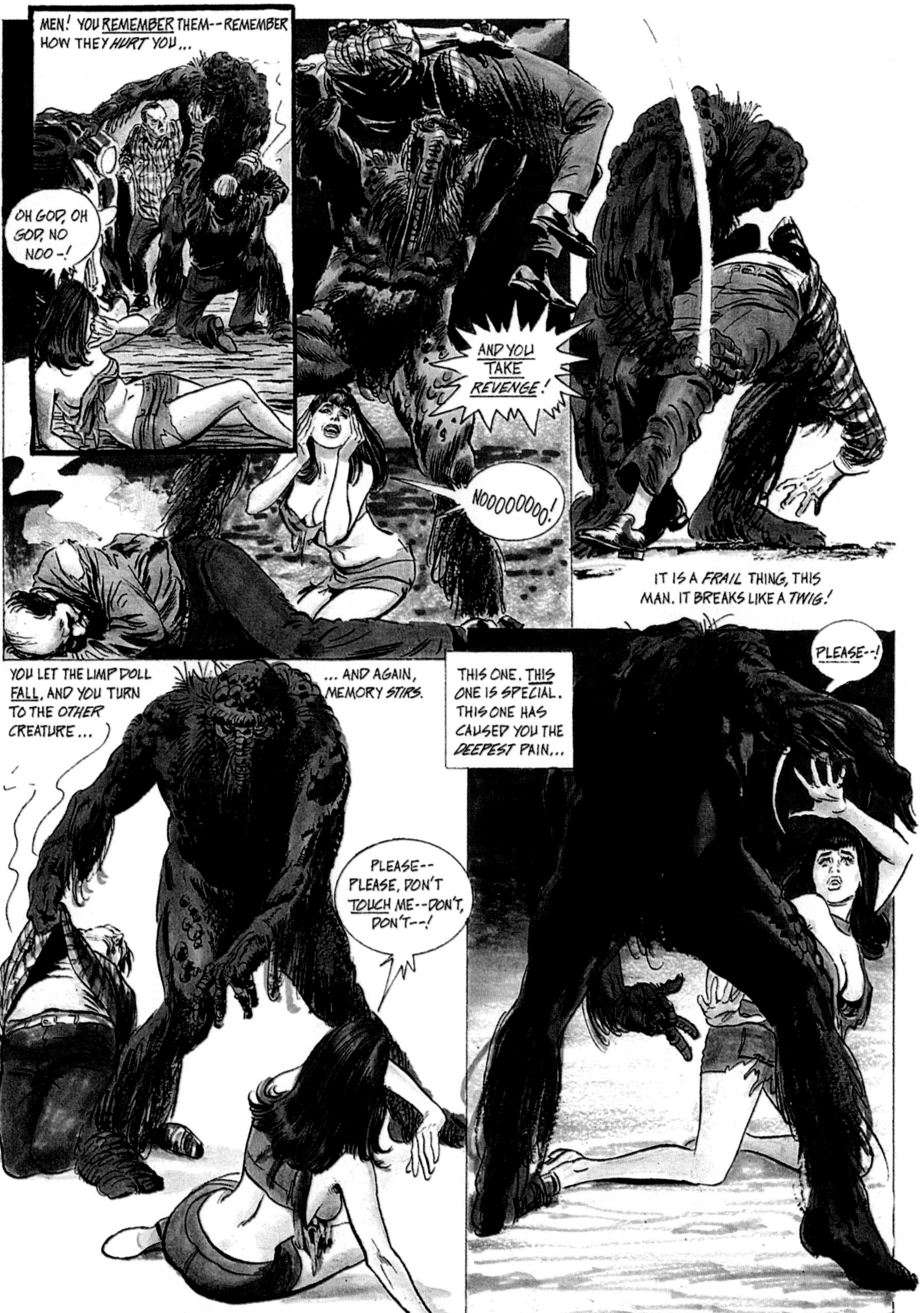
MEN! YOU REMEMBER THEM--REMEMBER HOW THEY HURT YOU...
OH GOD, OH GOD, NO NOO-!
AND YOU TAKE REVENGE!
NOOOOOOOO!
IT IS A FRAIL THING, THIS MAN. IT BREAKS LIKE A TWIG!
YOU LET THE LIMP DOLL FALL, AND YOU TURN TO THE OTHER CREATURE...
...AND AGAIN, MEMORY STIRS.
PLEASE--PLEASE, DON'T TOUCH ME--DON'T, DON'T--!
THIS ONE. THIS ONE IS SPECIAL. THIS ONE HAS CAUSED YOU THE DEEPEST PAIN...
PLEASE--!
10

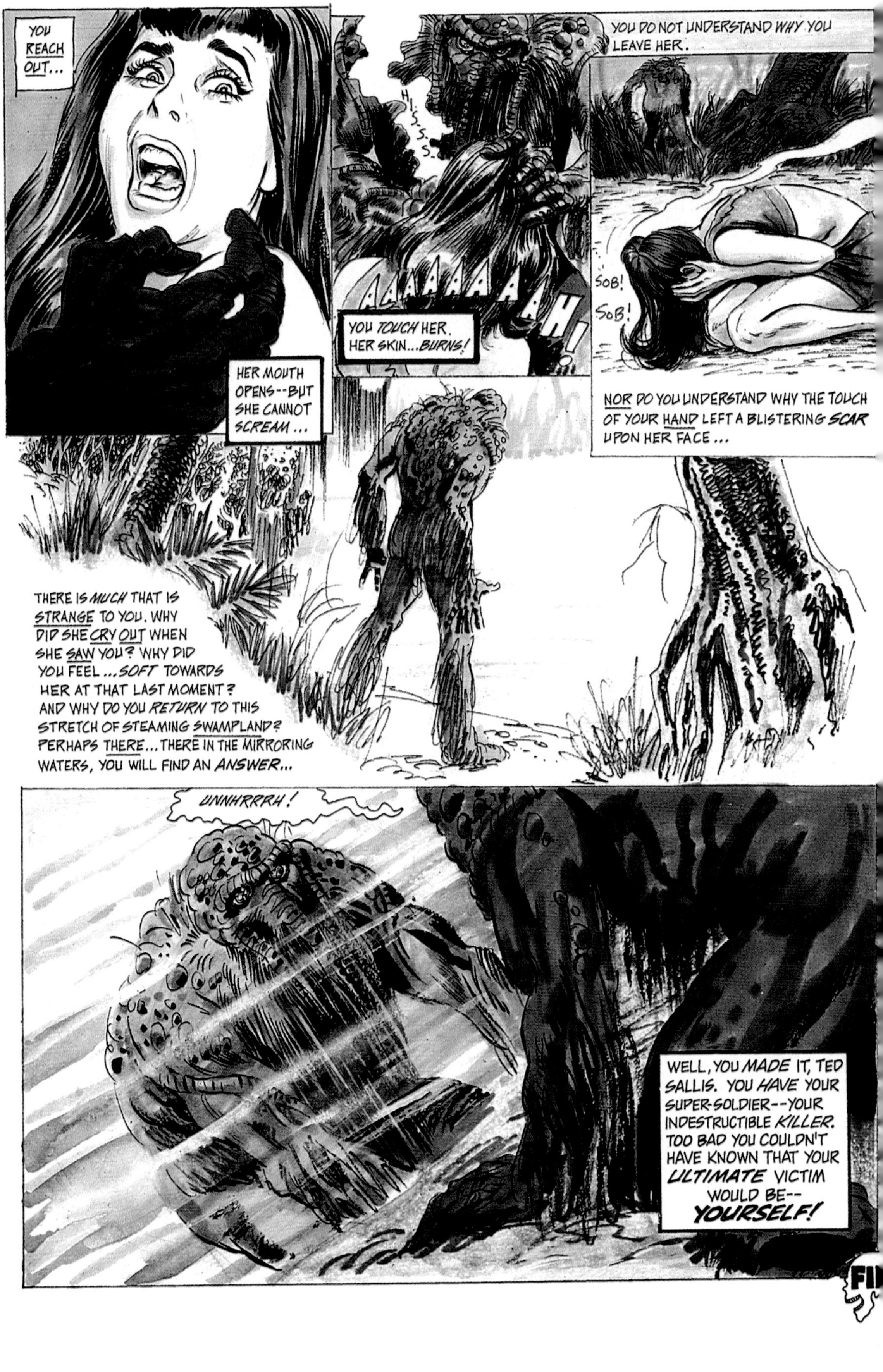
YOU REACH OUT...
HER MOUTH OPENS--BUT SHE CANNOT SCREAM...
HISSS
AAAAAAAAAH!
YOU TOUCH HER. HER SKIN...BURNS!
YOU DO NOT UNDERSTAND WHY YOU LEAVE HER.
SOB! SOB!
NOR DO YOU UNDERSTAND WHY THE TOUCH OF YOUR HAND LEFT A BLISTERING SCAR UPON HER FACE...
THERE IS MUCH THAT IS STRANGE TO YOU. WHY DID SHE CRY OUT WHEN SHE SAW YOU? WHY DID YOU FEEL...SOFT TOWARDS HER AT THAT LAST MOMENT? AND WHY DO YOU RETURN TO THIS STRETCH OF STEAMING SWAMPLAND? PERHAPS THERE...THERE IN THE MIRRORING WATERS, YOU WILL FIND AN ANSWER...
UNNHRRRH!
WELL, YOU MADE IT, TED SALLIS. YOU HAVE YOUR SUPER-SOLDIER--YOUR INDESTRUCTIBLE KILLER. TOO BAD YOU COULDN'T HAVE KNOWN THAT YOUR ULTIMATE VICTIM WOULD BE--YOURSELF!

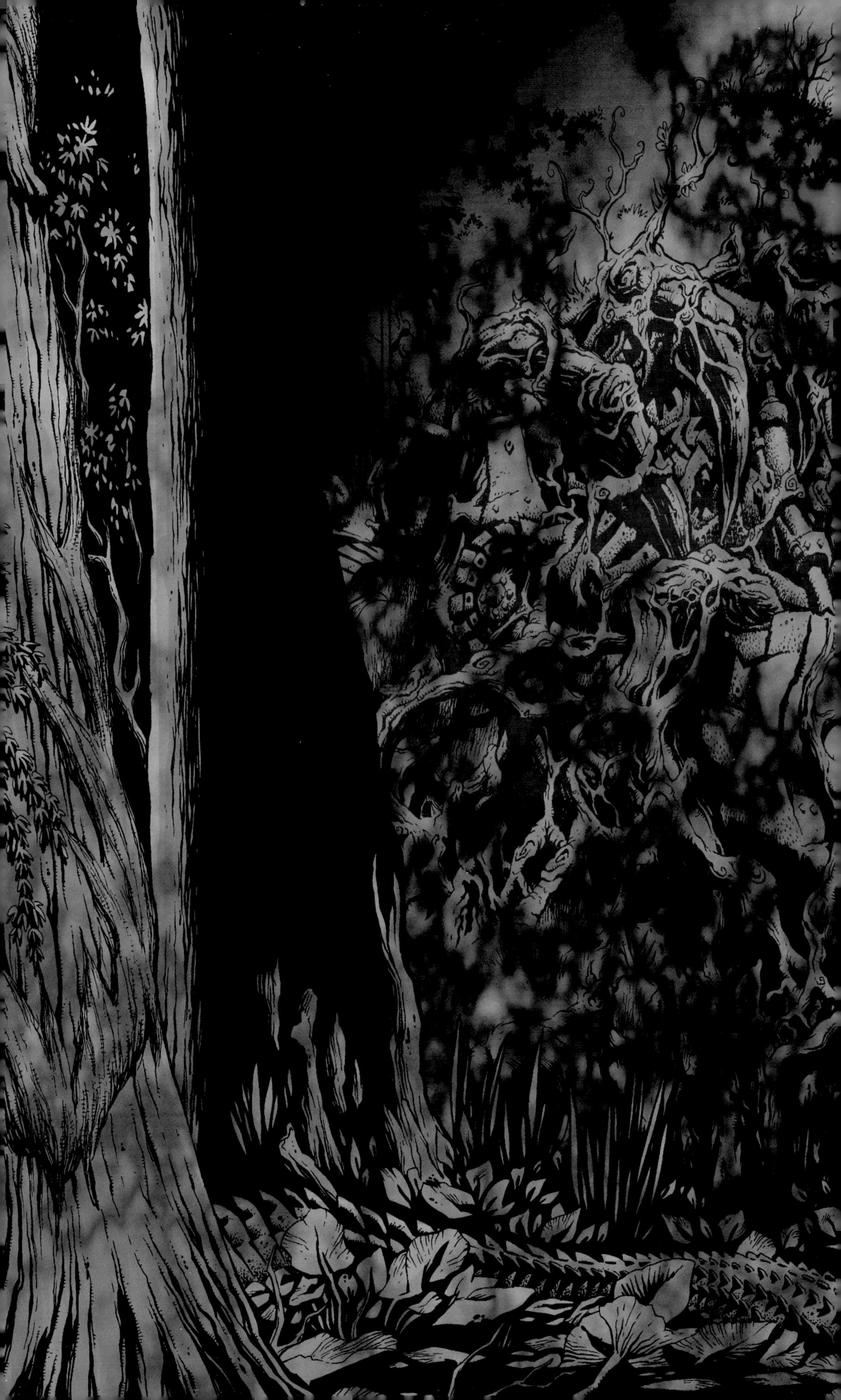

Adventure into Fear #16 (1973)

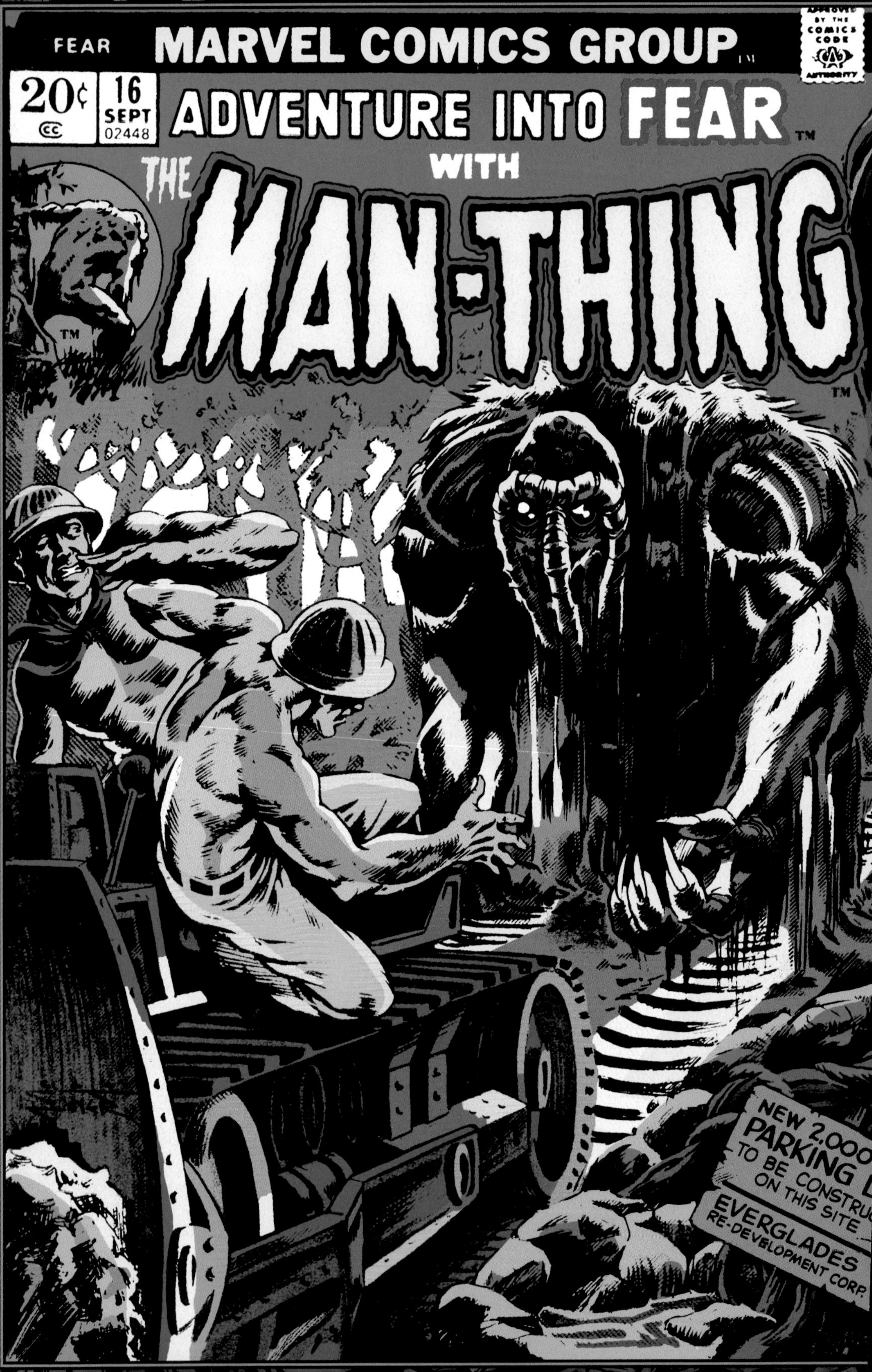
FEAR
MARVEL COMICS GROUP
20¢
16
SEPT
02448
ADVENTURE INTO FEAR
WITH
THE
MAN-THING
NEW 2,000
PARKING
ON THIS SITE
EVERGLADES
RE-DEVELOPMENT CORP.

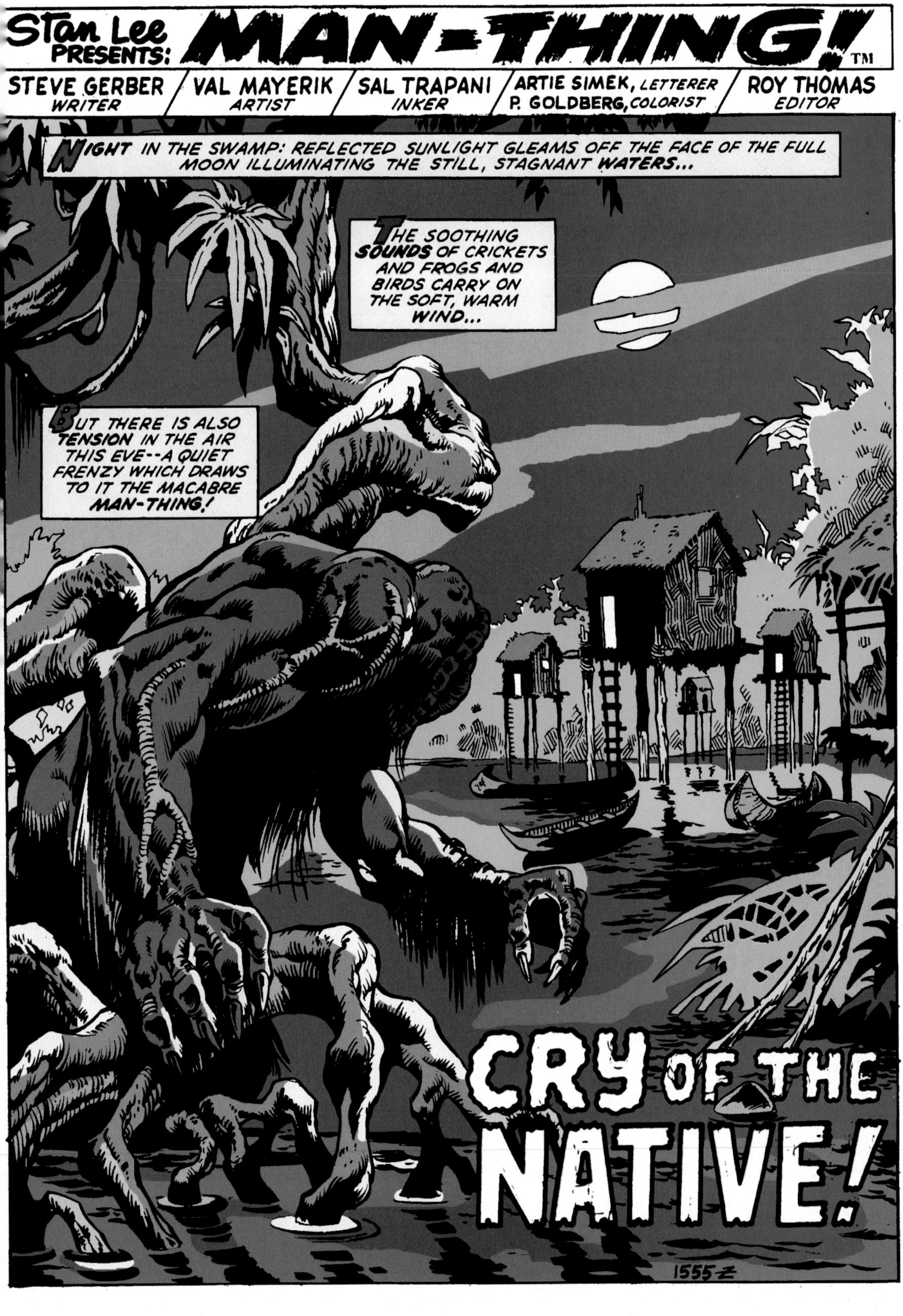
Stan Lee PRESENTS: MAN-THING! TM
STEVE GERBER WRITER
VAL MAYERIK ARTIST
SAL TRAPANI INKER
ARTIE SIMEK, LETTERER
P. GOLDBERG, COLORIST
ROY THOMAS EDITOR
NIGHT IN THE SWAMP: REFLECTED SUNLIGHT GLEAMS OFF THE FACE OF THE FULL MOON ILLUMINATING THE STILL, STAGNANT WATERS...
THE SOOTHING SOUNDS OF CRICKETS AND FROGS AND BIRDS CARRY ON THE SOFT, WARM WIND...
BUT THERE IS ALSO TENSION IN THE AIR THIS EVE--A QUIET FRENZY WHICH DRAWS TO IT THE MACABRE MAN-THING!
CRY OF THE NATIVE!
1555-Z

SILENTLY, HE SLOUCHES CLOSER TO ITS SOURCE...

...TO THIS CURIOUS VILLAGE BUILT ON STILTS.

AND HE PAUSES TO LISTEN...

...NOT TO THE WORDS OF THIS YOUNG BRAVE, RATHER--

--TO THE TONE IN WHICH HE SPEAKS THEM.

FOR THAT IS ALL THE CREATURE CAN UNDER-STAND.

I TELL YOU, FATHER, WE HAVE NO CHOICE!

THE EXCAVATION BEGINS TOMORROW --UNLESS WE STOP IT!

AND IF WE FAIL, WE HAVE ONLY MONTHS--

--BEFORE THE SWAMP--OUR HOMELAND--IS GONE-- REPLACED BY AN AIRPORT!

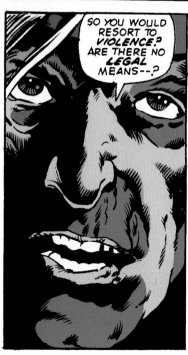

SO YOU WOULD RESORT TO VIOLENCE? ARE THERE NO LEGAL MEANS--?

FATHER, THE WHITE MEN HAVE NEVER EVEN SIGNED A TREATY WITH OUR TRIBE--!

NOT THAT IT MATTERS.

EVERY INDIAN TREATY THEY HAVE SIGNED--THEY HAVE BROKEN.

I RESPECT THE WORD OF MY FATHER--MY CHIEFTAIN--BUT I ALSO RESPECT THIS LAND!

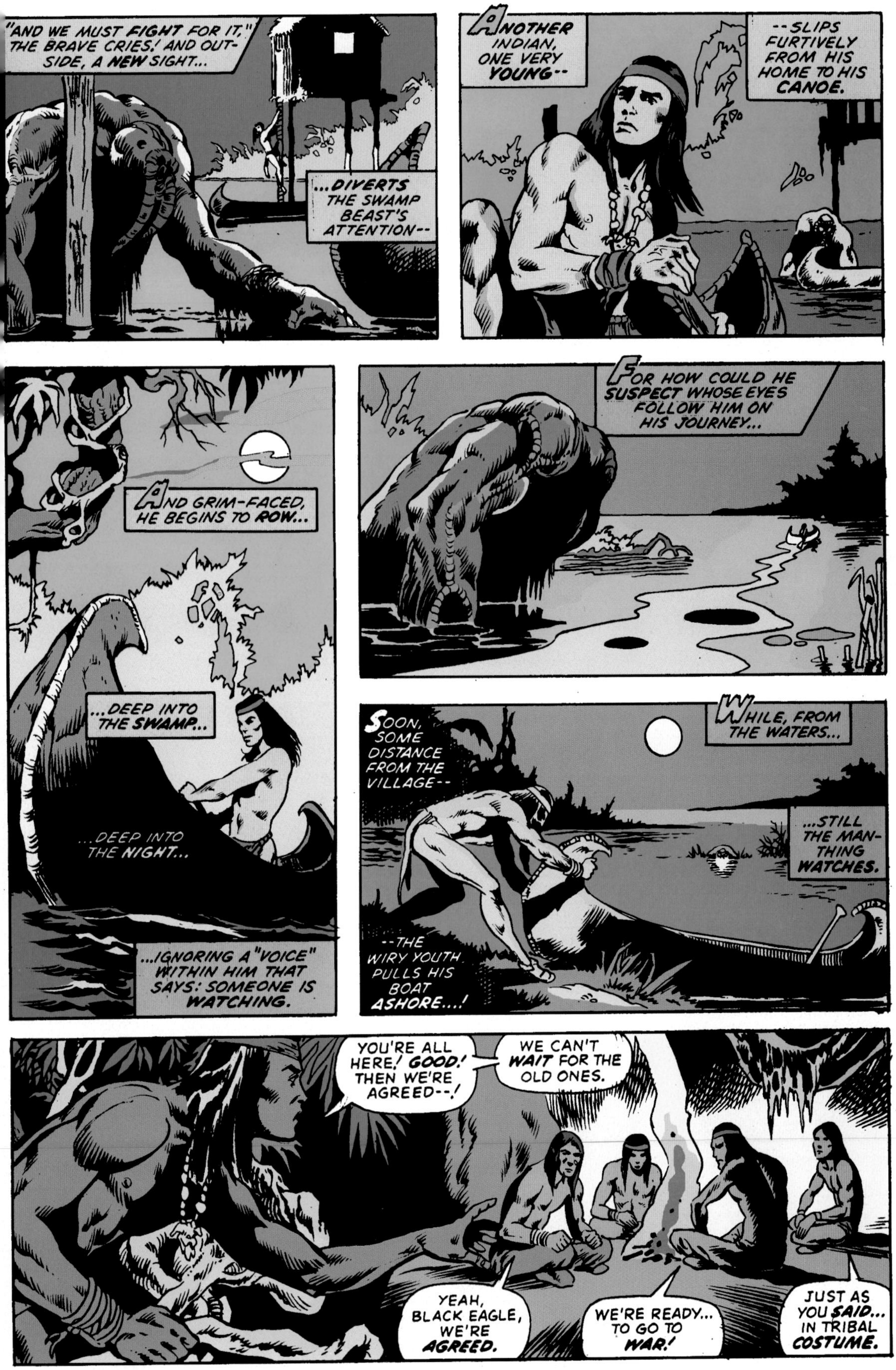
"AND WE MUST FIGHT FOR IT," THE BRAVE CRIES! AND OUTSIDE, A NEW SIGHT...
...DIVERTS THE SWAMP BEAST'S ATTENTION--
ANOTHER INDIAN, ONE VERY YOUNG--
--SLIPS FURTIVELY FROM HIS HOME TO HIS CANOE.
AND GRIM-FACED, HE BEGINS TO ROW...
...DEEP INTO THE SWAMP...
...DEEP INTO THE NIGHT...
...IGNORING A "VOICE" WITHIN HIM THAT SAYS: SOMEONE IS WATCHING.
FOR HOW COULD HE SUSPECT WHOSE EYES FOLLOW HIM ON HIS JOURNEY...
SOON, SOME DISTANCE FROM THE VILLAGE--
--THE WIRY YOUTH PULLS HIS BOAT ASHORE...!
WHILE, FROM THE WATERS...
...STILL THE MAN-THING WATCHES.
YOU'RE ALL HERE! GOOD! THEN WE'RE AGREED--!
WE CAN'T WAIT FOR THE OLD ONES.
YEAH, BLACK EAGLE, WE'RE AGREED.
WE'RE READY... TO GO TO WAR!
JUST AS YOU SAID... IN TRIBAL COSTUME.

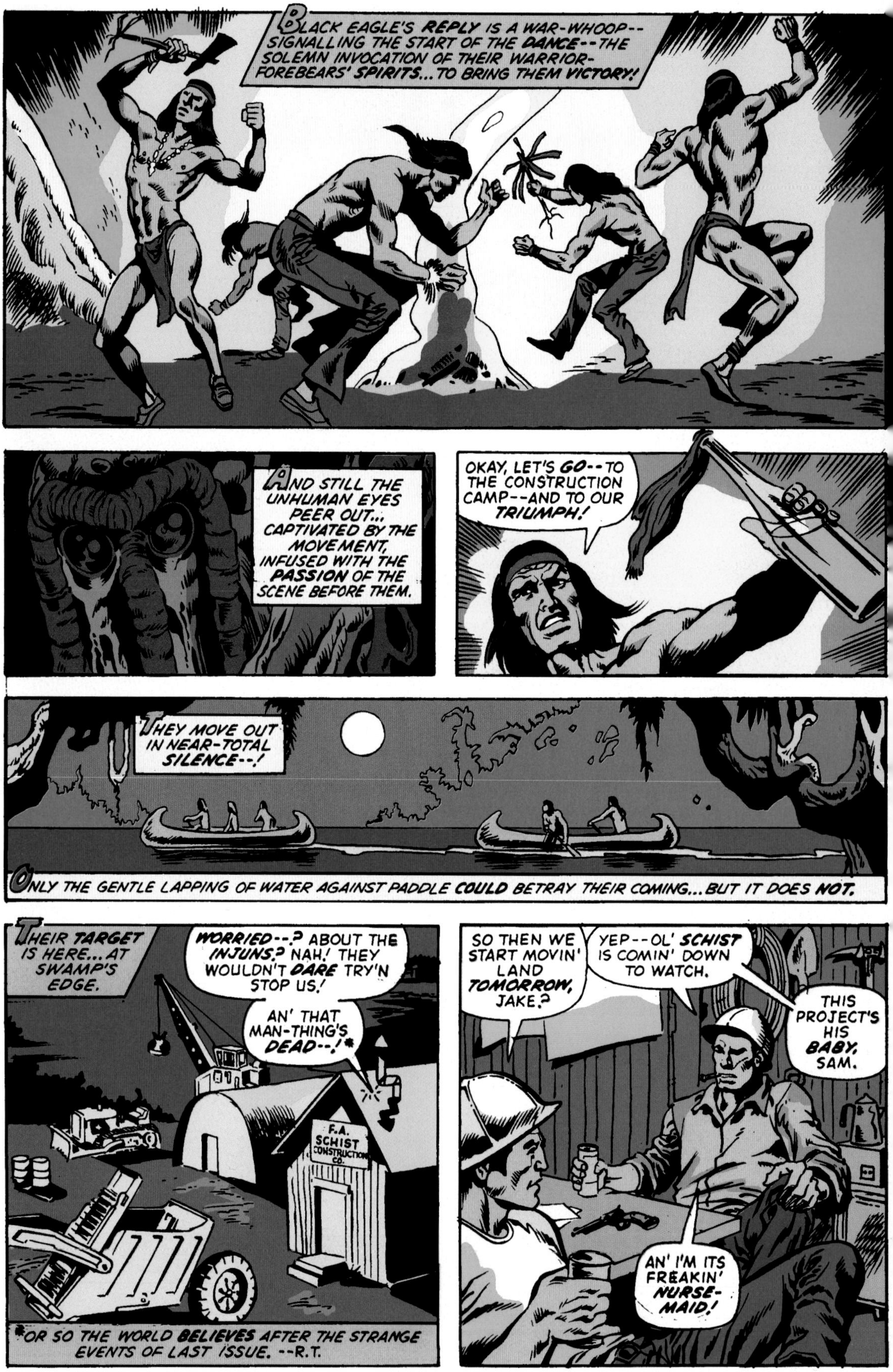
BLACK EAGLE'S REPLY IS A WAR-WHOOP-- SIGNALLING THE START OF THE DANCE--THE SOLEMN INVOCATION OF THEIR WARRIOR-FOREBEARS' SPIRITS...TO BRING THEM VICTORY!
AND STILL THE UNHUMAN EYES PEER OUT... CAPTIVATED BY THE MOVEMENT, INFUSED WITH THE PASSION OF THE SCENE BEFORE THEM.
OKAY, LET'S GO--TO THE CONSTRUCTION CAMP--AND TO OUR TRIUMPH!
THEY MOVE OUT IN NEAR-TOTAL SILENCE--!
ONLY THE GENTLE LAPPING OF WATER AGAINST PADDLE COULD BETRAY THEIR COMING...BUT IT DOES NOT.
THEIR TARGET IS HERE...AT SWAMP'S EDGE.
WORRIED--? ABOUT THE INJUNS? NAH! THEY WOULDN'T DARE TRY'N STOP US!
AN' THAT MAN-THING'S DEAD--!*
F.A. SCHIST CONSTRUCTION CO.
*OR SO THE WORLD BELIEVES AFTER THE STRANGE EVENTS OF LAST ISSUE. --R.T.
SO THEN WE START MOVIN' LAND TOMORROW, JAKE?
YEP--OL' SCHIST IS COMIN' DOWN TO WATCH.
THIS PROJECT'S HIS BABY, SAM.
AN' I'M ITS FREAKIN' NURSE-MAID!

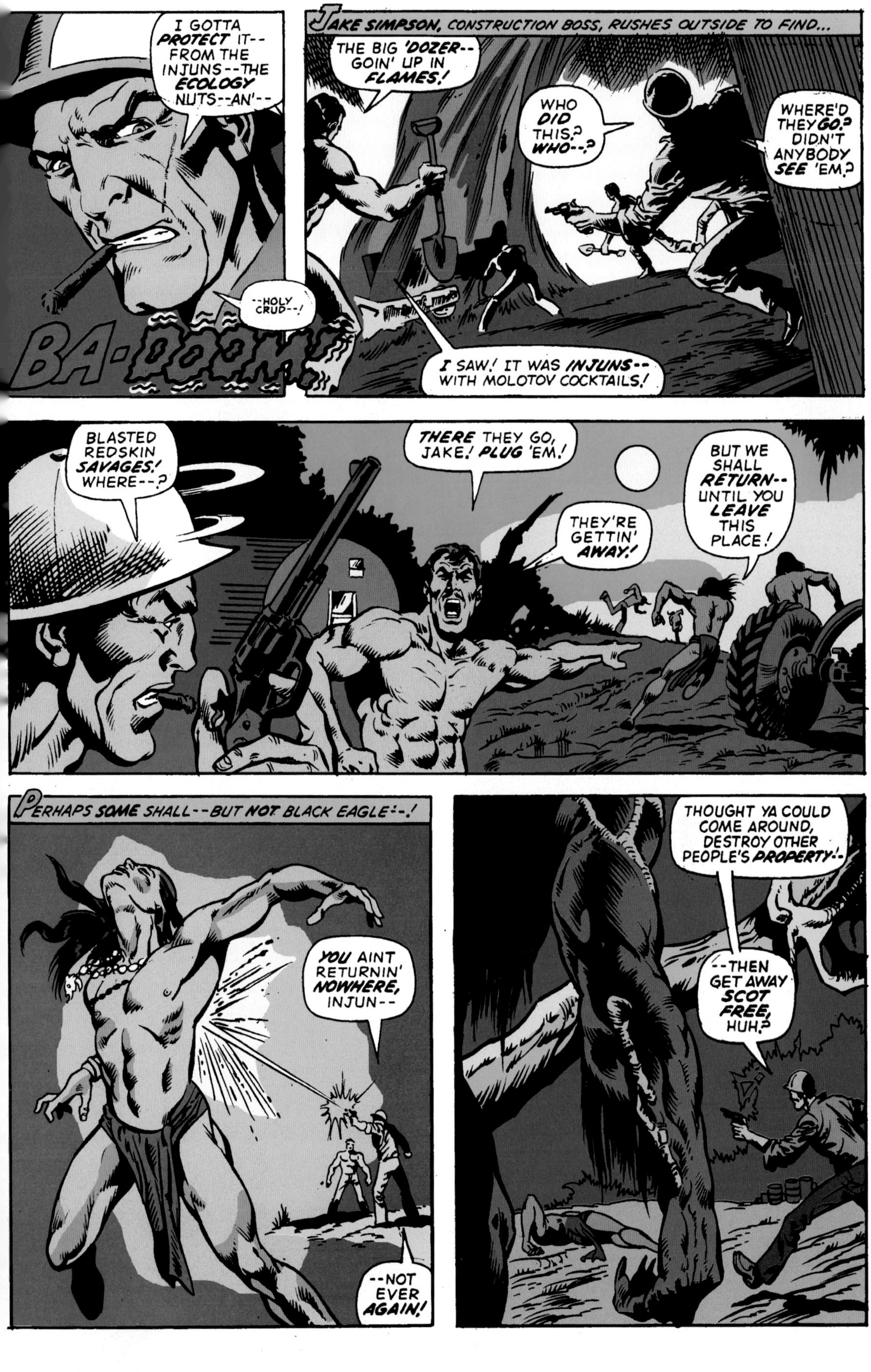
I GOTTA PROTECT IT-- FROM THE INJUNS--THE ECOLOGY NUTS--AN'--
--HOLY CRUD--!
BA-DOOM!
JAKE SIMPSON, CONSTRUCTION BOSS, RUSHES OUTSIDE TO FIND...
THE BIG 'DOZER-- GOIN' UP IN FLAMES!
WHO DID THIS? WHO--?
WHERE'D THEY GO? DIDN'T ANYBODY SEE 'EM?
I SAW! IT WAS INJUNS-- WITH MOLOTOV COCKTAILS!
BLASTED REDSKIN SAVAGES! WHERE--?
THERE THEY GO, JAKE! PLUG 'EM!
THEY'RE GETTIN' AWAY!
BUT WE SHALL RETURN-- UNTIL YOU LEAVE THIS PLACE!
PERHAPS SOME SHALL--BUT NOT BLACK EAGLE--!
YOU AINT RETURNIN' NOWHERE, INJUN--
--NOT EVER AGAIN!
THOUGHT YA COULD COME AROUND, DESTROY OTHER PEOPLE'S PROPERTY--
--THEN GET AWAY SCOT FREE, HUH?

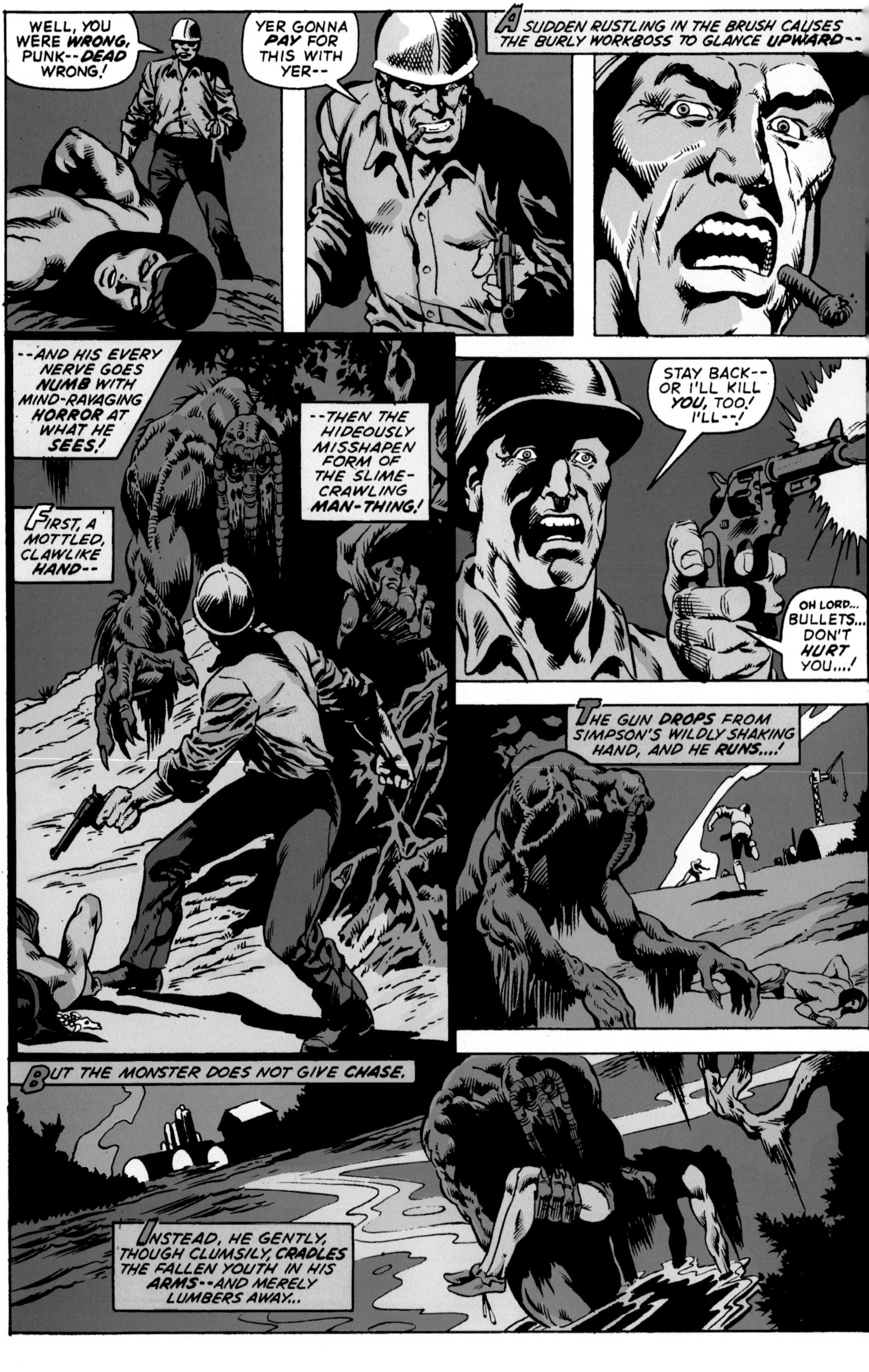

WELL, YOU WERE WRONG, PUNK--DEAD WRONG!
YER GONNA PAY FOR THIS WITH YER--
A SUDDEN RUSTLING IN THE BRUSH CAUSES THE BURLY WORKBOSS TO GLANCE UPWARD--
--AND HIS EVERY NERVE GOES NUMB WITH MIND-RAVAGING HORROR AT WHAT HE SEES!
FIRST, A MOTTLED, CLAWLIKE HAND--
--THEN THE HIDEOUSLY MISSHAPEN FORM OF THE SLIME-CRAWLING MAN-THING!
STAY BACK--OR I'LL KILL YOU, TOO! I'LL--!
OH LORD... BULLETS... DON'T HURT YOU....!
THE GUN DROPS FROM SIMPSON'S WILDLY SHAKING HAND, AND HE RUNS...!
BUT THE MONSTER DOES NOT GIVE CHASE.
INSTEAD, HE GENTLY, THOUGH CLUMSILY, CRADLES THE FALLEN YOUTH IN HIS ARMS--AND MERELY LUMBERS AWAY...

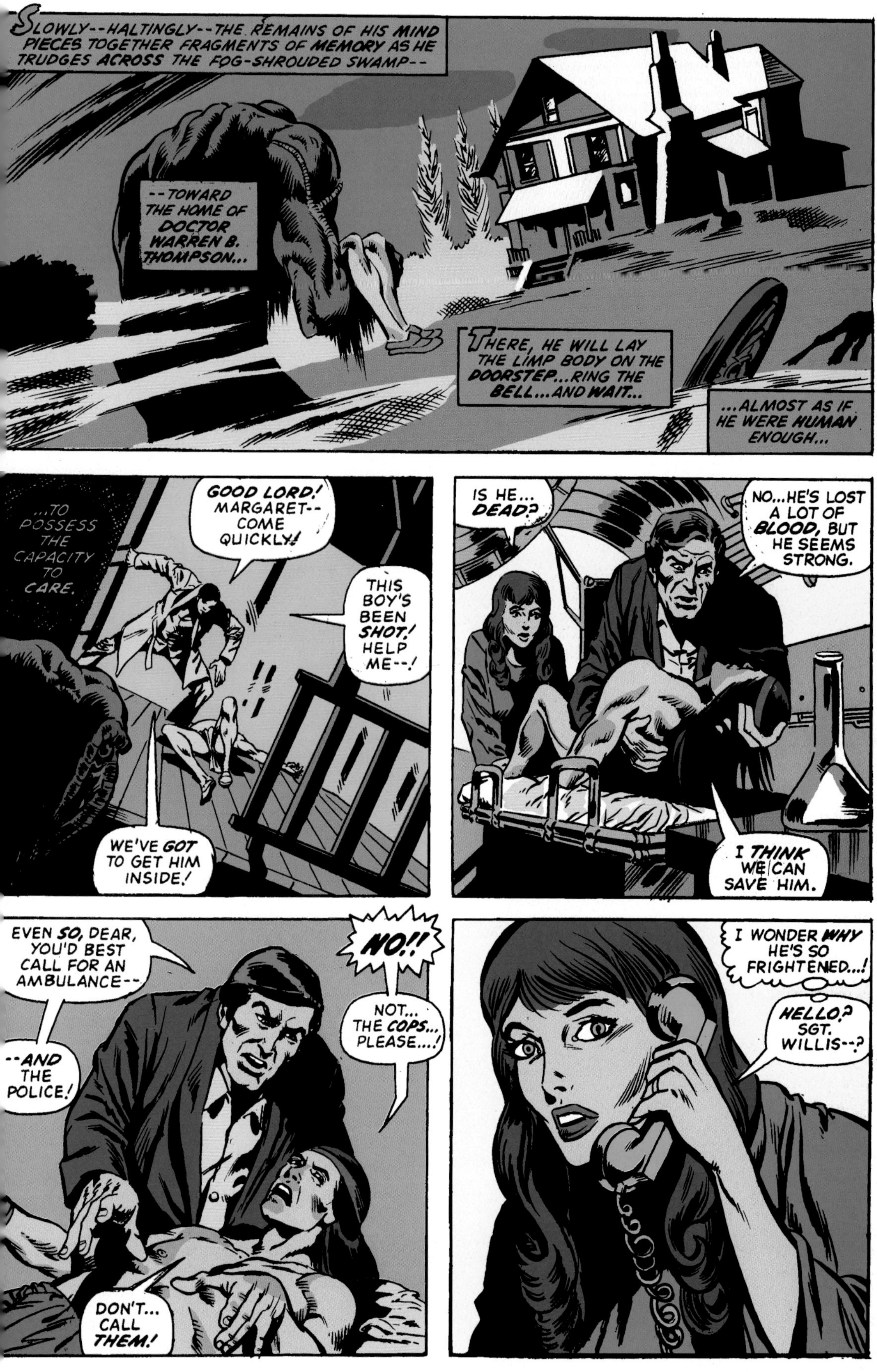
SLOWLY--HALTINGLY--THE REMAINS OF HIS MIND PIECES TOGETHER FRAGMENTS OF MEMORY AS HE TRUDGES ACROSS THE FOG-SHROUDED SWAMP--
--TOWARD THE HOME OF DOCTOR WARREN B. THOMPSON...
THERE, HE WILL LAY THE LIMP BODY ON THE DOORSTEP...RING THE BELL...AND WAIT...
...ALMOST AS IF HE WERE HUMAN ENOUGH...
...TO POSSESS THE CAPACITY TO CARE.
GOOD LORD! MARGARET--COME QUICKLY!
THIS BOY'S BEEN SHOT! HELP ME--!
WE'VE GOT TO GET HIM INSIDE!
IS HE... DEAD?
NO...HE'S LOST A LOT OF BLOOD, BUT HE SEEMS STRONG.
I THINK WE CAN SAVE HIM.
EVEN SO, DEAR, YOU'D BEST CALL FOR AN AMBULANCE--
--AND THE POLICE!
NO!!
NOT... THE COPS... PLEASE...!
DON'T... CALL THEM!
I WONDER WHY HE'S SO FRIGHTENED...!
HELLO? SGT. WILLIS--?

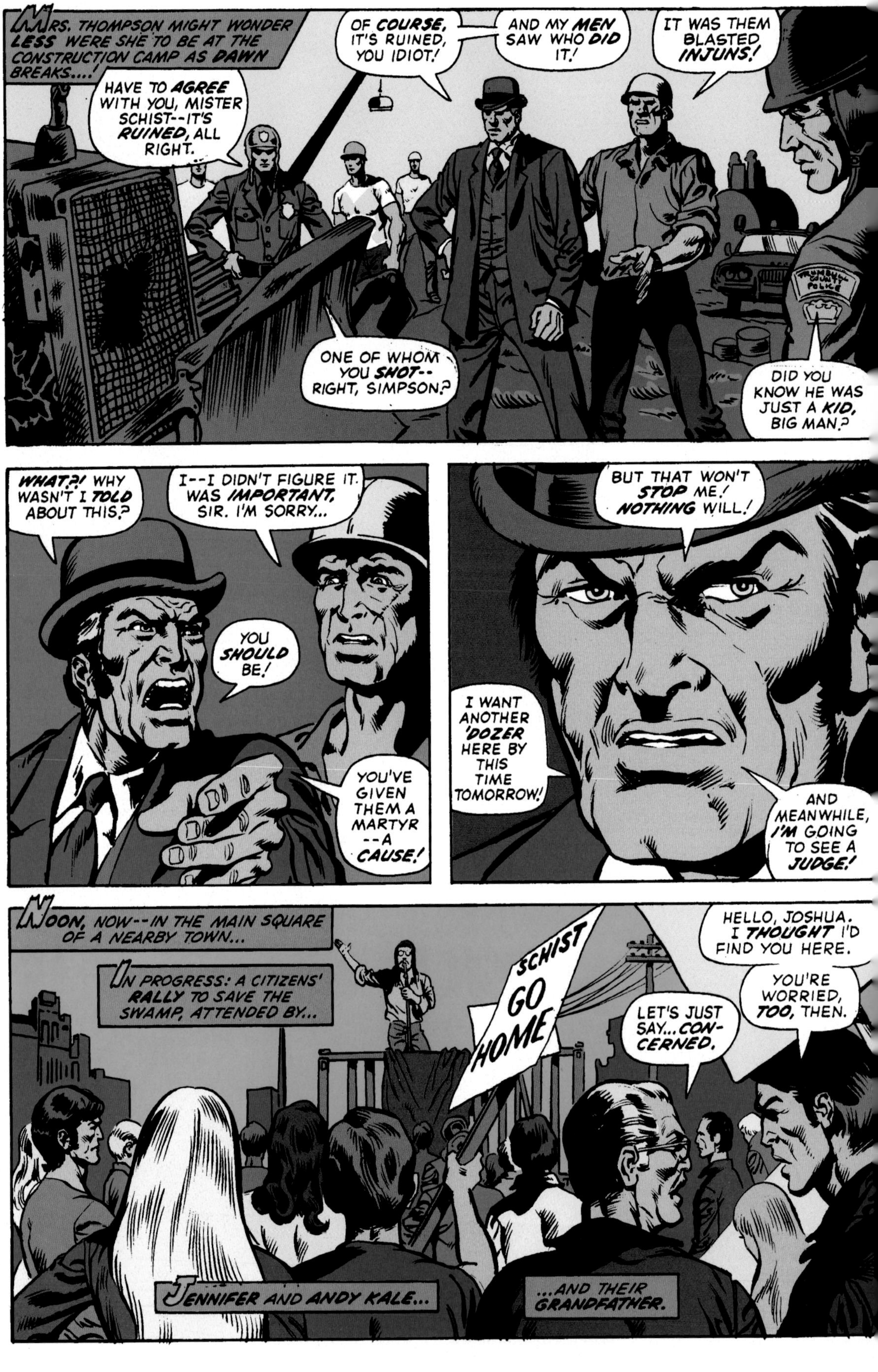
MRS. THOMPSON MIGHT WONDER LESS WERE SHE TO BE AT THE CONSTRUCTION CAMP AS DAWN BREAKS....!
HAVE TO AGREE WITH YOU, MISTER SCHIST--IT'S RUINED, ALL RIGHT.
OF COURSE, IT'S RUINED, YOU IDIOT!
AND MY MEN SAW WHO DID IT!
IT WAS THEM BLASTED INJUNS!
ONE OF WHOM YOU SHOT--RIGHT, SIMPSON?
DID YOU KNOW HE WAS JUST A KID, BIG MAN?
TRUMBULL COUNTY POLICE
WHAT?! WHY WASN'T I TOLD ABOUT THIS?
I--I DIDN'T FIGURE IT WAS IMPORTANT, SIR. I'M SORRY...
YOU SHOULD BE!
YOU'VE GIVEN THEM A MARTYR--A CAUSE!
BUT THAT WON'T STOP ME! NOTHING WILL!
I WANT ANOTHER 'DOZER HERE BY THIS TIME TOMORROW!
AND MEANWHILE, I'M GOING TO SEE A JUDGE!
NOON, NOW--IN THE MAIN SQUARE OF A NEARBY TOWN...
IN PROGRESS: A CITIZENS' RALLY TO SAVE THE SWAMP, ATTENDED BY...
SCHIST GO HOME
HELLO, JOSHUA. I THOUGHT I'D FIND YOU HERE.
YOU'RE WORRIED, TOO, THEN.
LET'S JUST SAY...CONCERNED.
JENNIFER AND ANDY KALE...
...AND THEIR GRANDFATHER.

IT'S *POSSIBLE,* ISN'T IT--THAT ALL THE ACTIVITY IN THE SWAMP...

...COULD REOPEN THE *GATE* TO THE *NETHER-WORLD?*

YES... POSSIBLE. BUT *UNLIKELY,* I THINK.

I'M UPSET OVER SOMETHING ELSE: *JENNIFER.*

SINCE THE PSYCHIC *BOND* BETWEEN HER AND THE MAN-THING WAS *BROKEN...**

WHAT, KALE? TELL ME.

I *CAN'T...* NOT YET...

*LAST ISSUE, --R.T.

*S*UDDENLY, JOSHUA'S TRAIN OF THOUGHT IS VIOLENTLY DERAILED BY:

STAND ASIDE, *PUNK!* WE'VE HEARD *ENOUGH!*

HEY--!

SAVE THE SWAMP

NOW IT'S *OUR* TURN TO TALK!

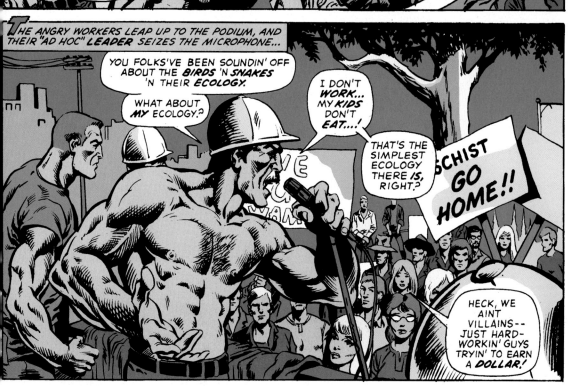

*T*HE ANGRY WORKERS LEAP UP TO THE PODIUM, AND THEIR "AD HOC" *LEADER* SEIZES THE MICROPHONE...

YOU FOLKS'VE BEEN SOUNDIN' OFF ABOUT THE *BIRDS* 'N *SNAKES* 'N THEIR *ECOLOGY.*

WHAT ABOUT *MY* ECOLOGY?

I DON'T *WORK...* MY *KIDS* DON'T *EAT...!*

THAT'S THE SIMPLEST ECOLOGY THERE *IS,* RIGHT?

SCHIST GO HOME!!

HECK, WE AINT VILLAINS-- JUST HARD-WORKIN' GUYS TRYIN' TO EARN A *DOLLAR!*

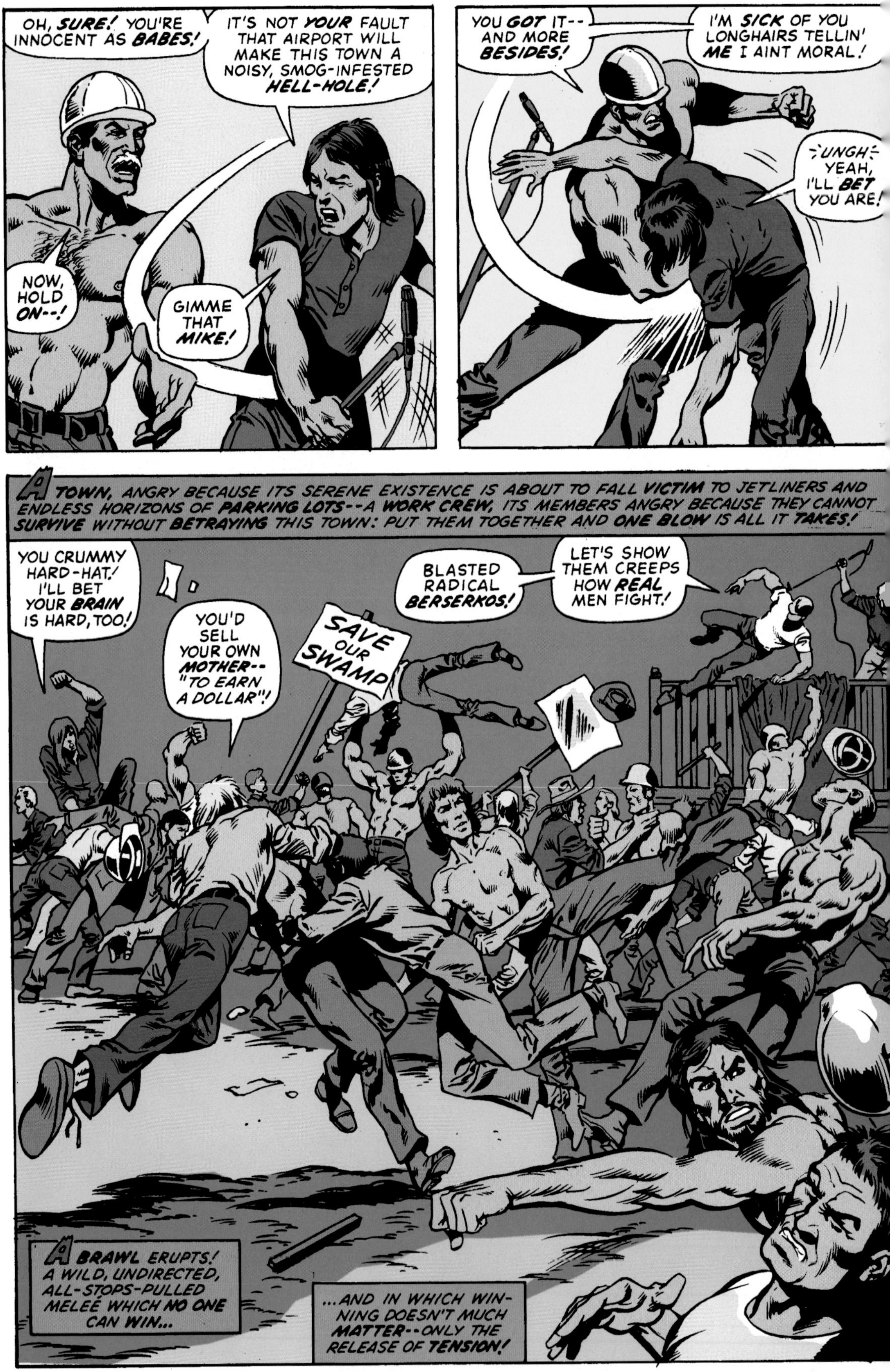
OH, SURE! YOU'RE INNOCENT AS BABES!
IT'S NOT YOUR FAULT THAT AIRPORT WILL MAKE THIS TOWN A NOISY, SMOG-INFESTED HELL-HOLE!
NOW, HOLD ON--!
GIMME THAT MIKE!
YOU GOT IT-- AND MORE BESIDES!
I'M SICK OF YOU LONGHAIRS TELLIN' ME I AINT MORAL!
UNGH YEAH, I'LL BET YOU ARE!
A TOWN, ANGRY BECAUSE ITS SERENE EXISTENCE IS ABOUT TO FALL VICTIM TO JETLINERS AND ENDLESS HORIZONS OF PARKING LOTS--A WORK CREW, ITS MEMBERS ANGRY BECAUSE THEY CANNOT SURVIVE WITHOUT BETRAYING THIS TOWN: PUT THEM TOGETHER AND ONE BLOW IS ALL IT TAKES!
YOU CRUMMY HARD-HAT! I'LL BET YOUR BRAIN IS HARD, TOO!
YOU'D SELL YOUR OWN MOTHER-- "TO EARN A DOLLAR"!
SAVE OUR SWAMP
BLASTED RADICAL BERSERKOS!
LET'S SHOW THEM CREEPS HOW REAL MEN FIGHT!
A BRAWL ERUPTS! A WILD, UNDIRECTED, ALL-STOPS-PULLED MELEE WHICH NO ONE CAN WIN...
...AND IN WHICH WINNING DOESN'T MUCH MATTER--ONLY THE RELEASE OF TENSION!

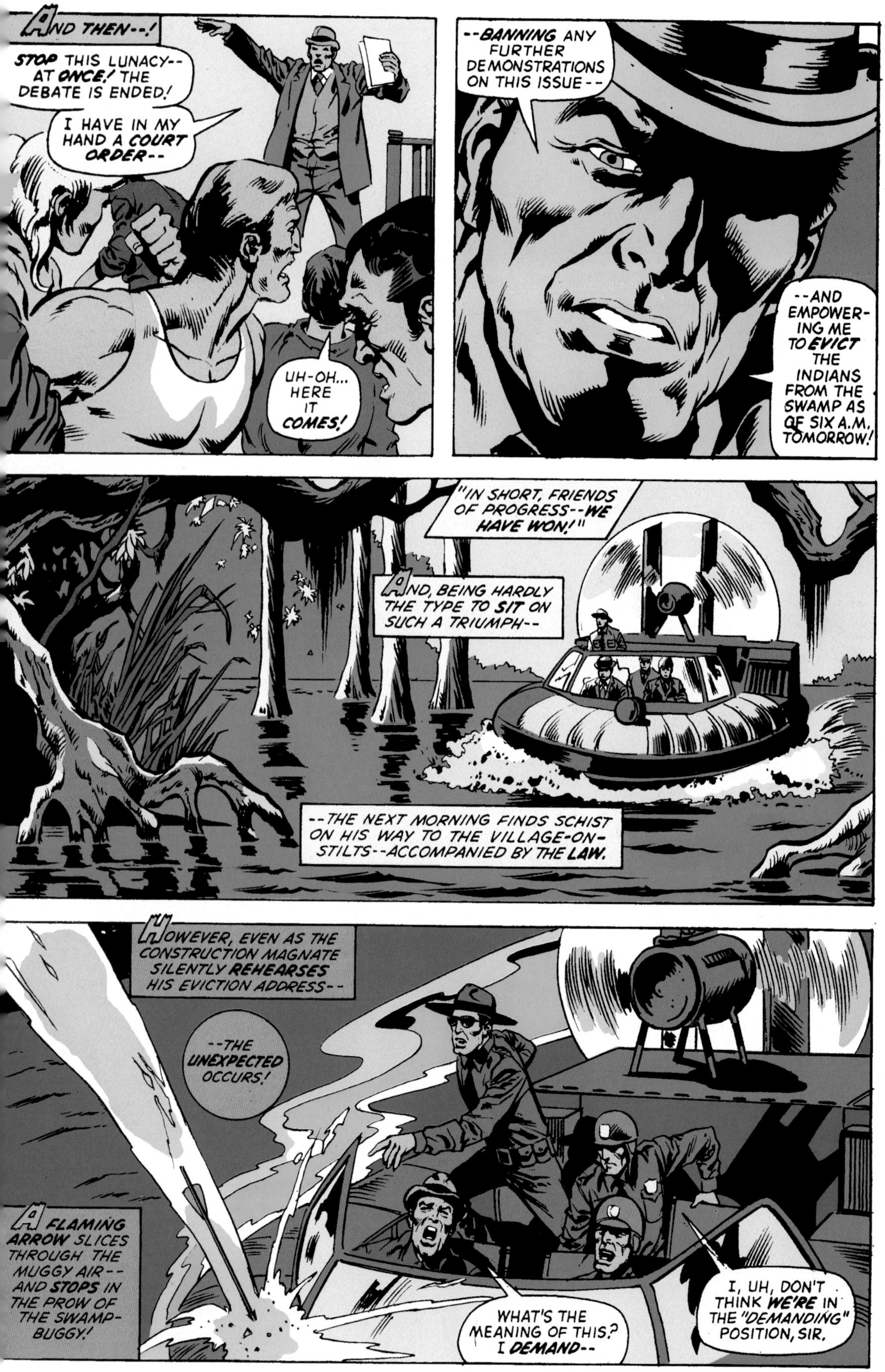
AND THEN--!
STOP THIS LUNACY-- AT ONCE! THE DEBATE IS ENDED!
I HAVE IN MY HAND A COURT ORDER--
UH-OH... HERE IT COMES!
--BANNING ANY FURTHER DEMONSTRATIONS ON THIS ISSUE--
--AND EMPOWERING ME TO EVICT THE INDIANS FROM THE SWAMP AS OF SIX A.M. TOMORROW!
"IN SHORT, FRIENDS OF PROGRESS--WE HAVE WON!"
AND, BEING HARDLY THE TYPE TO SIT ON SUCH A TRIUMPH--
--THE NEXT MORNING FINDS SCHIST ON HIS WAY TO THE VILLAGE-ON-STILTS--ACCOMPANIED BY THE LAW.
HOWEVER, EVEN AS THE CONSTRUCTION MAGNATE SILENTLY REHEARSES HIS EVICTION ADDRESS--
--THE UNEXPECTED OCCURS!
A FLAMING ARROW SLICES THROUGH THE MUGGY AIR--AND STOPS IN THE PROW OF THE SWAMP-BUGGY!
WHAT'S THE MEANING OF THIS? I DEMAND--
I, UH, DON'T THINK WE'RE IN THE "DEMANDING" POSITION, SIR.

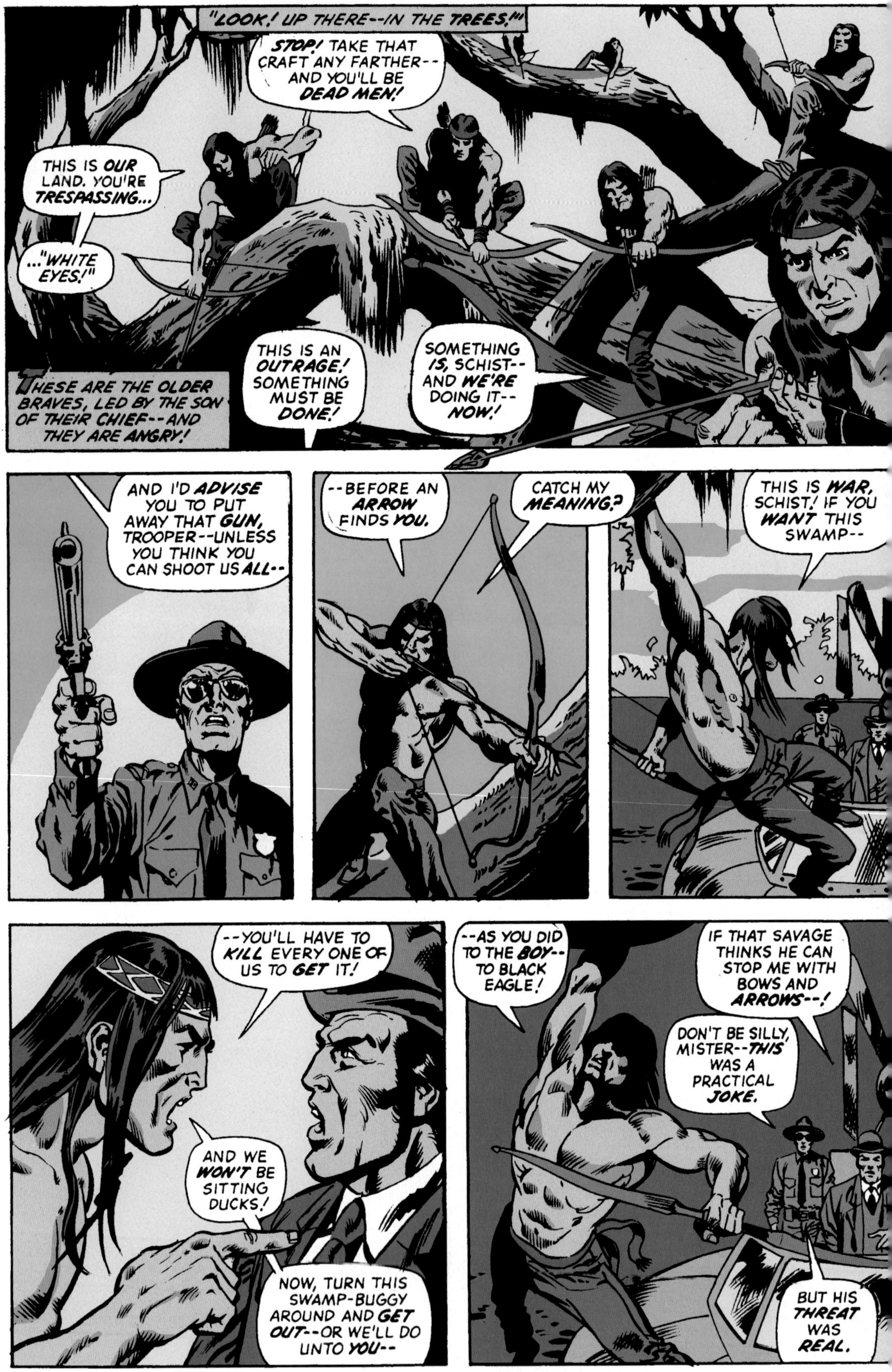
"LOOK! UP THERE--IN THE TREES!"
STOP! TAKE THAT CRAFT ANY FARTHER-- AND YOU'LL BE DEAD MEN!
THIS IS OUR LAND. YOU'RE TRESPASSING...
..."WHITE EYES!"
THESE ARE THE OLDER BRAVES, LED BY THE SON OF THEIR CHIEF--AND THEY ARE ANGRY!
THIS IS AN OUTRAGE! SOMETHING MUST BE DONE!
SOMETHING IS, SCHIST-- AND WE'RE DOING IT-- NOW!
AND I'D ADVISE YOU TO PUT AWAY THAT GUN, TROOPER--UNLESS YOU THINK YOU CAN SHOOT US ALL--
--BEFORE AN ARROW FINDS YOU.
CATCH MY MEANING?
THIS IS WAR, SCHIST! IF YOU WANT THIS SWAMP--
--YOU'LL HAVE TO KILL EVERY ONE OF US TO GET IT!
AND WE WON'T BE SITTING DUCKS!
NOW, TURN THIS SWAMP-BUGGY AROUND AND GET OUT--OR WE'LL DO UNTO YOU--
--AS YOU DID TO THE BOY-- TO BLACK EAGLE!
IF THAT SAVAGE THINKS HE CAN STOP ME WITH BOWS AND ARROWS--!
DON'T BE SILLY, MISTER--THIS WAS A PRACTICAL JOKE.
BUT HIS THREAT WAS REAL.

MEANWHILE, MASSIVE MACHINES *ROAR* TO LIFE AT THE SWAMP'S EDGE, AS SCHIST'S *CREW* BEGINS ITS EARTH-RENDING WORK.

BUT THEY DO NOT GO *UNOBSERVED.*

AND THOUGH THE MONSTER'S MENTAL LANDSCAPE RESEMBLES NOTHING SO MUCH AS *PUZZLE PARTS STREWN* OVER A BARE FLOOR--

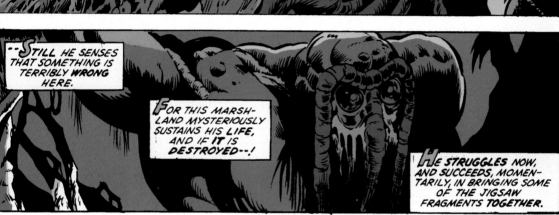

--STILL HE SENSES THAT SOMETHING IS TERRIBLY *WRONG* HERE.

FOR THIS MARSH-LAND MYSTERIOUSLY SUSTAINS HIS LIFE, AND IF *IT* IS *DESTROYED*--!

HE STRUGGLES NOW, AND *SUCCEEDS,* MOMENTARILY, IN BRINGING SOME OF THE JIGSAW FRAGMENTS *TOGETHER.*

A *NAME* HERE, A *FACE* THERE--HIS *OWN* FACE?--*YES,* IT *WAS!*--AND CURIOUS *BLUE FLAME*--AND A *WORD: KE--KELM--NO, KEM!--KEMSTREE!*

CHEMISTRY! IT WAS HIS WORD ONCE--WHEN HE WAS STILL--*WHO?*--YES, *SALLIS!* *TED SALLIS!*

BUT THE IMAGES *FADE* AS RAPIDLY AS THEY *COME*--AND WE CAN *CULL* MORE MEANING FROM THEM THAN HE...

DON'T CONGRATULATE ME, GENERAL-- *HATE* ME!

I'M AFRAID I'VE *FOUND* IT.

A SERUM TO *ALTER* HUMANS-- MAKE THEM ABLE TO BREATHE *POLLUTANTS.*

I'VE GIVEN YOU THE MEANS TO SACRIFICE OUR *HUMANITY* TO THE CAUSE OF *PROFIT!*

AND IF YOU *USE* IT-- YOU'RE A *FOOL!*

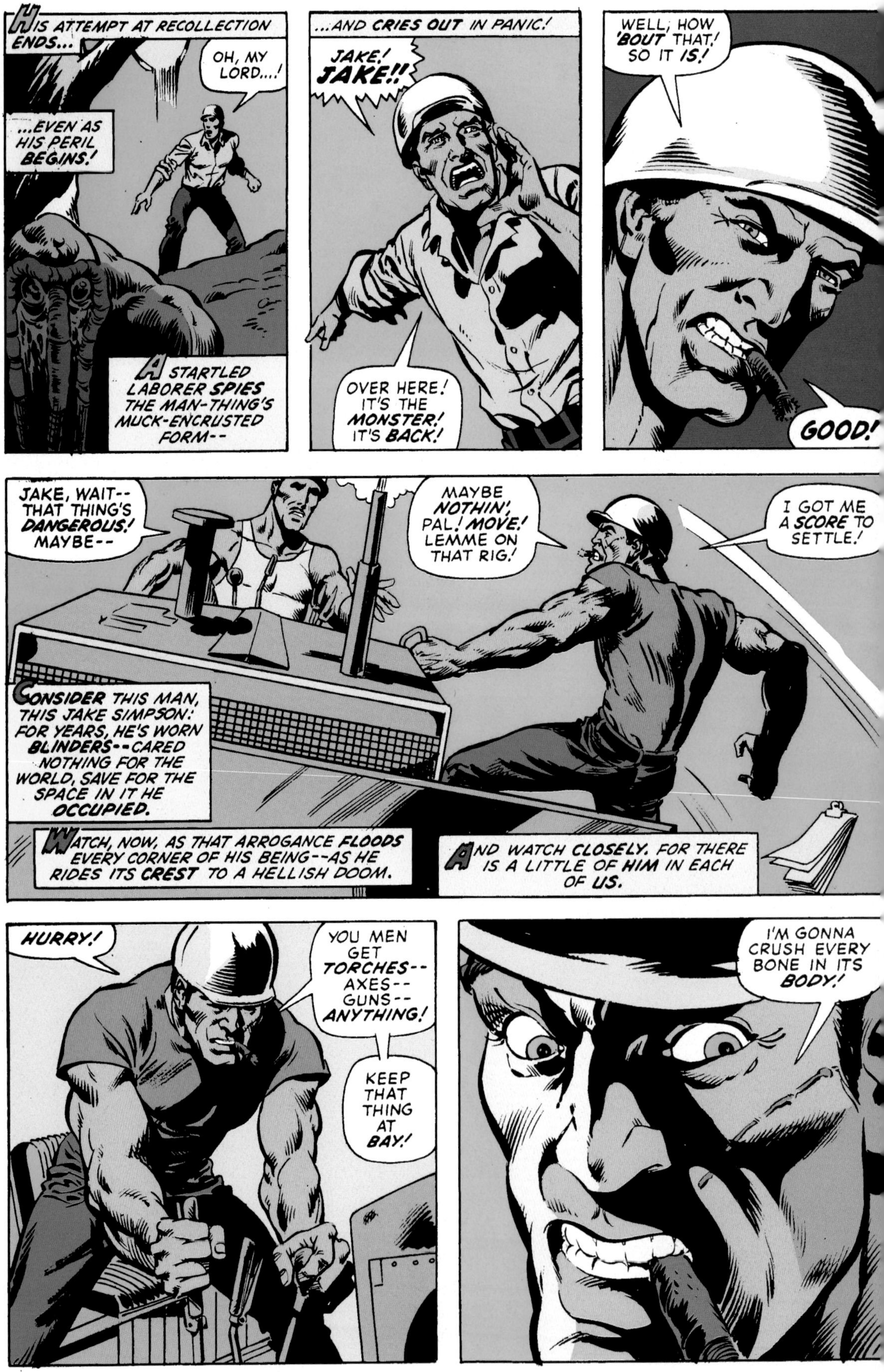
HIS ATTEMPT AT RECOLLECTION ENDS...
OH, MY LORD...!
...EVEN AS HIS PERIL BEGINS!
A STARTLED LABORER SPIES THE MAN-THING'S MUCK-ENCRUSTED FORM--
...AND CRIES OUT IN PANIC!
JAKE! JAKE!!
OVER HERE! IT'S THE MONSTER! IT'S BACK!
WELL, HOW 'BOUT THAT! SO IT IS!
GOOD!
JAKE, WAIT-- THAT THING'S DANGEROUS! MAYBE--
MAYBE NOTHIN', PAL! MOVE! LEMME ON THAT RIG!
I GOT ME A SCORE TO SETTLE!
CONSIDER THIS MAN, THIS JAKE SIMPSON: FOR YEARS, HE'S WORN BLINDERS--CARED NOTHING FOR THE WORLD, SAVE FOR THE SPACE IN IT HE OCCUPIED.
WATCH, NOW, AS THAT ARROGANCE FLOODS EVERY CORNER OF HIS BEING--AS HE RIDES ITS CREST TO A HELLISH DOOM.
AND WATCH CLOSELY. FOR THERE IS A LITTLE OF HIM IN EACH OF US.
HURRY!
YOU MEN GET TORCHES-- AXES-- GUNS-- ANYTHING!
KEEP THAT THING AT BAY!
I'M GONNA CRUSH EVERY BONE IN ITS BODY!

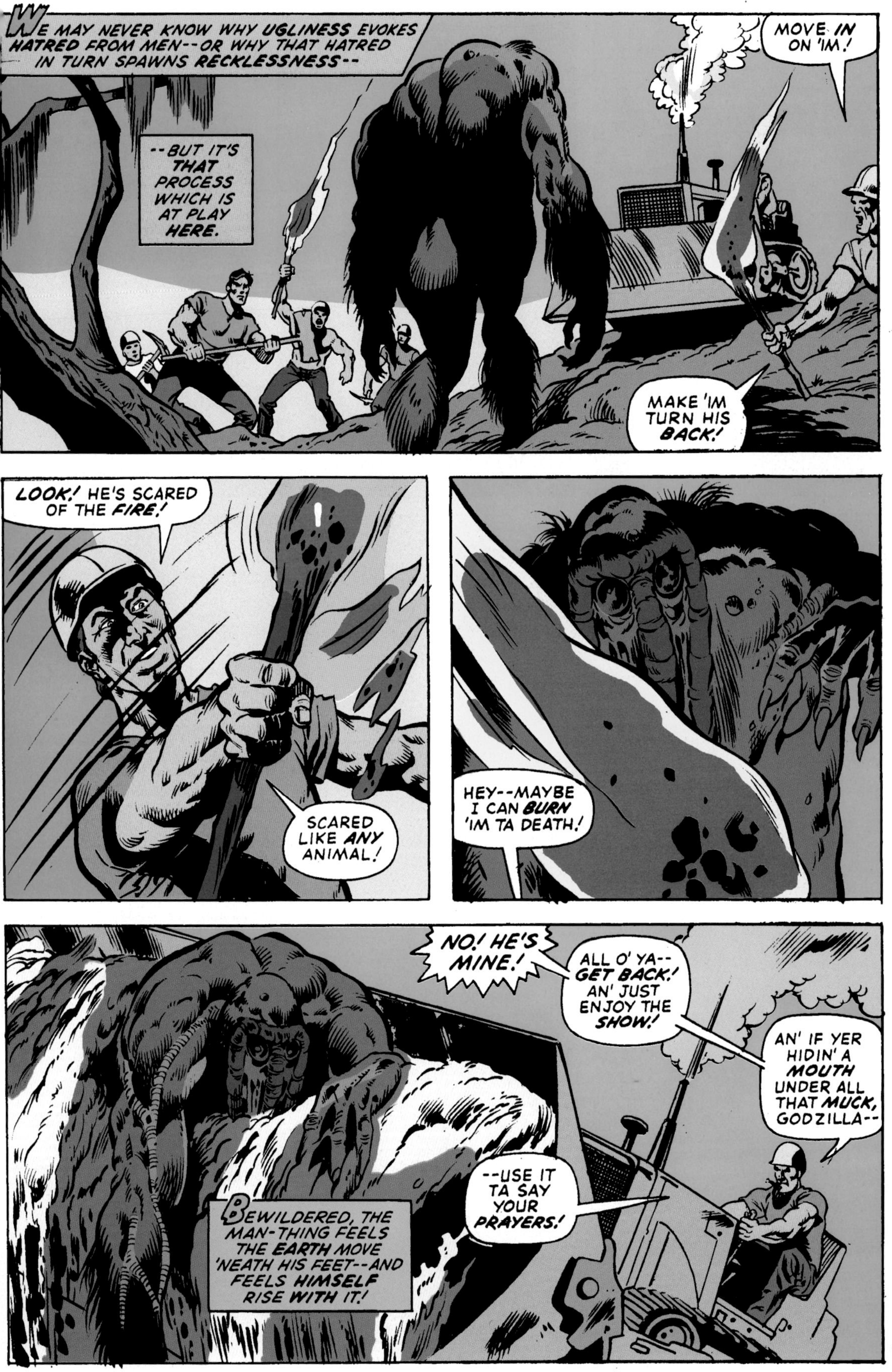
WE MAY NEVER KNOW WHY UGLINESS EVOKES HATRED FROM MEN--OR WHY THAT HATRED IN TURN SPAWNS RECKLESSNESS--
--BUT IT'S THAT PROCESS WHICH IS AT PLAY HERE.
MOVE IN ON 'IM!
MAKE 'IM TURN HIS BACK!
LOOK! HE'S SCARED OF THE FIRE!
SCARED LIKE ANY ANIMAL!
HEY--MAYBE I CAN BURN 'IM TA DEATH!
NO! HE'S MINE!
ALL O' YA--GET BACK! AN' JUST ENJOY THE SHOW!
AN' IF YER HIDIN' A MOUTH UNDER ALL THAT MUCK, GODZILLA--
--USE IT TA SAY YOUR PRAYERS!
BEWILDERED, THE MAN-THING FEELS THE EARTH MOVE 'NEATH HIS FEET--AND FEELS HIMSELF RISE WITH IT!

AN INSTANT LATER, IT COMES CRASHING DOWN UPON HIM--BURIES HIM!

THEN PICKS AND AXES STAB AND TEAR AT HIS MUD-COVERED, UNMOVING FORM...

UNTIL--

ENOUGH! YOU GUYS STAND CLEAR!

I'M GONNA ROLL THIS FOUR-TON BABY RIGHT OVER HIM!

SIMPSON'S HARD, CALLOUSED HAND SHOVES THE LEVER THAT SETS THE PONDEROUS TREADS IN MOTION!

PLACE A TOMATO IN THE PALM OF YOUR HAND. SQUEEZE IT-- SLOWLY--UNTIL THE SKIN BREAKS AND IT BURSTS...

...AND YOU WILL UNDERSTAND WHAT THIS MACHINE HAS DONE TO THE MAN-THING!

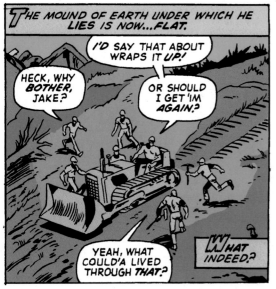

THE MOUND OF EARTH UNDER WHICH HE LIES IS NOW...FLAT.

I'D SAY THAT ABOUT WRAPS IT UP!

HECK, WHY BOTHER, JAKE?

OR SHOULD I GET 'IM AGAIN?

YEAH, WHAT COULD'A LIVED THROUGH THAT?

WHAT INDEED?

WE WILL NOT ATTEMPT TO DESCRIBE THE HORROR THAT SURGES THROUGH THIS MAN--

--AS HE LEARNS THE ANSWER TO THAT QUESTION.

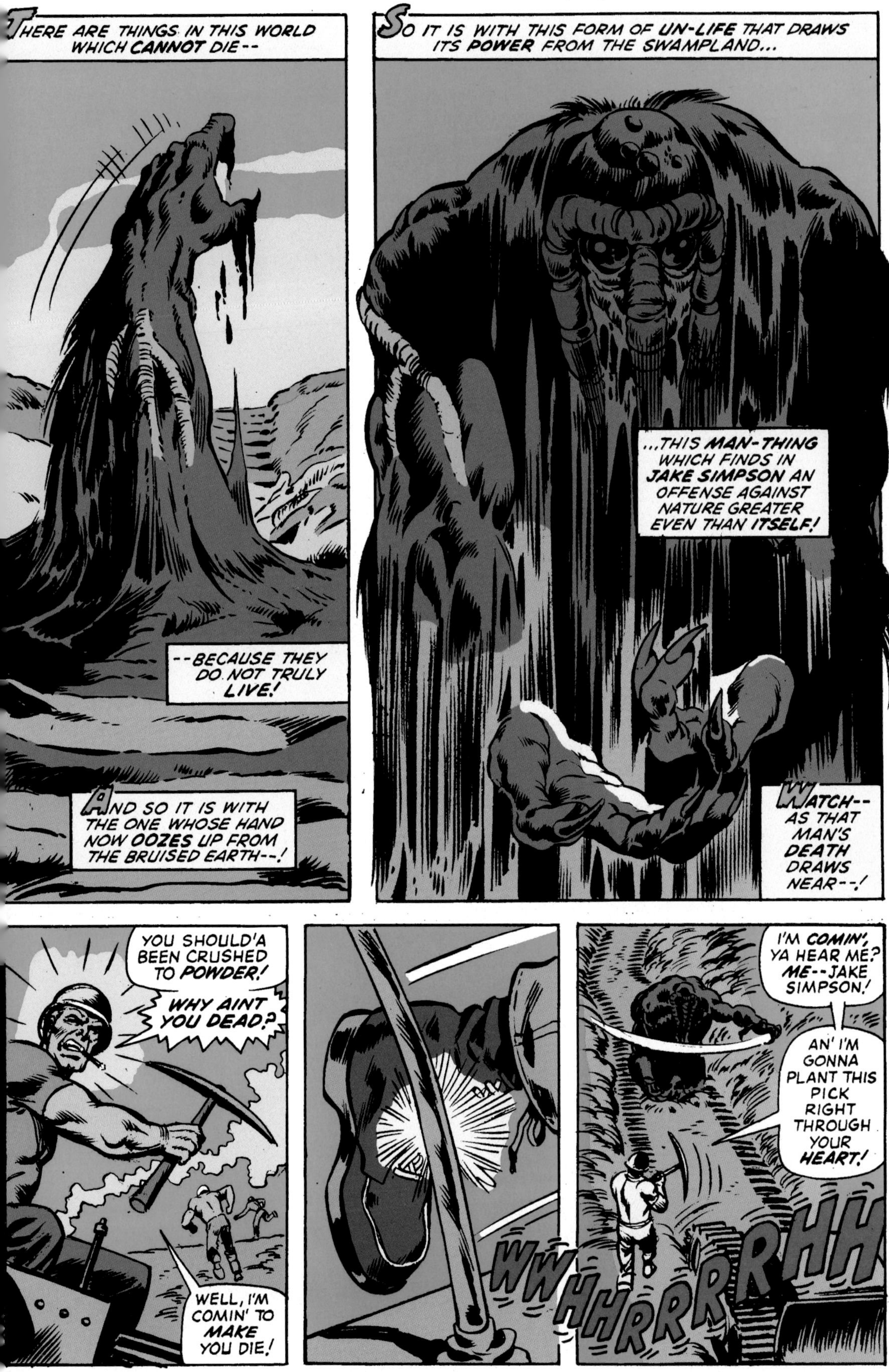
THERE ARE THINGS IN THIS WORLD WHICH CANNOT DIE--
--BECAUSE THEY DO NOT TRULY LIVE!
AND SO IT IS WITH THE ONE WHOSE HAND NOW OOZES UP FROM THE BRUISED EARTH--!
SO IT IS WITH THIS FORM OF UN-LIFE THAT DRAWS ITS POWER FROM THE SWAMPLAND...
...THIS MAN-THING WHICH FINDS IN JAKE SIMPSON AN OFFENSE AGAINST NATURE GREATER EVEN THAN ITSELF!
WATCH--AS THAT MAN'S DEATH DRAWS NEAR--!
YOU SHOULD'A BEEN CRUSHED TO POWDER!
WHY AINT YOU DEAD?
WELL, I'M COMIN' TO MAKE YOU DIE!
I'M COMIN', YA HEAR ME? ME--JAKE SIMPSON!
AN' I'M GONNA PLANT THIS PICK RIGHT THROUGH YOUR HEART!
WWHHRRRRRHH

THERE! NOW *DIE!* *DIE! DIE!*

DIE.

AND THEN IT COMES: FEAR! FEAR--FOR HE KNOWS NOW THE THING HE FACES IS IN NO WAY HUMAN!

NO--STAY BACK!!

AND IT *GROWS*, THIS FEAR, LIKE *CANCER*--EATING UP ALL ELSE WITHIN HIM. UNTIL THERE IS ONLY FEAR--

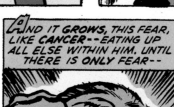

--THE SINGLE EMOTION THE MAN-THING HATES!

AND WHAT JAKE SIMPSON FEARS HE *HIDES* FROM-- HIDES HIS EYES--!

AND THIS TIME HE HIDES THEM FOREVER--!

FOR WHATEVER KNOWS FEAR--*BURNS* AT THE MAN-THING'S TOUCH.!!

*T*HE FLESH OF FINGERTIPS MELTS AND *FUSES* WITH THAT OF FOREHEAD AND CHEEK--

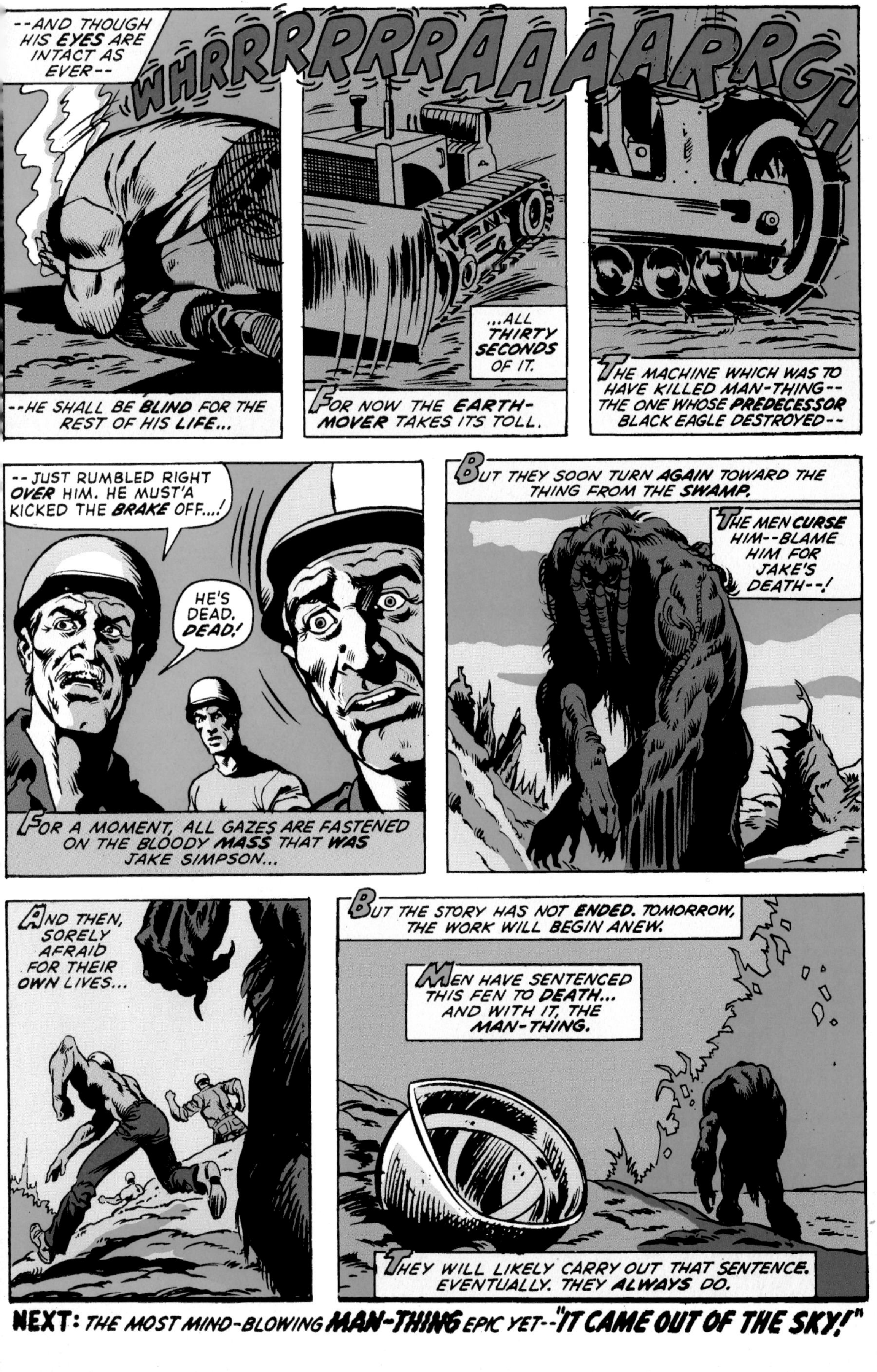
--AND THOUGH HIS EYES ARE INTACT AS EVER--
WHRRRRRRAAAAARRGH
--HE SHALL BE BLIND FOR THE REST OF HIS LIFE...
...ALL THIRTY SECONDS OF IT.
FOR NOW THE EARTH-MOVER TAKES ITS TOLL.
THE MACHINE WHICH WAS TO HAVE KILLED MAN-THING--THE ONE WHOSE PREDECESSOR BLACK EAGLE DESTROYED--
--JUST RUMBLED RIGHT OVER HIM. HE MUST'A KICKED THE BRAKE OFF...!
HE'S DEAD. DEAD!
FOR A MOMENT, ALL GAZES ARE FASTENED ON THE BLOODY MASS THAT WAS JAKE SIMPSON...
BUT THEY SOON TURN AGAIN TOWARD THE THING FROM THE SWAMP.
THE MEN CURSE HIM--BLAME HIM FOR JAKE'S DEATH--!
AND THEN, SORELY AFRAID FOR THEIR OWN LIVES...
BUT THE STORY HAS NOT ENDED. TOMORROW, THE WORK WILL BEGIN ANEW.
MEN HAVE SENTENCED THIS FEN TO DEATH... AND WITH IT, THE MAN-THING.
THEY WILL LIKELY CARRY OUT THAT SENTENCE. EVENTUALLY. THEY ALWAYS DO.
NEXT: THE MOST MIND-BLOWING MAN-THING EPIC YET--"IT CAME OUT OF THE SKY!"

Pencils for Man-Thing #1, Pages 8 & 9

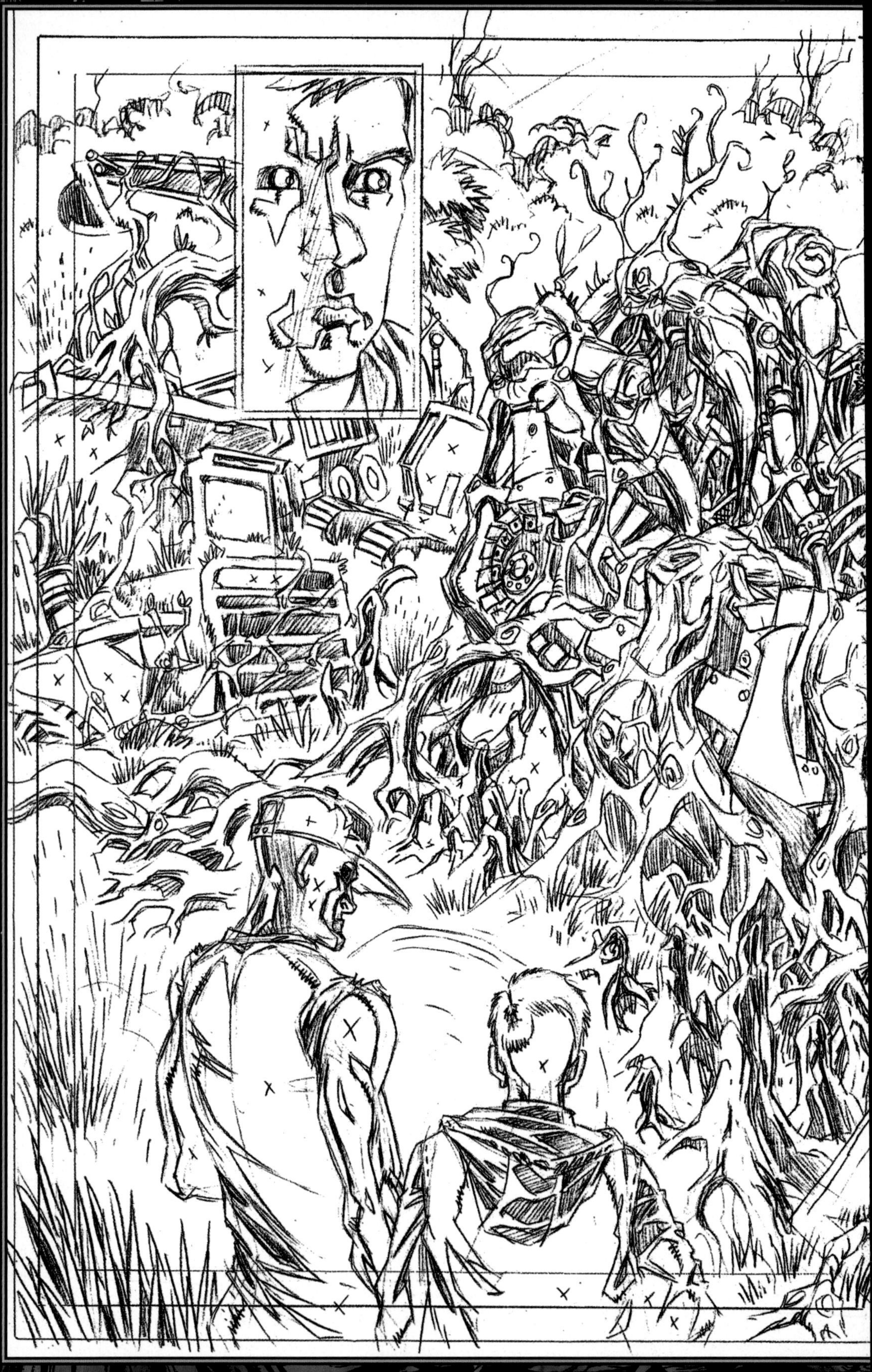

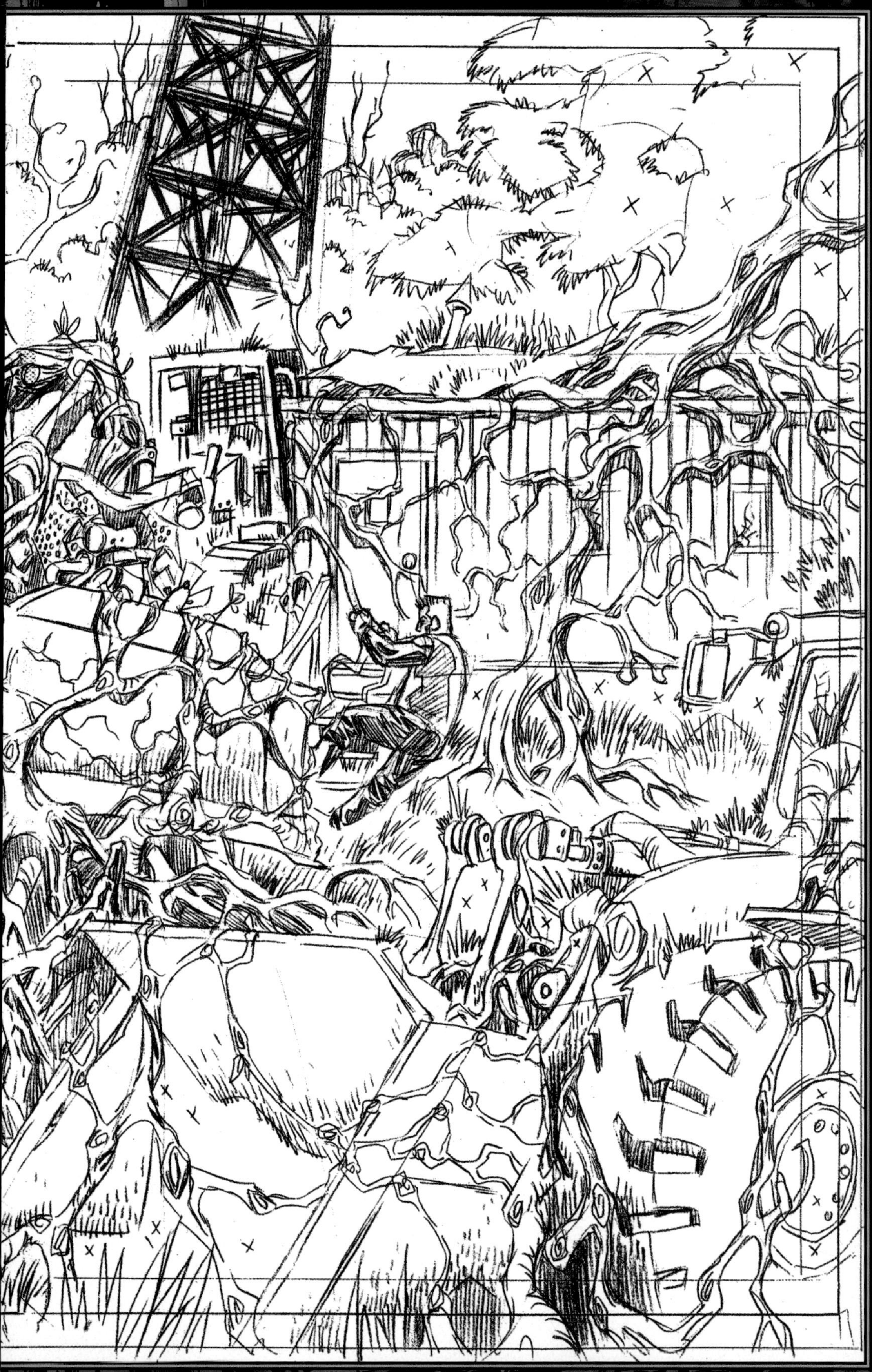

Pencils for Man-Thing #2, Page 22

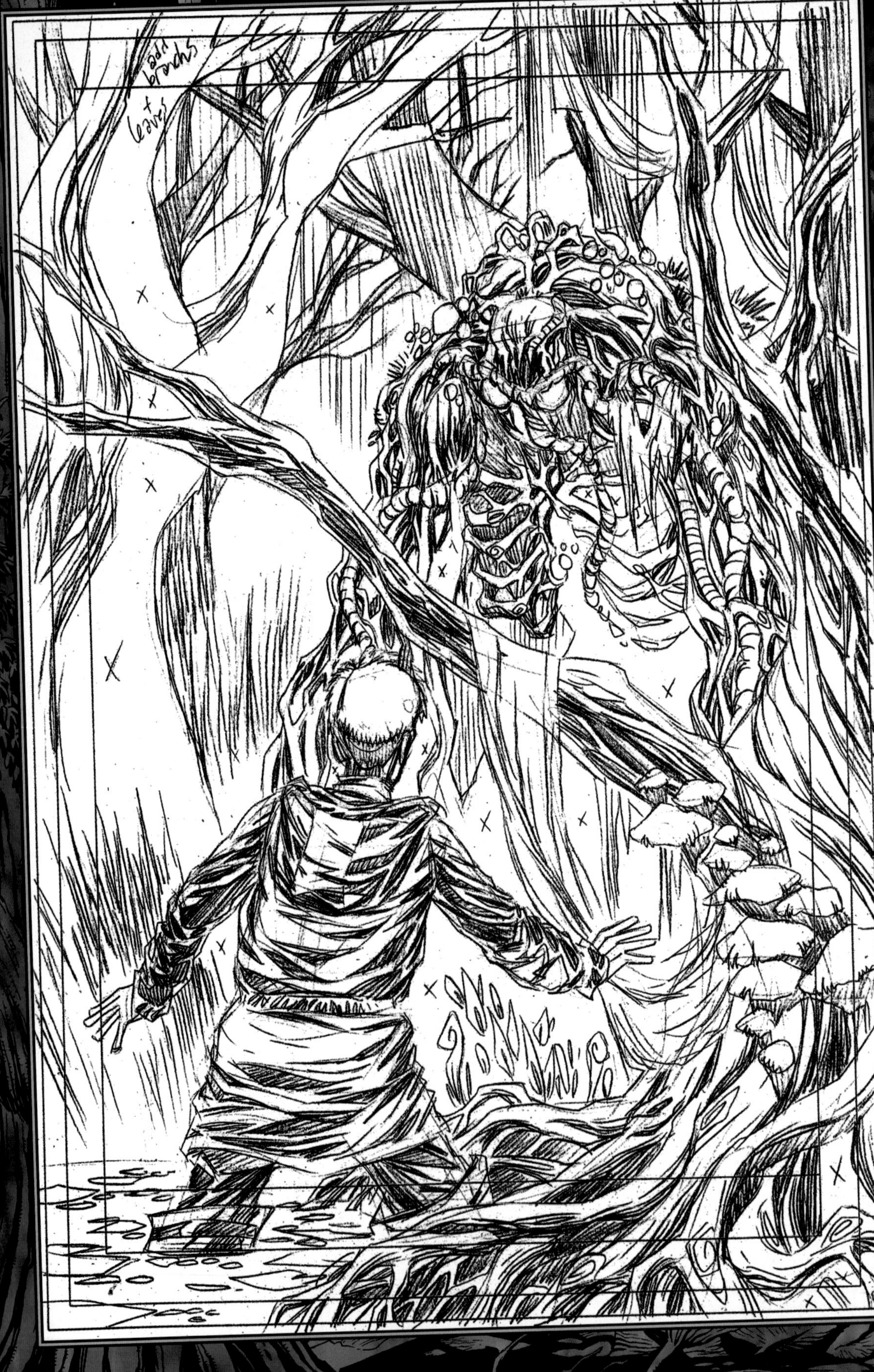
add branchs
+ leaves

Pencils for Man-Thing #3, Page 14

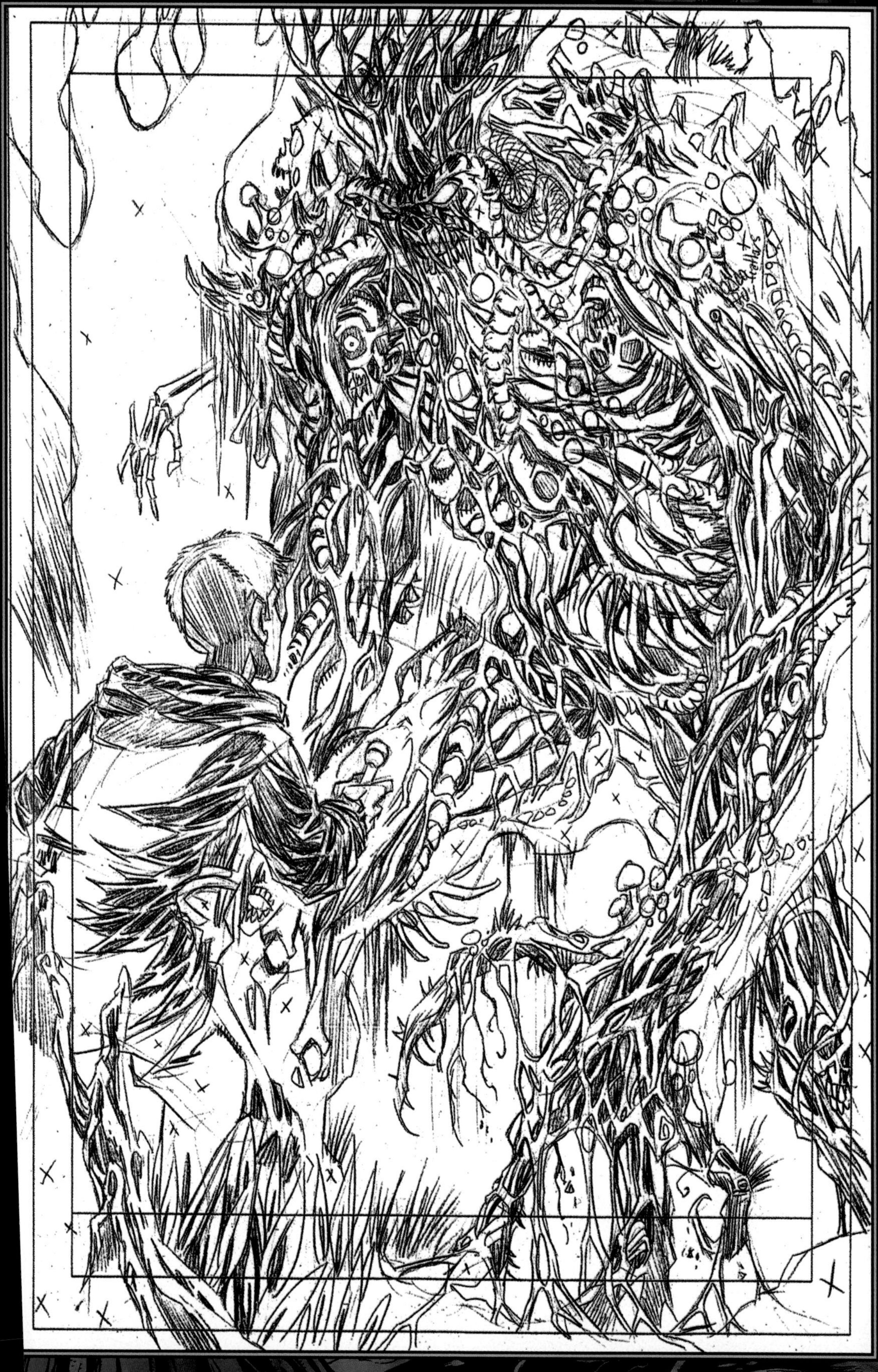

Cover Pencils for Man-Thing #2

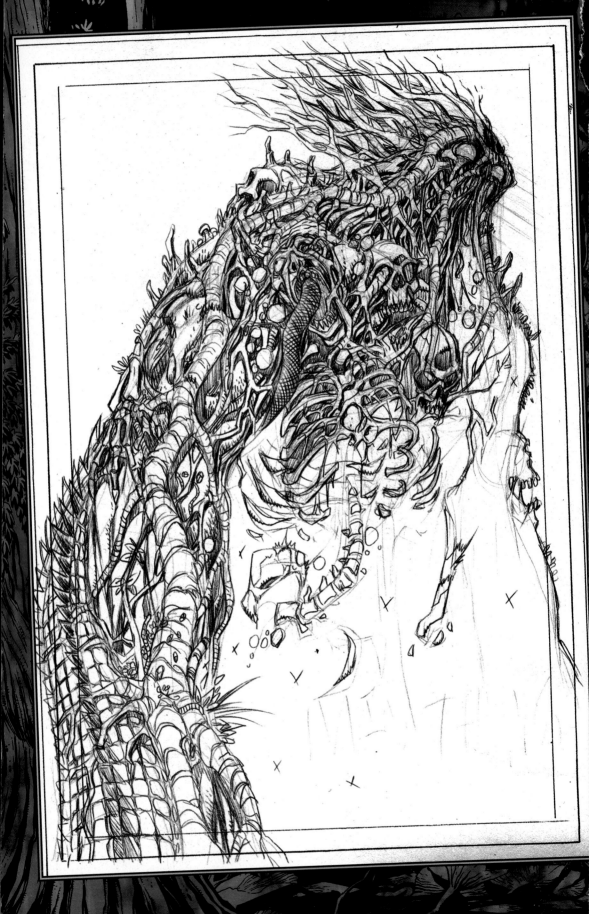